THE DAILY STUDY BIBLE

(OLD TESTAMENT)

General Editor: John C.L. Gibson

GENESIS

Volume 2

GENESIS

Volume 2

JOHN C.L. GIBSON

THE WESTMINSTER PRESS
PHILADELPHIA

Scripture quotations from the Revised Standard Version of the Bible are copyrighted 1946, 1952, © 1971, 1973 by the Division of Christian Education of the National Council of the Churches of Christ in the U.S.A., and are used by permission of the National Council of Churches, New York, and William Collins Sons & Co., Ltd., Glasgow.

Published by
The Saint Andrew Press
Edinburgh, Scotland
and
The Westminster Press®
Philadelphia, Pennsylvania

Printed in the United States of America

5   6   7   8   9   10

Library of Congress Cataloging in Publication Data

Gibson, John C. L.
  Genesis.

  (The Daily study Bible series)
  Bibliography: p.
  1. Bible. O.T. Genesis—Commentaries. I. Title.
II. Series: Daily study Bible series (Westminster Press)
BS1235.3.G53 1981   222'.11077   81-7477
                                            AACR2

ISBN (U.S.A.) 0-664-21804-0 (v. 2)
ISBN (U.S.A.) 0-664-24571-4 (pbk. : v. 2)

GENERAL PREFACE

The series of commentaries on the Old Testament, to which this second volume on *Genesis* belongs, has been planned as a companion series to the much-acclaimed New Testament series of the late Professor William Barclay. As with that series, each volume is arranged in successive headed portions suitable for daily study. The Biblical text followed is that of the Revised Standard Version or Common Bible. Eleven contributors share the work, each being responsible for from one to three volumes. The series is issued in the hope that it will do for the Old Testament what Professor Barclay's series succeeded so splendidly in doing for the New Testament—make it come alive for the Christian believer in the twentieth century.

Its two-fold aim is the same as his. Firstly, it is intended to introduce the reader to some of the more important results and fascinating insights of modern Old Testament scholarship. Most of the contributors are already established experts in the field with many publications to their credit. Some are younger scholars who have yet to make their names but who in my judgment as General Editor are now ready to be tested. I can assure those who use these commentaries that they are in the hands of competent teachers who know what is of real consequence in their subject and are able to present it in a form that will appeal to the general public.

The primary purpose of the series, however, is *not* an academic one. Professor Barclay summed it up for his New Testament series in the words of Richard of Chichester's prayer—to enable men and women "to know Jesus Christ more clearly, to love Him more dearly, and to follow Him more nearly." In the case of the Old Testament we have to be a little more circumspect than that. The Old Testament was completed long before the time of Our Lord, and it was (as it still is) the sole Bible of the Jews, God's first people, before it became part of the Christian Bible. We must take this fact seriously.

Yet in its strangely compelling way, sometimes dimly and sometimes directly, sometimes charmingly and sometimes embarrassingly, it holds up before us the things of Christ. It should not be forgotten that Jesus Himself was raised on this Book, that He based His whole ministry on what it says, and that He approached His death with its words on His lips. Christian men and women have in this ancient collection of Jewish writings a uniquely illuminating avenue not only into the will and purposes of God the Father, but into the mind and heart of Him who is named God's Son, who was Himself born a Jew but went on through the Cross and Resurrection to become the Saviour of the world. Read reverently and imaginatively the Old Testament can become a living and relevant force in their everyday lives.

It is the prayer of myself and my colleagues that this series may be used by its readers and blessed by God to that end.

New College   JOHN C.L. GIBSON
Edinburgh   General Editor

CONTENTS

Introduction   1

ABRAHAM: AN EPIC OF FAITH

Call (12:1–3)   5
Separation (12:1–3) *(cont'd)*   8
Promise (12:1–3) *(cont'd)*..   11
Pilgrimage I (12:1–3) *(cont'd)*   15
Pilgrimage II (12:1–3) *(cont'd)*   16
Pilgrimage III (12:1–3) *(cont'd)*   19
Pilgrimage IV (12:1–3) *(cont'd)*   23
Pilgrimage V (12:1–3) *(cont'd)*   26
Obedience (12:4–9)   28
Expediency (12:10–20)   32
A Note on Genesis Chapters 12ff. as "History"   36
Magnanimity (13:1–18)   38
Victory (14:1–24)   42
Blessing (14:1–24) *(cont'd)*   45
A Note on the Title "Hebrews"   48
Righteousness (15:1–6)   49
Covenant (15:7–21)   52
Jealousy (16:1–6)   56
Providence (16:7–16)   60
Laughter I (17:1–27)   64
Circumcision (17:1–27) *(cont'd)*   69
Warning (18:1–19:29)   71
Laughter II (18:1–15) *(cont'd)*   75
Intercession (18:16–33) *(cont'd)*   79
Vice (19:1–11) *(cont'd)*   82
Prevarication (19:12–23) *(cont'd)*   85
Judgment (19:24–29) *(cont'd)*   88
Incest (19:30–38)   91
"*Experience*" (20:1–18)   93
"*Fulfilment*" I: *A Son* (21:1–21)   97
Grace (21:1–21) *(cont'd)*   102

"Fulfilment" II: The Blessing (21:22–34)   105
Sacrifice I: Man's Sacrifice (22:1–19)   107
Sacrifice II: God's Sacrifice (22:1–19) *(cont'd)*   111
"Fulfilment" III: The Land (22:20–23:20)   115
Matchmaking I (24:1–67)   119
Matchmaking II (24:1–67) *(cont'd)*   123
Genealogy (25:1–18)   127
Death (25:1–18) *(cont'd)*   131

JACOB: AN EPIC OF CONFLICT

Conflict (25:19–34)   136
A Note on the Names Jacob and Esau   140
Birthright (25:19–34) *(cont'd)*   141
Timidity (26:1–33)   144
Blessing (26:34–27:40)   149
Effrontery (26:34–27:40) *(cont'd)*   153
Flight (27:41–28:9)   157
Bethel I: Jacob's Bethel (28:10–22)   161
Bethel II: Our Bethel (28:10–22) *(cont'd)*   165
Exile (29:1–31:55)   169
Nemesis (29:1–30) *(cont'd)*   176
Sons (29:31–30:24) *(cont'd)*   179
Success (30:25–43) *(cont'd)*   183
Hypocrisy (31:1–16) *(cont'd)*   185
Vindication (31:17–55) *(cont'd)*...   ...   ·...   ...   188
Foreboding I (32:1–21)   191
Foreboding II (32:1–21) *(cont'd)*   194
Peniel I: Jacob's Peniel (32:22–32)   196
Peniel II: Our Peniel (32:22–32) *(cont'd)*   200
Peniel III: Israel's Peniel (32:22–32) *(cont'd)*   202
Reconciliation (33:1–17)   207
Rape and Revenge (33:18–34:31)   211
Triumph to Tragedy (35:1–22)   215
The Parting of the Ways (35:23–36:43)   220

JOSEPH: AN EPIC OF DESTINY

Discord (37:1–4)   225
Dreams (37:5–11)   228
Revenge (37:12–36)   231
Silence (37:12–36) *(cont'd)*.   235

CONTENTS

Interlude (38:1–30) 237
Justice (38:1–30) *(cont'd)* 241
Temptation (39:1–23) 245
A Note on Structure and Style in the Joseph Epic 248
Inspiration (40:1–41:45) 250
Wisdom (40:1–41:45) *(cont'd)* 254
Ingratitude (40:1–41:45) *(cont'd)* 258
Forgetfulness (41:46–57) 261
Not You but God (42:1–45:28) 265
Remorse (42:1–25) *(cont'd)* 273
Grief (42:26–43:15) *(cont'd)* 276
A Note on "Sources" in Chapters 42 and 43 279
The Calm... (43:16–34) *(cont'd)* 280
...Before the Storm (44:1–17) *(cont'd)* 283
Reconciliation (44:18–45:28) *(cont'd)* 286
Providence (45:4–8) *(cont'd)* 289
Into Egypt (46:1–27) 294
The Pharaoh Upstaged (46:28–47:12) 296
Tyranny (47:13–27) 299
A Note on Dating the Patriarchal Age 302
Death-bed Scenes I (47:28–49:32) , ... 304
Death-bed Scenes II (47:28–49:32) *(cont'd)* 310
Nothing is Here for Tears (49:33–50:14) 314
All Passion Spent (50:15–26) 317

Further Reading 321

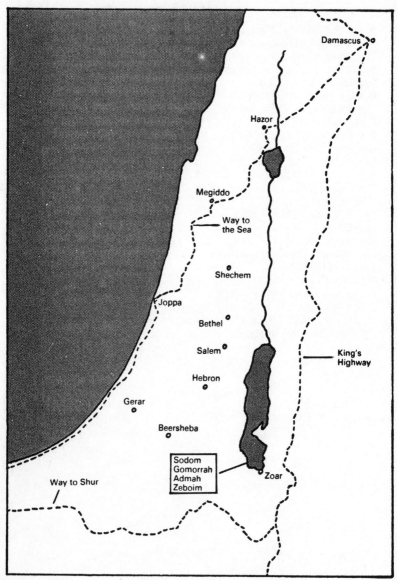

Map 1 The Way to the Sea

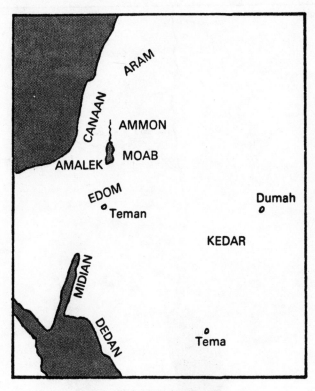

Map 2   Neighbouring Peoples

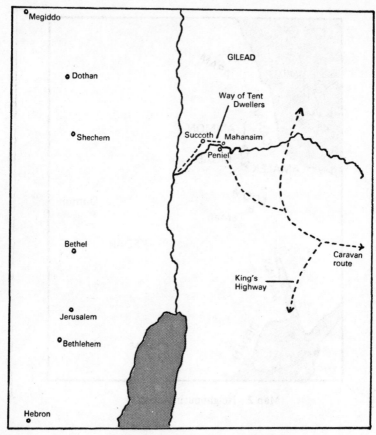

Map 3   The Way of the Tent-Dwellers

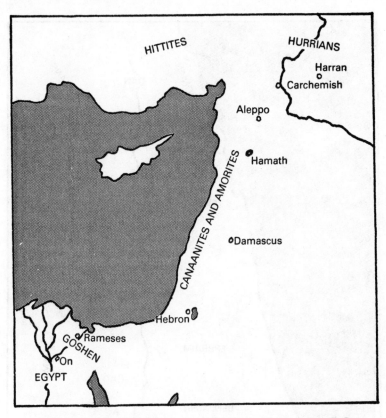

Map 4   The Near East in the Mid-Second Millennium B.C.

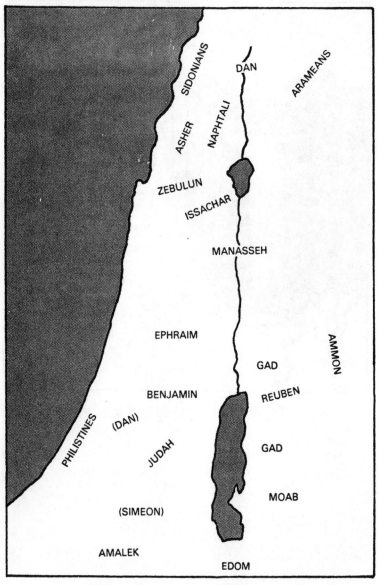

Map 5   The Tribes in Palestine

INTRODUCTION

THE NAME OF THE BOOK AND THE KIND OF LITERATURE

On the name Genesis, which means "beginning" or "origin", and on older traditional and more recent views of its authorship—the book itself gives no direct information—the reader is referred to the Introduction to Volume 1. There I gave my own opinion that if anyone deserves the accolade of Genesis' "author", it is the people of Israel itself or, to be more precise, the anonymous bards or "singers of tales" who in its early tribal days first gave literary expression in their oral stories to the insights and aspirations, and the hopes and fears of the infant nation. The stories they retailed by word of mouth have reached us in a later written dress, but they still carry about them the flavour and atmosphere of folk literature. I also suggested there that if we in this sophisticated age wish to get on the "wavelength" of these old tales, we must be willing to set aside our predilections and presuppositions and try by an effort of the imagination to approach them with the eyes of ancient wonder and ancient wisdom.

PROBLEMS MET IN INTERPRETING THE FIRST ELEVEN CHAPTERS

But of course that is only the start. We may be ready to admit that Genesis comes to us from a bygone age when people did their thinking in the form of stories, but we have still to restate its lessons in terms acceptable to our own age. We saw in Volume 1 how difficult this could be in the case of the book's opening chapters, and how many tricky distinctions had to be made—between scientific truth and religious truth, for instance, or between a naive outward form and an anything but naive inner meaning, or between the words of men in Scripture and the Word of God, or between what an ancient Hebrew would have got from the text and what, often without realizing it, later generations of Jews and Christians have read into it. We had also to pay careful attention to the differing emphases of the source documents which the scholars identify by the labels "J" and "P".

Our conclusion in the end was that the chapters were not to be regarded as a historical account of the world's and of mankind's beginnings. But there was a compensation. By that very conclusion we were freed to see them as their first audiences must have seen them, and to find in them an imaginative analysis of the Creator's will for his Creation, and of what inevitably ensues when an arrogant humanity rebels against that will, so penetrating in its judgments and so devastating in its scope that far from being time-bound it is timeless. Genesis 1-11 did not tell us the "facts" of what happened at Creation, but it did something infinitely more necessary and valuable. It confronted us with our dire peril *here and now* and with our desperate need *here and now* of a Saviour.

THE DIFFERENT PROBLEMS PRESENTED BY CHAPTERS 12-50

Chapters 12-50 of Genesis, with which this second volume is concerned, relate how at a certain moment in the remote past in a certain area of the world's surface God moved to meet that timeless need of men and to defend them from that timeless peril. The call to Abraham to leave Mesopotamia and migrate to Palestine was in effect the first act of the Gospel. Many centuries were to pass before the final act took place in the Incarnation of God's own Son and his Crucifixion and Resurrection. But God had begun the process of the world's salvation, and the second part of Genesis records that beginning.

It follows from this that the stories in Genesis 12-50 are in one very important respect different from those in Genesis 1-11. They are still folk stories, composed to appeal to unlettered people, and therefore not at all like the carefully dated and annotated history books we are used to nowadays. But they are stories that tell of things that actually happened. It is possible to ask historical questions of them and to make use of the discoveries of archaeology and the chronicles of contemporary nations in attempting our answers. We could not ask such questions of Genesis 1–11.

We will meet with tricky problems in this part of Genesis too. One is that small groups of wandering semi-nomads like Abraham and his clan do not often leave tangible traces of their presence for future scholars to mull over, and that such evidence as we possess will therefore concern the background to the Patriarchal era more often than it will the Patriarchs as individuals. Another is that traditions about ethnic or tribal history have tended to get mixed up with stories about individuals, and it is not always easy to disentangle the two. Moreover, there is the penchant of folk literature the world over for painting heroes of the past somewhat larger than life, or for seeing the prejudices of a later age reflected in what these heroes say and do, or even on occasion for indulging in a little make-believe. It would not be right of us to expect Hebrew folk stories to be exempt from such interference, and we will therefore need to exercise a modicum of scepticism from time to time. We will also have to take note here and there of differences among the documents "J", "P" and (appearing for the first time in Genesis 12ff.) "E".

OUR MAIN TASK IN THIS COMMENTARY

Fortunately, however, these problems are not nearly so worrying as their counterparts in Volume 1, and it will not be so essential in this volume to take up space dealing with them at length. We will be able to concentrate more exclusively on our central task, which is surely not to argue about what the scholars say, interesting as that may be, but to make the acquaintance of the real live Abraham and Isaac and Jacob and Joseph and to profit as we can from their experience. They were among the first human beings to meet with the living God in the round of their daily lives. Their strengths and weaknesses, their glories and shames, their moments of assurance and despair, are ours too, though writ larger. As, perhaps more carefully than we have done before, we study these remarkable old stories of the Hebrew Patriarchs, so full of vigour and reality and truth, so simple yet so profound, so attractive yet at the same time so disturbing, our faith cannot but be deepened and our vision of God and his ways with men enlarged.

ABRAHAM: AN EPIC OF FAITH

CALL

Genesis 12:1-3

1 Now the Lord said to Abram, "Go from your country and your
  kindred and your father's house to the land that I will show you.
2 And I will make of you a great nation, and I will bless you, and make
3 your name great, so that you will be a blessing. I will bless those who
  bless you, and him who curses you I will curse; and by you all the
  families of the earth shall bless themselves."

At some point in the early or mid-second millennium B.C. a
nomadic Semite called Abraham left Harran in Upper Mesopotamia and went to Palestine. On the face of it a quite unremar-
kable event—yet both Jews and Christians believe that it
marked a moment fraught with destiny for the whole human
race, indeed for the whole created universe. For God was
behind it. Both Jews and Christians believe that by his call to
this one individual God was setting in motion a series of acts of
grace and judgment which would fashion a special people for
him, who would lead a lost mankind back to their true home. It
is our claim as Christians that we belong to that special people,
and with our Jewish brethren we look back today to Abraham
as father of the faithful. If he had not answered that call, Israel
would not have reached her Promised Land, the Church we
love would not exist, there would be no Scriptures for us to
study and write commentaries on, and our lives would be
emptied of everything that makes them worth while.

Our first reaction to this event ought therefore to be one of
wonder, wonder that God should choose so seemingly undramatic a way of opening the story of the world's redemption, and
wonder that this single man in those far-off days should have
grasped, however dimly, what it was about.

(i)

The first eleven chapters of Genesis set the scene for the call,
and a dark and sombre scene it is. (For a detailed study of these
chapters see Volume 1.)

God had created a good world and filled it with his creatures
so that he might lavish on them the love and affection he had to
spare and that would otherwise have gone to waste. But that
good world was in disarray. His highest creation, his supreme
masterpiece—we human beings—had gone horribly wrong.
Made to govern his universe in justice, we had mercilessly
exploited it and turned his fair earth into a desert. Made to live
in harmony with our fellows, we were now scattered to the four
winds and hopelessly fragmented. Made to serve our Creator
and worship him, we had forgotten our creatureliness and laid
usurping hands on a divinity to which we had no right. God
could of course, being God, have compelled us to keep our
place and do our duty. But that was not his way. So as the
chapters draw to their close, we catch a glimpse of him—if we
may so phrase it—puzzling over what to do next, as resolutely
but with a heavy heart he staved off the final disaster which
would undo all his creative work and leave him alone in eternal
and rueful silence. In short, because of human sin the world was
in a state of mortal danger.

(ii)

Such was the fearful problem with which according to Genesis
1–11 God was faced. Having forsworn compulsion he had, if all
was not to be forever lost, to begin again, to try a new initiative
and once more attempt to get through to proud and sinful men.
So as chapter 12 approaches (see 11:26ff.) he encompassed with
his grace and favour a small group of wandering Semites, a
family who by their way of life would not, he hoped, be overly
impressed by what the world called greatness. He detached
Terah, his son Abraham, his grandson Lot (Abraham's nephew), and his daughter-in-law Sarah (Abraham's wife), from
their contact with Ur of the Chaldeans (or as the AV has it,

Chaldees—the name is later than Abraham's time) in Babylonia and led them back to their ancestral homeland around Harran in Northern Mesopotamia. And there he left them for a while continuing their age-long nomadic existence as they moved slowly from pasture to pasture with their servants and their flocks and herds. There, too, as the years passed, they all grew older and, as we are ominously reminded (11:30), Sarah remained childless.

But then suddenly, after Terah's death, God decided that the hour had arrived, and issued his call to Abraham, speaking for the second time a Word "out of the blue" that would, if it were heard, bring light into the darkness of chaos and eventually form peace out of present discord (see commentary on 1:3–5, *And God said*).

(iii)

Let us ponder a little this marvellous occasion. Before we even look at what God said in his call or what it involved for the human beings to whom it was addressed, there are a number of lessons to be learned from its setting and circumstances.

Firstly, it was centred on a group of people who, if we except slaves, were among the weakest in the society of that time, people who were already fully aware of the precariousness of the human condition, knowing nothing of that feeling of security engendered by settled city life. They had the freedom to move about that slaves did not have, but not a great deal more. Significantly, also, Abraham and his wife were getting on in years and had no issue. But this was exactly the situation God wanted them to be in, cast adrift and with no apparent future. In his providence they were, in so far as any human beings could be, in the right frame of mind to hear and answer the call that really mattered.

Secondly, God's initiative was so engineered that it implicitly but powerfully condemned the security of civilized life—and its pomp and achievements and philosophy as well. It cannot have been by chance that, as the chosen people emerge from the mists of pre-history, we find them in Babylonia, the cradle of one of the most advanced cultures that ancient world had yet known. Nor can it have been by chance that before God could do anything with them, he had to get them out from there to the wide and open spaces of the ruder, nomadic north.

Thirdly, there is the tremendous risk God was taking. His providence had prepared the way. He had chosen—and chosen carefully—the time, the place, and the people. He had done all that he could do without using a force on mankind that would have made a mockery of his love. But now he had to depend on these people responding, to "put his money", as it were, on representatives of the very creatures who had already let him down so badly. "Love conquers all", we say. But does it? It is not certainty that tells us that, but faith. In that one moment— did we call it undramatic?—everything God had planned hung in the balance.

Which brings us *fourthly* to Abraham himself. According to Hebrew tradition the Patriarchs had "lived beyond the Euphrates and served other gods" (Josh. 24:2). This reminds us that up to his very call Abraham was a pagan. The gods he worshipped would not be the great deities of Babylonia, for whom as a free nomadic spirit he probably had very little stomach. What then did he think of his own nomadic gods, the gods of his own clan and tribe? We cannot say, and it is idle to speculate. All that we can say is that he answered the call of the one true God when it was issued. We have spoken about God's hand guiding Abraham to this hour. But though, looking back on his life later, he himself would undoubtedly have acknowledged this, he knew nothing of it at the time. He simply recognized that his life had been changed, and obeyed. The call of this God was self-authenticating. In the last analysis it needed no other explanation beyond itself.

SEPARATION

Genesis 12:1–3 *(cont'd)*

God said to Abraham, "Go!" or, as the AV, more in tune with

the drama of the moment, has it, "Get thee out!" There could have been no more radical summons. He commanded this man, already a wanderer on the face of the earth, to leave behind him for good the only area he had ever settled in for any length of time. The few certainties he knew had to be abandoned for something still more uncertain.

(i)

Abraham is not asked to renounce his "country" in the sense of giving up his citizenship. He was already stateless. "Country" here means simply the place where he lived. The emphasis is more on leaving his "kindred" and his "father's house", the first of these terms signifying the larger tribal group to which he belonged and the second his immediate blood relatives. He was to take only his wife and his fatherless nephew with him.

Did those among whom he lived think it was only the old nomadic urge reasserting itself and, as he left, wish him well and say, "See you in a month or two"? Or did they sense that this was a more permanent parting and try to dissuade him, pointing out to him that he was getting too old for that sort of thing? Did, for that matter, his wife and his nephew understand what was happening, and acquiesce happily? Or did they too try to dissuade him, reminding him of his duty to his kith and kin? As so often in the Bible, we are not told. We are given only the bare essential facts, God's summons to break with the past and begin a new life under his control, and Abraham's positive response. The rest we have to infer.

(ii)

It seems reasonable, however, to assume from their behaviour later that neither Sarah nor Lot would have been too keen on the move. And certainly if Abraham had made any attempt to explain to his other kinsmen why he was going, we can well imagine their ridicule and opposition.

If that were the case, there is a very perturbing parallel in the Gospels, which underscores the radical nature of the crisis facing Abraham. It concerns what happened the first time Jesus returned to Nazareth.

Jesus was reared at Nazareth in Galilee, where he was probably apprenticed to Joseph and after his death became the village carpenter. Until he was about thirty his days would be passed making ploughs for the local farmers and furniture for the villagers' homes. But he was more than a carpenter, and when the clarion call of John the Baptist sounded, he downed his tools and left his bench and went out to announce that God's Kingdom had arrived. The crowds in the beginning flocked to listen, and to marvel at his miracles.

But when in due course he came back to his home village and preached from the pulpit of the local synagogue, it was not admiration that he elicited, but a galling repulse. The folks among whom he had been brought up, with whom maybe he had played when they were youngsters together, whose ploughs he had mended, whose homes he had furnished, were scandalised at his arrogance, even attempting violence to his person and coming near to lynching him. Little wonder that Jesus was driven to say (in words that are strangely reminiscent of our verses in Genesis), "A prophet is not without honour, except in his own country, and among his own kin, and in his own house" (Mark 6:4)! And little wonder that he could do no mighty work there "because of their unbelief" (Matt. 13:58)! It was a shattering experience but only, alas, the prelude of much more to come.

(iii)

Faith has always had the disconcerting habit of causing separations, of cutting across family and community ties. The things of home are regarded as sacrosanct by the majority of mankind, but to the few who are the true children of faith there is something higher and holier, the call of God, and there is no certainty that the two will not clash. Abraham was commanded to separate himself from his "country" and his "kindred" and his "father's house". Bunyan's pilgrim had to leave his wife and family to seek his own salvation. In the early Church converts had to suffer insult and sometimes betrayal from relatives and friends who remained pagans. In the service of God a man's foes may well be those of his own household (Matt. 10:36).

In the quiet and uneventful life that is the lot of most of us, there is not much chance of a conflict. But what if the cards were down? How would *we* choose? We will never probably be called upon to choose, as some great souls in the past have been and as not a few of our fellow Christians in totalitarian lands are being called upon to do even today. But what if we were?

We are all of us wrapped up in the things and folk around us, and not many can make the leap of faith required to see them as good and lovely but as by no means the most vital part of life, to see them as something which *may*—if it is God's will—have to be given up.

Our Lord has some perplexing, even repellent words to say on this matter. They constitute one of the "hard sayings" of the Gospel, and it is not difficult to believe that they arose out of the distressing experience at Nazareth which we have been looking at. They also bear very uncomfortably on how we ought to understand God's call to us and to apply Abraham's experience to our own littler lives:

> If any one comes to me and does not hate his own father and mother and wife and children and brothers and sisters, yes, and even his own life, he cannot be my disciple.
>
> (Luke 14:26)

PROMISE

Genesis 12:1-3 *(cont'd)*

Only after the call to separate himself from all that he had previously held dear does God give Abraham a promise of something to replace it. It is a three-fold promise:

(a) of a land which God would show him;

(b) of descendants who would grow into a great nation;

(c) of a special blessing which would in the immediate future afford him protection against anyone opposing him, but which would eventually bring all the nations of the earth within its scope.

(i)

It is natural for us to place the emphasis on the third of these promises, since it is the one that particularly involves us. I would guess that for Abraham himself, however, it was the least relevant of the three, or rather that the second part of it was. That part told him that his God was much more than a tribal god, that he was indeed the God of the whole earth, and that he desired every nation on it to worship him. But Abraham was an unlettered nomad, and it would be foolish of us to think of him having more than the sketchiest awareness of what this would ultimately mean. He would, at the beginning at any rate, be much more interested in the protection which the first part of the third promise held out to him, since that was more immediately and practically applicable to his situation.

But that necessary note of caution having been sounded, namely that we ought not to expect Abraham to have understood the promises as we now understand them, it is beyond dispute that these promises are what gave purpose and meaning to Abraham's life. Everything he does following his call and everything that happens to him are either directly related to them in the narratives or may be brought into connection with them by the exercise of a little imagination. Will he be able to settle in Canaan? Will he have a son? How will his contacts with the peoples already in the land turn out? If we keep these questions in our minds as we read through chapters 12–25, we will see how the working out of the promises supplies both the main element of tension in the plot of the stories and the primary key to their interpretation.

(ii)

Most obviously there is the specific renewal of one or more of the promises at moments of perplexity or crisis in his life:

—of the promise of land in 12:7 when he first arrives in Canaan

—of the promise of land and descendants in 13:14–17 after Lot has chosen the best territory and he is left with the least attractive

—of the promise of descendants in 15:4–5 after he has complained that he was still childless

—of the same promise in 17:19–21 after he has laughed at the thought of his aged wife bearing a son

—of the promise of descendants and blessing in 22:16–18 after his faith has been tested by the command to sacrifice Isaac.

Moreover, in at least one place the story itself makes a connection between the promise of blessing and what is about to happen, when in 18:17–19 God in a soliloquy speaks of it just before the destruction of Sodom and Gomorrah.

These specific references should encourage us to look for links elsewhere, for instance:

—between the promise of descendants and Abraham's attempt on two occasions (12:10–20 in Egypt and chapter 20 in Gerar) to pass his wife off as his sister

—between the promise of blessing and (a) Abraham's warlike victory over the four great kings in chapter 14; and (b) his more peaceable agreement with the king of Gerar in chapter 21

—between the promise of land and (a) the several occasions on which Abraham builds an altar and calls upon God's name (12:8; 13:4, 18; 21:33); and (b) the occasion on which he purchases from some Hittites an actual piece of Canaanite territory in order to bury his wife (chapter 23).

(iii)

There can be no doubt that these promises mattered vitally to Abraham and that it was his ardent desire to see some signs that they were coming true that sustained him in his wanderings and gave him both strength and hope in hours of despair and darkness. And he was granted his signs—and they were apparently enough to convince him that his God was no liar and that his waiting and suffering had not been in vain.

Yet when all is said and done, what tiny signs they were! Escape from danger here, a rare victory over the great ones of the earth there, a son at last—at long last—in his old age, a small plot of land to receive the dead body of his wife! Most men would have demanded much more evidence that things were moving in the right direction before they could have died contentedly and in peace. There is a long way to go from a single son to a great nation or from a field to a country. The plain fact is that Abraham remained a homeless wanderer to the end, with nowhere of his own to lay his head, and in the end there were not many more people around him than at the beginning. In the last analysis only faith told him that he would not have been better off staying with his kindred at Harran. And such faith cannot have come easily to him.

The writer of the Epistle to the Hebrews finely catches that sense of "How long, O Lord?" which must have nagged at Abraham all his days when he says of him in his famous eleventh chapter

> By faith . . . he went out, not knowing where he was to go (verse 8)

or

> By faith he sojourned in the land of promise, as in a foreign land (verse 9)

or

> . . . from [this] one man, and him as good as dead, were born descendants as many as the stars of heaven (verse 12)

or when he says of the Patriarchs as a whole, including Abraham

> These all died in faith, not having received what was promised, but having seen it and greeted it from afar, and having acknowledged that they were strangers and exiles on the earth (verse 13).

PILGRIMAGE I

Genesis 12:1-3 *(cont'd)*

(i)

There was, then, a huge gap between promise and fulfilment in Abraham's life, which was only bridged by his remarkable faith. There ought not to be so huge a gap in our lives for, as the Epistle to the Hebrews reminds us at the close of chapter 11, "All these [i.e. Abraham and the other Patriarchs and all the heroes and martyrs of Old Testament times] did not receive what was promised" (verse 39). *We* did. Because (verse 40) "God had foreseen something better for us, that apart from us they should not be made perfect" or, as Dr. Barclay translates it, "God had some better plan for us, that they, without us, should not find all his purposes fulfilled". It was a way of saying that the promises first given to Abraham and so very fitfully fulfilled in his own lifetime were finally and magnificently fulfilled in the Church which grew out of ancient Israel and of which we are members. The Church of Jesus Christ is the real Canaan of Abraham's dreams, the real nation which he fathered, the real defence of the faithful in time of trial, the real channel of blessing to all the peoples of the earth.

(ii)

But there is a lot more to be said than that. We must not in the slightest underestimate the stupendous claims of the New Testament that by the Incarnation God's rule over men took a visible shape among them in Jesus of Nazareth, a shape it had not previously taken, or that by his Cross and Resurrection God won so decisive a victory over his ancient enemies of sin and evil that never again would they be able to plunge his Creation into chaos and disaster. As Christians these must be our claims too. In the truest of senses the strife which the first eleven chapters of Genesis had so eloquently described *is* over and the battle to which they had so unerringly pointed *is* won. In that sense the journey on which God had embarked when he called on Abraham to cross the great river and enter the unknown *was* at an end.

Yet we must at the same time be realists. As we survey the world around us, it does not look that way. Nor will it look any more that way simply because we keep exultantly repeating that it is. It is faith, not the present state of the world, that speaks to us of God's and Christ's triumph and of the fulfilment in our day and in our midst of the promises so long ago spoken to Abraham.

(iii)

The New Testament is in no doubt about this either. In continuous counterpoint with the proclamation that the Kingdom's day has dawned is the growing realization that it is still only its early morning and that its noontide not to mention its evening are a long way off. Even as it celebrates joyously Christ's first coming it looks forward expectantly—and sometimes desperately—to his second coming. In that sense—and it is just as true a sense—faithful Christians are still with Abraham in Harran and still with Israel in the wilderness, Pharaoh's Egypt is still strong, the Jordan has still to be crossed, and Canaan still to be possessed. In that sense faith is still for us, as in the words of Hebrews chapter 11 it was for the Patriarchs and heroes of God's first people, "the assurance of things hoped for, the conviction of things not seen" (verse 1). In that sense there *is* still a gap between promise and fulfilment and Abraham's descendants are still "strangers and exiles on the earth".

PILGRIMAGE II

Genesis 12:1–3 *(cont'd)*

(iv)

"Strangers and exiles on the earth". The Jews, Abraham's

descendants after the flesh, know this in their heart of hearts. They have in our lifetime entered their Promised Land for a third time, and on the surface they seem quite powerful enough to keep it for as long into the future as one cares to look. And they hardly need God's help! But is this to be a permanent fulfilment of God's promise to the patriarch? Their history will not, if they consider it, fill them with confidence.

The first occasion on which they gained the land, it was by military force under Joshua and they kept it for more than half a millennium. But Nebuchadnezzar removed them into exile in Babylon, and from his time onwards there have always been more Jews outside Palestine than in it. There was a return after the Exile, but it was not to the glories of the old kingdom, but to a life of domination by Persians and after them by Greeks and Romans. And when not long after the age of the New Testament they rebelled against Rome and tried to win their freedom, Jerusalem and her Temple were razed to the ground, and the Jews were homeless once more. Will the third return in the present century be any different, or will the suspicion and enmity of other nations one day drive them out again? Will the world, after a suitable interval, forget the Nazi gas-chambers and resume its old ways of hounding this people from pillar to post?

Let us pray that nothing like that ever happens again. But even if it does not, no thinking Jew can ever be sure that he has finally come home. Even in possession of his ancestral country he is still in his heart the wandering Jew, still awaiting the Messiah of his Scriptures, still searching for the land that flows with milk and honey.

(v)

A proud Christendom has also to learn this lesson of uncertainty and fragility. The success of God's cause must not be equated with the success of his Church nor must his imperial claims be arrogated by his followers—as far too often in the past they have been. Take the following extracts from some well-known hymns about the Church:

John Newton's

> On the Rock of Ages founded,
>   What can shake thy sure repose?
> With salvation's walls surrounded,
>   Thou may'st smile at all thy foes.

or Samuel Johnson's

> In vain the surge's angry shock,
>   In vain the drifting sands:
> Unharmed upon the eternal Rock
>   The eternal City stands.

or Frances Ridley Havergal's

> Fierce may be the conflict,
>   Strong may be the foe,
> But the King's own army
>   None can overthrow.

or Sabine Baring-Gould's

> Crowns and thrones may perish,
>   Kingdoms rise and wane,
> But the Church of Jesus,
>   Constant will remain.

or even, though it uses the figure of pilgrimage, the same writer's

> Through the night of doubt and sorrow,
>   Onward goes the pilgrim band,
> Singing songs of expectation,
>   Marching to the promised land.
>
> Clear before us, through the darkness,
>   Gleams and burns the guiding light;
> Brother clasps the hand of brother,
>   Stepping fearless through the night.

In the expansive days when Europe and America dominated the world scene and their missionaries were gathering the heathen by the million into the Church's fold, these hymns struck a responsive chord. Empire and science and Christianity were together ushering in the millennium. I would not like to suggest that we give up singing such hymns, but are they not too triumphalist by half? For if the truth were told, the Church of Jesus is not in our day constant; it is in retreat. As often as not its foes are smiling at it, not the other way round. It is not unharmed, but badly buffeted by all sorts of tempests. The King's own army is in fact in grave danger of being overthrown.

(vi)

The chief lesson we Christians have to learn from this part of Genesis describing Abraham's call is, I would suggest, that the Church is a vulnerable, not a solid institution. To be really faithful to her Lord, who himself won his greatest victory on a Cross, she should be silencing her erstwhile superior and triumphalist tones and recognizing herself as she in fact is, a serving, suffering Church, a scorned Church, maybe a persecuted Church, certainly a pilgrim Church, travelling in the midst of a hostile world with only God knows how long a journey to traverse before the eternal City is reached, still very much in the "night of doubt and sorrow" but not, if she is wise, "stepping fearless" through it. Faith like Abraham's can lead to great endeavour and it can bring much assurance and comfort, but it is not faith but arrogance that uses words like "fearless" and "unharmed".

PILGRIMAGE III

Genesis 12:1-3 *(cont'd)*

(vii)

And what is true of the believing community is true of the individual believer too. It is well worth our while thinking some more on this idea of pilgrimage; for the Bible is full of it, and it is full of it because it so aptly describes not only the Church's situation in the world but the perennial human condition.

There are first of all a veritable host of comparisons of life to a *road* or *journey*. These images are perhaps not directly drawn from the theme of pilgrimage, but rather from the more general circumstances of daily living in a country and in an era without cars or trains, when not even animals but walking on foot was the usual manner of getting from one place to another. But they are not unconnected. I list some from the Old Testament:

Noah walked with God

(Gen. 6:9)

You shall be careful to do as the Lord your God has commanded you; you shall not turn aside to the right hand or to the left. You shall walk in all the way which the Lord your God has commanded you.

(Deut. 5:32–33)

And now I am about to go the way of all the earth

(Josh. 23:14)

Blessed is the man
  who walks not in the counsel of the wicked
nor stands in the way of sinners.

(Ps. 1:1)

He leads me in the paths of righteousness
  for his name's sake.
Even though I walk through the valley of the shadow of death,
  I fear no evil;
for thou art with me.

(Ps. 23:3,4)

Thou searchest out my path and my lying down,
  and art acquainted with all my ways

. . . .
Whither shall I go from thy Spirit?
  Or whither shall I flee from thy presence?
. . . .
  Try me and know my thoughts!
And see if there be any wicked way in me,
  and lead me in the way everlasting!

                       (Ps. 139:3, 7, 23–24)

(of folly)

  . . . her house sinks down to death,
    and her paths to the shades;
  none who go to her come back
    nor do they regain the paths of life.

                         (Prov. 2:18–19)

(of wisdom)

Her ways are ways of pleasantness,
  and all her paths are peace.

                           (Prov. 3:17)

Even youths shall faint and be weary,
  and young men shall fall exhausted;
but they who wait for the Lord shall renew their strength,
  they shall mount up with wings like eagles,
they shall run and not be weary,
  they shall walk and not faint.

                         (Isa. 40:30–31)

Stand by the roads, and look,
  and ask for the ancient paths,
where the good way is; and walk in it,
  and find rest for your souls.

                           (Jer. 6:16)

I know, O Lord, that the way of man is not in himself,
  that it is not in man who walks to direct his steps.

                         (Jer. 10:23)

Why does the way of the wicked prosper?

(Jer. 12:1)

Can two walk together unless they be agreed?

(Amos 3:3)

(viii)

Such language is also richly employed in the New Testament, in the epistles, but particularly in the teaching of Jesus. The following are examples:

Enter by the narrow gate; for the gate is wide and the way is easy, that leads to destruction, and those who enter it are many. For the gate is narrow and the way is hard, that leads to life, and those who find it are few.

(Matt. 7:13–14)

Walk while you have the light, lest the darkness overtake you; he who walks in the darkness does not know where he goes.

(John 12:35)

"You know the way where I am going." Thomas said to him, "Lord, we do not know where you are going; how can we know the way?" Jesus said to him, "I am the way, and the truth, and the life; no one comes to the Father, but by me."

(John 14:4–6)

Whoever brings back a sinner from the error of his way will save his soul from death.

(James 5:20)

He who hates his brother is in the darkness, and does not know where he is going, because the darkness has blinded his eyes.

(1 John 2:11)

PILGRIMAGE IV

Genesis 12:1-3 *(cont'd)*

(ix)

More closely linked with the verses from Genesis which we are studying, however, are the many forceful and colourful descriptions of the journeyings of Israel's ancestors and of Israel's own forty years' wandering in the wilderness. Here are just a few from the rest of Genesis and later:

And they went forth to go into the land of Canaan; and into the land of Canaan they came

(Gen. 12:5, AV)

And Abram journeyed on, still going toward the Negeb

(Gen. 12:9)

Then Jacob went on his journey, and came to the land of the people of the east

(Gen. 29:1)

So Israel took his journey with all that he had, and came to Beersheba

(Gen. 46:1)

God led the people round by the way of the wilderness toward the Red Sea.... And the Lord went before them by day in a pillar of cloud to lead them along the way, and by night in a pillar of fire to give them light, that they might travel by day and by night.

(Exod. 13:18, 21)

Not one of these men of this evil generation shall see the good land which I swore to give to your fathers ... [but] your little ones, who you said would become a prey, and your children, who this day have no knowledge of good or evil, shall go in there. . . . But as for you, turn, and journey into the wilderness.

(Deut. 1:35, 39–40)

And you shall remember all the way which the Lord your God has led you these forty years in the wilderness, that he might humble you, testing you to know what was in your heart.

(Deut. 8:2)

A wandering Aramean [AV: a Syrian ready to perish] was my father; and he went down into Egypt . . . and the Lord brought us out of Egypt with a mighty hand and an outstretched arm . . . and he brought us into this place and gave us this land, a land flowing with milk and honey.

(Deut. 26:5, 8–9)

Was it not thou that didst dry up the sea,
    the waters of the great deep;
that didst make the depths of the sea a way
    for the redeemed to pass over?

(Isa. 51:10)

(x)

A third idea related to our theme, which is met with especially in the Psalms, is that of the pilgrimage to Zion, the holy city. Examples are:

Who shall ascend the hill of the Lord?
    And who shall stand in his holy place?
He who has clean hands and a pure heart.

(Ps. 24:3–4)

My soul thirsts for God,
    for the living God.
When shall I come and behold
    the face of God?

(Ps. 42:2)

> Oh send out thy light and thy truth;
>> let them lead me,
> let them bring me to thy holy hill,
>> and to thy dwelling!

(Ps. 43:3)

> Blessed are the men whose strength is in thee
>> in whose heart are the highways to Zion
>
> . . . . . .
> They go on from strength to strength;
>> the God of gods will be seen in Zion.

(Ps. 84:5, 7)

> I was glad when they said to me,
>> "Let us go to the house of the Lord!"
> Our feet have been standing
>> within your gates, O Jerusalem!

(Ps. 122:1–2)

> How shall we sing the Lord's song
>> in a foreign land?
> If I forget you, O Jerusalem,
>> let my right hand wither!
> Let my tongue cleave to the roof of my mouth,
>> if I do not remember you,
> if I do not set Jerusalem
>> above my highest joy!

(Ps. 137:4–6)

(xi)

In some passages we even find this idea of the pilgrimage to Jerusalem finely interwoven with that of the wilderness wandering, as in the two excerpts below from Isaiah, in which the prophet is looking forward to the return to Zion after the Exile in Babylon:

> The wilderness and the dry land shall be glad,
>> the desert shall rejoice and blossom;

like the crocus it shall blossom abundantly,
  and rejoice with joy and singing
......
And a highway shall be there,
  and it shall be called the Holy Way
......
The ransomed of the Lord shall return,
  and come to Zion with singing;
everlasting joy shall be upon their heads;
  they shall obtain joy and gladness,
  and sorrow and sighing shall flee away.

(Isa. 35:1, 8, 10)

You shall go out in joy,
  and be led forth in peace;
the mountains and the hills before you
  shall break forth into singing,
  and all the trees of the field shall clap their hands.

(Isa. 55:12)

PILGRIMAGE V

Genesis 12:1–3 *(cont'd)*

(xii)

The imagery of pilgrimage in the preciser sense is not so prominent in the New Testament. There is in the prologue to John's Gospel a very imaginative reminiscence of the wilderness wandering in the phrase translated "dwelt among us" (1:14), but which literally means "pitched his tent, tabernacled among us", i.e. as God had once dwelt with his people on the journey to the Promised Land. And we have already noted the reverberating phrases used in Hebrews chapter 11 of Abraham going out, not knowing where he was to go but seeking a city which had foundations, and of the Patriarchs as a whole catching sight of the fulfilment of God's promise from afar and acknowledging therefore that they were but strangers and exiles on the earth.

But if the New Testament—which is after all not a large book—does not make an extensive use of the figure of pilgrimage, Christian literature and hymnology down the ages are replete with it. We meet it in many guises, in theological classics like Augustine's *City of God* or Bunyan's *Pilgrim's Progress,* and in hymns like "O God of Bethel! by whose hand" (a paraphrase of Gen. 28:20–22) or (already cited) "Through the night of doubt and sorrow", like Bunyan's own "Who would true valour see" or Blake's "And did those feet in ancient time". An especially favourite use is to illumine faith in the face of death, as in hymns like Bernard of Cluny's "Jerusalem the golden", or Isaac Watts' "There is a land of pure delight", or Charles Wesley's "Let saints on earth in concert sing". Happily not all of these by any means show the triumphalism we were criticizing earlier.

(xiii)

Put all these passages and compositions and poems together— those about life as a path or a road, those about Israel's journey to the Promised Land, those about the pilgrimage to Zion— and we have a very potent and marvellous *pot-pourri* of images and symbols with which to strengthen and inspire both the believing community and the believing individual in matters of faith and conduct.

They bring it forcibly to our attention that the Christian life is an ongoing process, with both a beginning or a setting out which calls for courage and commitment and a goal or a journey's end to which we look forward eagerly but which we have not yet reached. They warn us that there are all the time choices to be made, wrong turnings to be avoided, a right path to be kept. They remind us too that we are not alone but have a protector and guide on the way, who has brought us to where we are now and who will help us to circumvent the dangers that still lie before us.

The whole Bible in fact is governed more by this symbol of journeying and pilgrimage than by any other. It begins with Paradise Lost, from which man has been driven out, and ends with a new heaven and a new earth, a Paradise Regained which we shall enter at the end of the age. It speaks of a Canaan our predecessors won, but which is not to be compared with the Canaan still to be attained. It tells of a Jordan that was once crossed but also of many other Jordans looming ahead. It dwells joyously on the fact that Our Lord once "tabernacled" among us so that we could see his glory, yet its last words are still of faith, not sight—"Come, Lord Jesus" (Rev. 22:20). The movement of the Gospel story is, in short, inexorably forward.

(xiv)

And the story had its start in the three verses that open chapter 12 of Genesis! These three verses not only encapsulate the lost condition of humanity and supply the first indication of God's answer to it. They also enshrine the hope that constantly tugs at man's breast that one day his wanderings shall cease and he shall reach his Father's abode in peace. But—and this, as I suggested before, is their chief message to us—that day is not yet. Tiredness and elation, shame and purpose, striving and expectation, responsibility and dependence—these are the contrary thoughts and emotions the verses should engender in us, but not—and I repeat not—notions of victory and triumph, or even of rest and contentment. These things we believe shall be ours too, but that is for the future, and the future is God's. They can only be enjoyed in this life by faith, and that still means for us, as it did for Abraham, fleetingly and in foretaste.

OBEDIENCE

Genesis 12:4–9

4 So Abram went, as the Lord had told him; and Lot went with him. Abram was seventy-five years old when he departed from Haran.
5 And Abram took Sarai his wife, and Lot his brother's son, and all their possessions which they had gathered, and the persons that they had gotten in Haran; and they set forth to go to the land of Canaan. When they had come to the land of Canaan, Abram passed through
6 When they had come to the land of Canaan, Abram passed through

the land to the place at Shechem, to the oak of Moreh. At that time
7 the Canaanites were in the land. Then the Lord appeared to Abram,
and said, "To your descendants I will give this land." So he built
8 there an altar to the Lord, who had appeared to him. Thence he
removed to the mountain on the east of Bethel, and pitched his tent,
with Bethel on the west and Ai on the east; and there he built an altar
9 to the Lord and called on the name of the Lord. And Abram
journeyed on, still going toward the Negeb.

In this terse little passage we are given simply a list of happenings. It is left to us to sense its drama—and there is a good deal
of drama about it—by using our imaginations.

(i)

First there is Abraham's *obedience,* communicated in a single
short sentence: he went as he had been told.

He left Harran with his wife and nephew, their possessions
and their slaves ("the persons—AV, souls—that they had
gotten"). The mention of slaves tells us that it was not a tiny
family that went out from Harran but a sizeable caravan, and
prepares us for the three hundred and eighteen men who in
chapter 14 Abraham was able to put into the field for a military
raid. We have not, therefore, to think in the chapters ahead of
Abraham as a poverty-stricken refugee on the model of Cain in
chapter 4. Certainly he was not one of the great men of the
earth, but he was a chief of a clan, though as yet a small one. He
had no landed property and lived in nomadic encampments,
but with his flocks and herds and the people required to tend
and protect them he would have been considered quite prosperous in his time and probably enjoyed for that time a reasonably
comfortable standard of living (compare 13:2). When he left
Harran he was not abandoning a life of ease for one of physical
deprivation and asceticism. Neither of these extremes was
relevant in his case.

But all this kind of background information is unimportant
to the story-teller. With their frugality of language these verses
home in on what was essential, the urgency of God's call and the
immediate response it evoked. We get the same feelings of

urgency and immediacy when we read the equally terse stories
of how Jesus got himself a band of disciples (and how little of
the background we are given there too!):

> And passing along by the Sea of Galilee, he saw Simon and Andrew
> the brother of Simon casting a net in the sea; for they were
> fishermen. And Jesus said to them, "Follow me and I will make you
> become fishers of men". And immediately they left their nets and
> followed him.
>
> (Mark 1:16–18)

> And as he passed on, he saw Levi the son of Alphaeus sitting at the
> tax office, and he said to him, "Follow me". And he rose and
> followed him.
>
> (Mark 2:14)

> Another of the disciples said to him, "Lord, let me first go and bury
> my father". But Jesus said to him, "Follow me, and leave the dead to
> bury their own dead" (or more crisply still with the AV, "let the dead
> bury their dead!").
>
> (Matt. 8:21–22)

The lesson for the reader is clear. There can be no gainsaying
the call of God or God's Son. No excuses are allowed. It must be
obeyed in the moment it is issued, for to do otherwise is to
misunderstand what it is about. In such a vital matter this God
does not give a second chance, and the Son of this God will not
pass the same way again.

(ii)

Next, Abraham and his family set out to go to the land of
Canaan—as we know and as they afterwards knew, but of
course they did not know it at the time; but the story-teller
cannot even spare a moment to point that out. Then—as the
AV, again with a nicer sense of the drama of the occasion,
translates—"into the land of Canaan they came".

Not a word is said of the long journey that intervened.

Probably the travellers kept near to the great international caravan route from Mesopotamia to Egypt, which is called in Isa. 9:1 "the way of [or rather, to] the sea". Harran was a staging-post on this route, which crossed the Euphrates at Carchemish and turned southwestwards through Aleppo and Hamath to Damascus and thence across Galilee and the plain of Sharon to reach the coast at Joppa (see Map 1). Abraham may have left it at Damascus and continued south along the "King's Highway", entering Palestine from the east across the Jordan (as Jacob was later to do on his return from Mesopotamia), or he may have remained on it till Hazor or Megiddo, then turned south into the hill-country of Ephraim. We do not know. All we know is that the first place mentioned after Harran is Shechem. There, following a laconic reference to the indigenous inhabitants, the Canaanites, Abraham is given in a vision the news—and once more a single short sentence is enough—that this was the land of promise.

So in a mere phrase or two is Abraham transported from the old to the new, and the first forefather of the chosen people stands for the first time on the sacred soil of Palestine. The hazards of the way—the bandits that attacked the caravans, the fierce desert sections, the awesome defiles of the eastern Lebanon range—are not reported at all. The powerful Canaanites, who built the great fortresses of Hazor and Megiddo uncovered by the archaeologists and who in centuries to come were to fight bitterly with the Hebrews for possession of this very land, are brought in almost in the passing. All Abraham is told is: "You have arrived, and your descendants shall one day settle permanently in this territory".

(iii)

But how he must have needed that message with its renewal of the promise and its reminder that God was still with him! For his immediate reaction is to build an altar to the Lord to commemorate the occasion.

Again only a few words are used. It is not said that Abraham prayed to God for guidance. Rather it is said—or more accurately, hinted at—that in his servant's loneliness and his apprehension at his new surroundings and the ominously strong people who were now his neighbours God drew near to him to offer him hope. Only then does Abraham express his gratitude in an act of worship.

The original audience would note that this act of worship, the first recorded of a Hebrew in the Holy Land, took place at Shechem, a centre where later the twelve tribes used regularly to meet to renew their allegiance to the Lord (see, for example, Joshua chapter 24). But perhaps more important for us is that *worship* is not mentioned until verse 7 of this crucial chapter. The order of events is God's call—man's obedience—man's perplexities—God's comfort—and only then man's address to God. It is an order which is maintained throughout Scripture. God seeks us out, we do not seek for him. He does things for us and asks us to do things for him, and that is the way we find out what he is like. And that experience and that knowledge, not what we think up by our own arguing and philosophizing, then become the proper subject-matter of our prayers and praises.

Presumably after his exhausting travels Abraham remained for a while at Shechem, but he was not allowed to stay too long. Soon he was on the move again, and reached Bethel (also renowned as a centre of worship in later Israel) where he built another altar. And there he is in verse 9 still journeying on, "still going towards the Negeb". It was to be generations yet to be born, not he himself, who would settle down in this land and enjoy the full fruit of the promise first given to him.

Perhaps it were best if we too, as we "journey on" in life's pilgrimage, concentrate on the two things emphasized in this frugal passage—obedience and worship—and do not pretend that we are near our goal.

EXPEDIENCY

Genesis 12:10–20

10 Now there was a famine in the land. So Abram went down to Egypt

11 to sojourn there, for the famine was severe in the land. When he was about to enter Egypt, he said to Sarai his wife, "I know that you are
12 a woman beautiful to behold; and when the Egyptians see you, they will say, 'This is his wife'; then they will kill me, but they will let you
13 live. Say you are my sister, that it may go well with me because of
14 you, and that my life may be spared on your account." When Abram entered Egypt the Egyptians saw that the woman was very beautiful.
15 And when the princes of Pharaoh saw her, they praised her to
16 Pharaoh. And the woman was taken into Pharaoh's house. And for her sake he dealt well with Abram; and he had sheep, oxen, he-asses, menservants, maidservants, she-asses, and camels.
17 But the Lord afflicted Pharaoh and his house with great plagues
18 because of Sarai, Abram's wife. So Pharaoh called Abram, and said, "What is this you have done to me? Why did you not tell me
19 that she was your wife? Why did you say, 'She is my sister,' so that I took her for my wife? Now then, here is your wife, take her, and be
20 gone." And Pharaoh gave men orders concerning him; and they set him on the way, with his wife and all that he had.

The next little tale of Abraham and Sarah in Egypt is scarcely less taut in its composition than the one preceding it. To know what the story-teller is getting at we have to do a lot of reading between the lines.

(i)

Many commentators interpret it positively as showing how Abraham gets the better of none other than Egypt's Pharaoh and acquires considerable wealth at his expense. He thus makes his "name great" in accordance with the third of God's promises (12:2), and God's "blessing" on him is given a quick confirmation at the first whiff of serious danger in his life. Famine has forced him out of the land of promise soon after reaching it, and the attractiveness of his wife to the Egyptians faces him with a real problem if he and she are to survive to start a family. That he uses rather dubious means to safeguard their future may be regrettable but is in the circumstances understandable.

(ii)

But I find a negative interpretation more in keeping with the laconic tones of the narrative. The very first words of the story may indeed contain an implicit rebuke to Abraham for quitting Canaan so hastily, even though it be to escape a famine. That is perhaps to read in too much, but what does not seem to be in doubt is that behind Abraham's suggestion to his wife when they arrive in Egypt to pretend that she was his sister was simple cowardice, a desire to save his own skin. He may also have had the promise of progeny in mind, but what he says is "When the Egyptians see you . . . they will kill me, but they will let you live".

His subterfuge appears to work, and Sarah is taken into Pharaoh's house. In reality this is a euphemism for into his harem, not at all a pleasant fate. But the story says nothing about Abraham being appalled at what might happen to her there. Didn't he care? Or was he carried away by the generous gifts of sheep and cattle and servants which Pharaoh bestowed on him and on which the story does dwell? Was he congratulating himself that not only had he secured his safety but made a profit out of the deal as well?

We cannot answer these questions with any certainty, but it is significant that from this point in the story onwards it is Pharaoh who takes the initiative. Abraham has no choice but to go along with what he does. Plagues come upon Pharaoh's house, which he must have put down to the arrival of the new woman and, suspecting the truth, he asks Abraham why he did not tell him that Sarah was his wife. In a similar quandary later on in Gerar Abraham advances the excuse to Gerar's king that Sarah was in fact his half-sister, with the same father but not the same mother (20:12). But on this occasion he makes no reply. The Pharaoh peremptorily commands him, "Take her, and be gone!" And as though still not sure that Abraham could be trusted, he orders his men to "set him on his way". He does not even ask for his gifts back, but in disdain lets Abraham take "all that he had" with him. It does look as if the patriarch is being unceremoniously bundled out of the country with his tail firmly between his legs.

(iii)

In my view that is exactly the impression the narrator wishes to give. I cannot see how this story can be taken as other than critical of Abraham. It is like many another Hebrew story terse and frugal in the extreme. But the irony that shines through it cannot but be felt if it is read over slowly and the right emphases put on the right phrases.

It is not, as a positive interpretation would suggest, a story of God's intervention to save his threatened people from a cruel overlord and turn the tables on him. That, we know, is what happened when his people were next in Egypt in Moses' time. Certainly God intervenes, and he does save Abraham and Sarah. But if the tables are turned on anyone, it is on Abraham for his scheming, and on this occasion Pharaoh does not "allow" the holy people to go and then change his mind and pursue them, but he "commands" them to go and appoints an escort of soldiers to see that they do. He is not this time God's enemy, but God's ally to punish his wayward servant.

Considering what Egypt was later to mean to the Hebrews as a symbol of oppression and slavery, the irony of Pharaoh's role in this story must have hurt. I think it was meant to. For the lesson that is being taught Abraham—and all God's people after him—is that it was not up to him—or to them—to plan victories for God's cause. Their task was to trust God, not to do God's job for him. Abraham was succumbing to fear and, worse, resorting to expediency—he was, if you like, trying to guarantee his own salvation—when he should have been leaving the outcome to God.

The Bible does not idealize its heroes and can at times turn a very jaundiced eye on their weaknesses. That it does so in Abraham's case even before the first chapter devoted to him is ended speaks volumes for its realistic opinion of man's ability to save himself.

I finish with a quote from a study of Genesis written nearly a century ago which finely sums up the frightening message of this story of Abraham's pathetic failure so soon after his magnificent start on a life of faith. The author knows his

Scottish history well, as both his allusion to my home city and his closing citation (from an essay by Thomas Chalmers, the leader of the Disruption) show:

> It is recorded in history that Edinburgh Castle was supposed to be inaccessible on the precipitous side, and there the defences were feeble and the outlook careless, while on the weaker sides the fortifications were strong and the watch was strictly kept. But it was at the strongest, not the weakest point that the entrance was effected and the citadel captured. It is also on the strongest side that the citadel of man's soul is often captured. The weakness of God's servants is most conspicuous where their strength lies. Abraham, the most faithful of men, sinned by unfaithfulness; Moses, the meekest of men, by anger; Solomon, the wisest, by folly; Elijah, the most valiant, by fear; John, one of the gentlest, by vindictiveness; Peter, one of the boldest, by cowardice. Unguarded strength is double weakness. "We are not to walk in all the footsteps of the saints, but only in the footsteps of their faith."
>
> (from Dr. Strahan's Hebrew Ideals)

A Note on Genesis Chapters 12ff. as "History"

I must confess to feeling uneasy about the historical trustworthiness of this story of Abraham and Sarah in Egypt. For one thing, it has Abraham passing off his wife as his sister because she was an attractive woman, which is hardly consistent with the fact stressed elsewhere (e.g. 18:11) that both he and she were old. We need not believe *literally* that Abraham was seventy-five and Sarah sixty-five (see 17:17) when they left Harran and a hundred and seventy-five and a hundred and twenty-seven respectively when they died (see 25:7 and 23:1). Such exaggerated numbers like the even more exaggerated ones used of Adam, Noah and the rest earlier in Genesis seem to have been conventional in Hebrew tradition when referring to the distant days at the edge of human memory and beyond (see the commentary on chapter 5 in Volume 1). If they had a significance, it was to contrast the great figures of the past with the puny men and women of the present day. But convention apart, it is difficult to avoid the impression throughout Gen. 12ff. that neither Abraham nor his wife were, to put it mildly, in the first bloom of youth.

But even more suspicious is the mention of the Lord afflicting Pharaoh and his house with *plagues*. Add to this that it was a *famine* that led Abraham to go down to Egypt and that in spite of his relative obscurity as a minor nomadic chieftain he is pictured in direct confrontation with the *Pharaoh* himself, and the parallels with what happened later to Israel in the time of Joseph and Moses become too striking for comfort. This does not mean that we have to dismiss the story as a fabrication, but it does seem as though a visit made by Abraham to Egypt (quite likely to escape famine in Canaan—there is no reason why that should not have happened twice) has been rather outrageously "written up" to catch the interest of later Hebrew audiences with a nose for intriguing comparisons.

We get quite a lot of this kind of "writing up" in Gen. 12ff. (there is another and rather less edifying example coming soon in chapter 14), and it is only honest to acknowledge the fact right at the start of our study of these chapters. Biblical scholars tend to connect it with the "documents" which they find behind our present Genesis and which they identify by the well known labels "J" and "P" and (appearing in chapters 12ff. but not in 1–11) "E". But though in Volume 1 I spent some time pointing out where "J" and "P" are present in chapters 1–11, it does not seem to me necessary to be so academically precise in the case of the Patriarchal narratives. Because of the unique problems Gen. 1–11 raise at all sorts of levels, a very detailed treatment of these chapters had to be given, even at the risk of bringing in refinements of analysis which would normally only interest the specialist. With chapters 12ff., however, it is usually enough that the reader be guided to recognize where later "hands" have been at work without being burdened with the question of which document such and such a passage should be assigned to. Such a broad distinction between early and late is one that we can all appreciate, for we know from our own experience how stories "grow" in the telling. By making it in Gen. 12ff. we not only put ourselves into closer touch with the "real live" Abraham and Isaac and Jacob and Joseph but are freed in our own interpretation of the stories from falling prey to the exaggeration (as in this chapter) or the prejudice (as in chapter 14) which as the centuries passed they have drawn to themselves.

MAGNANIMITY

Genesis 13:1-18

1 So Abram went up from Egypt, he and his wife, and all that he had, and Lot with him, into the Negeb.

2,3 Now Abram was very rich in cattle, in silver, and in gold. And he journeyed on from the Negeb as far as Bethel, to the place where his 4 tent had been at the beginning, between Bethel and Ai, to the place where he had made an altar at the first; and there Abram called on 5 the name of the Lord. And Lot, who went with Abram, also had 6 flocks and herds and tents, so that the land could not support both of them dwelling together; for their possessions were so great that 7 they could not dwell together, and there was strife between the herdsmen of Abram's cattle and the herdsmen of Lot's cattle. At that time the Canaanites and the Perizzites dwelt in the land.

8 Then Abram said to Lot, "Let there be no strife between you and me, and between your herdsmen and my herdsmen; for we are 9 kinsmen. Is not the whole land before you? Separate yourself from me. If you take the left hand, then I will go to the right; or if you take 10 the right hand, then I will go to the left." And Lot lifted up his eyes, and saw that the Jordan valley was well watered everywhere like the garden of the Lord, like the land of Egypt, in the direction of Zoar; 11 this was before the Lord destroyed Sodom and Gomorrah. So Lot chose for himself all the Jordan valley, and Lot journeyed east; thus 12 they separated from each other. Abram dwelt in the land of Canaan, while Lot dwelt among the cities of the valley and moved his tent as 13 far as Sodom. Now the men of Sodom were wicked, great sinners against the Lord.

14 The Lord said to Abram, after Lot had separated from him, "Lift up your eyes, and look from the place where you are, northward and 15 southward and eastward and westward; for all the land which you 16 see I will give to you and to your descendants for ever. I will make your descendants as the dust of the earth; so that if one can count the 17 dust of the earth, your descendants also can be counted. Arise, walk through the length and breadth of the land, for I will give it to you." 18 So Abram moved his tent, and came and dwelt by the oaks of Mamre, which are at Hebron; and there he built an altar to the Lord.

In stark contrast to the preceding story of Abraham in Egypt, in which his self-centredness is exposed and the irony of his punishment at Pharaoh's hand subtly underlined, this story of Abraham's renunciation of his right as the senior to choose where to settle shows him recovering the secret of his faith. Where in Egypt he had been unable to see beyond the needs of the moment, here at Bethel his vision is large again and he is prepared to leave the future to God. God rewards his magnanimity and faith with a renewal of the promise, and the ironies in the story are reserved for his younger kinsman Lot who is given the choice that Abraham refused, and chooses wrongly.

(i)

Verses 1–4 are introductory and could well be entitled a *pilgrimage of penitence*. Abraham was now relatively prosperous ("very rich" is probably a bit of an exaggeration), and we do not need to be reminded how he came by much of his new wealth. But it is his destination that is stressed. There is purpose in his "journeying on" this time, for he is aiming at the mountain east of Bethel "where his tent had been at the beginning" and "where he had made an altar at the first". And there he called on the name of the Lord.

The similar phrases "at the beginning" and "at the first" are strictly speaking inaccurate. For it was at Shechem further to the north that he had first experienced God's presence in the land of promise (12:6). But if anything the inaccuracy brings his urgency into greater prominence, an urgency caused earlier by an unceremonious Egyptian escort but now centred on God. For Bethel was nearer! The scene is redolent of the desire of the unquiet spirit to return from disgrace to grace, to be quit of life's compromises and breathe again the clean air of the place where faith had once been fresh and strong.

William Cowper catches the shame and the hope of it all in his hymn "O for a closer walk with God":

> Where is the blessedness I knew
>   When first I saw the Lord?
> Where is the soul-refreshing view
>   Of Jesus and his word?

(ii)

It is not certain that Lot had been with Abraham in Egypt, but
he is with him at Bethel. He is now a minor chieftain in his own
right, the famine is past, and he too is prospering.

The Patriarchs should not be thought of as camel-nomads
traversing vast areas of desert quickly like the Bedouin of
modern times (or the Midianites or Amalekites of the Bible).
They could use camels for special journeys when speed was of
the essence (as in chapter 24), but in general they followed a
pastoral economy based on flocks of sheep and goats and
sometimes herds of cattle. Their movements from place to place
would be measured and slow and largely dictated by the
availability of grass. They would go into the hilly and remoter
regions if they had to, but would prefer to stay in the lusher
valleys as long as they could arrange amicable terms with the
farming communities and townsmen who lived there permanently. On occasion they would quarrel with the settled population and be driven out, and frequently they must have quarrelled with each other, whether they were related by blood or
not. "We were here first!" "This is our bit of ground. We had it
last year!" The kind of scrapping which is described as taking
place between the retainers of Abraham and of Lot rings true to
the conditions of life in the Palestine of the time.

The two chiefs meet to try to reach an accommodation. They
agree that separation is the only solution. Abraham is distressed that members of the same tribal group should be
engaging in such unseemly strife and, though he is the senior, he
magnanimously allows Lot the prior choice of where to go.

Probably the place where they stood is a hill a little to the
south of the present-day village (Beitin) which is described by
Sir George Adam Smith as "one of the great view-points of
Palestine". From it the Jordan valley around Jericho and the
northern end of the Dead Sea are plainly visible. The implication of verse 10 is that at this period the Dead Sea did not yet
exist and that the valley extended as far south as Zoar, which
occupied a site now near the southern tip of the Sea. We shall be
looking later at the problems of the location and destruction of

the "cities of the plain" (see commentary on chapter 19). For the moment it is enough to note that Lot elected to go down into the valley and that he eventually ended up at Sodom. Abraham was left with the highlands, not by any means a barren area but certainly at first glance not nearly so attractive as the area chosen by Lot.

(iii)

But *at first glance* are the operative words, and the fatal consequences which were to flow from Lot's choice are cunningly foreshadowed in the story. The Jordan valley, we are told, was well watered like the garden of the Lord, in other words a veritable Eden. It is also compared with the land of Egypt, green and fructified by the gentle and beneficent Nile. But what had happened to Adam and Eve in Eden when they had made *their* false choice, and what to Abraham himself not long since in Egypt when he had made *his?* The paradox of the description would not be lost on a perceptive audience, and if it were, none but the most obtuse could miss the point of the naive-sounding sentence that follows the notice of Lot's arrival in Sodom. "Now the men of Sodom were wicked, great sinners against the Lord." Here begins the disintegration of Lot, his descent not to the valley of ease and luxury but to ignominy and disaster as he becomes history's first backslider from the faith, the man without the pilgrim spirit.

How different is the prospect which the story lovingly holds out for Abraham because once more he has put his hand in the hand of God! The Lord invites him to look around at the clean and vigorous hill-country of Judah to the south and of Ephraim to the north (Bethel straddled the two), not so luxuriant as the meadows below but perfectly capable of supplying his and his clan's every need. This was his inheritance, and he was entering upon it. Proudly he walks through it. We need not imagine him visiting every corner of what was later to become the Holy Land. It was the exhilarating experience of knowing that this land would belong to his descendants that mattered to him, not its exact dimensions, and of hearing that these descendants would be in number like the dust of the earth. There *may* be just a hint of a warning in the use of the word "dust", reminding the audience even as they relished this happy scene of man's creatureliness (see 2:7 and 3:19), but it is swallowed up in Abraham's joy as he moves about the land and finally settles in Hebron, some thirty miles south of Bethel right in the centre of the Judean hills.

And there again he builds an altar to the Lord. The last words of this story sum up its abiding message. Greatness of spirit and fellowship with God go together, as do their opposites, selfishness and apostasy.

VICTORY

Genesis 14:1-24

1 In the days of Amraphel king of Shinar, Ari-och king of Ellasar,
2 Ched-or-laomer king of Elam, and Tidal king of Goiim, these kings made war with Bera king of Sodom, Birsha king of Gomorrah, Shinab king of Admah, Shemeber king of Zeboiim, and the king of
3 Bela (that is, Zoar). And all these joined forces in the Valley of
4 Siddim (that is, the Salt Sea). Twelve years they had served Ched-or-
5 laomer, but in the thirteenth year they rebelled. In the fourteenth year Ched-or-laomer and the kings who were with him came and subdued the Rephaim in Ashteroth-karnaim, the Zuzim in Ham, the
6 Emim in Shaveh-kiriathaim, and the Horites in their Mount Seir as
7 far as El-paran on the border of the wilderness; then they turned back and came to En-mish-pat (that is, Kadesh), and subdued all the country of the Amalekites, and also the Amorites who dwelt in
8 Hazazon-tamar. Then the king of Sodom, the king of Gomorrah, the king of Admah, the king of Zeboiim, and the king of Bela (that is, Zoar) went out, and they joined battle in the Valley of Siddim
9 with Ched-or-laomer king of Elam, Tidal king of Goiim, Amraphel king of Shinar, and Ari-och king of Ellasar, four kings against five.
10 Now the Valley of Siddim was full of bitumen pits; and as the kings of Sodom and Gomorrah fled, some fell into them, and the rest fled
11 to the mountain. So the enemy took all the goods of Sodom and
12 Gomorrah, and all their provisions, and went their way; they also

took Lot, the son of Abram's brother who dwelt in Sodom, and his goods, and departed.

13 Then one who had escaped came, and told Abram the Hebrew, who was living by the oaks of Mamre the Amorite, brother of Eshcol

14 and of Aner; these were allies of Abram. When Abram heard that his kinsman had been taken captive, he led forth his trained men, born in his house, three hundred and eighteen of them, and went in

15 pursuit as far as Dan. And he divided his forces against them by night, he and his servants, and routed them and pursued them to

16 Hobah, north of Damascus. Then he brought back all the goods, and also brought back his kinsman Lot with his goods, and the women and the people.

17 After his return from the defeat of Ched-or-laomer and the kings who were with him, the king of Sodom went out to meet him at the

18 Valley of Shaveh (that is, the King's Valley). And Melchizedek king of Salem brought out bread and wine; he was priest of God Most

19 High. And he blessed him and said,

"Blessed be Abram by God Most High,
    maker of heaven and earth;

20   and blessed be God Most High,
    who has delivered your enemies into your hand!"

21 And Abram gave him a tenth of everything. And the king of Sodom said to Abram, "Give me the persons, but take the goods for

22 yourself." But Abram said to the king of Sodom, "I have sworn to

23 the Lord God Most High, maker of heaven and earth, that I would not take a thread or a sandal-thong or anything that is yours, lest

24 you should say, 'I have made Abram rich.' I will take nothing but what the young men have eaten, and the share of the men who went with me; let Aner, Eshcol, and Mamre take their share."

The next story shows Abraham still concerned about his errant nephew. The core of it is a raid mounted by him against a huge army which had invaded southern Palestine, defeated the king of Sodom and his allies, and carried off much booty and many prisoners. Among the latter was Lot, who was being given his first taste of what the pleasant life he had chosen could lead to. Abraham pursues the army as it withdraws northwards, puts it to flight, rescues Lot and the other prisoners, and recovers the captured booty. But it is what happens after this famous victory that really interests the story-teller, when Abraham on his return meets the king of the future Jerusalem. This confrontation puts a larger significance on a local event and forcibly makes us think of the promise of "blessing" in 12:2-3 and what it means for the world.

(i)

For once we are given in a story about Abraham the kind of specific detail that a historian likes to have. The first eleven verses read like a transcript from an ancient chronicle, one so ancient indeed that places and peoples in the area had to be identified by their later names so that those listening to the story would be able to follow what was going on.

It is unfortunate that so far none of the great monarchs, who came from as far away as Elam (Persia) and Shinar (Babylonia), has been certainly equated with any known ruler. But a careful analysis of the account shows that they did not come simply to put down a revolt among five petty kings in the region of Sodom and Gomorrah, but to subdue the whole area of Transjordan and southern Judah (see Map 1). It is probable that this expedition, like the one twelve years previously, had as its purpose the safeguarding of trade routes, particularly the great "King's Highway" south from Damascus (where it joined the "way to the sea" mentioned earlier) to the Gulf of Aqabah and so on to the fabled land of Sheba in southern Arabia; see Num. 20:17 and 21:22. Content that it had sufficiently "shown the flag", the imperial army turned back at the Gulf, made a detour through the Negeb and reached the Valley of Siddim, which according to verse 3 lay through what was later to be the Dead Sea. It was there that it defeated the forces of the local kings in a pitched battle.

Probably the old chronicle ended at this point and what follows is derived from Hebrew tradition. It tells how "one who had escaped", presumably one of Lot's men, took the news to Abraham at Hebron, not a great distance away, though up in the hills. With a mere three hundred or so men he hurried after the victorious army and did what the five minor kings had

been unable to do, smashed it and set it scurrying home-
wards.

(ii)

There is nothing odd in Abraham fighting when he had to. He
was a real man living in a real world and his kinsman was in
danger. But routing a whole army! This must be an exaggeration, designed to point up Abraham as the equal, indeed the
superior, of the four emperors. The audience would enjoy the
idea of it immensely and see in it a sign that the "blessing" was
working. But it is in fact much more likely that Abraham's
small band merely attacked the rear of the retiring column
where the prisoners and the booty would have been kept.
Hobah north of Damascus was probably therefore not where
they got tired of the pursuit but where after a number of
unsuccessful forays they finally managed to effect Lot's rescue.

It was a considerable feather in Abraham's cap, and reminds
us that his display of cowardice in Egypt was only one side of his
character. But though those hearing the story later may have
liked to think of him as such, he is hardly convincing as God's
warrior scattering alien powers and annihilating the enemies of
the faith.

BLESSING

Genesis 14:1-24 *(cont'd)*

(iii)

There follows the blessing pronounced on Abraham by Melchizedek, the king of Salem. The story speaks first of the king of
Sodom going out to congratulate an Abraham flushed with
success, and meeting him in a valley near Jerusalem which was
later called the King's Valley (it is mentioned in 2 Sam. 18:18).
But then suddenly Melchizedek appears, bringing refresh-
ments, and blesses Abraham in the name of God Most High, his
own pagan deity who it was, he claims, had given Abraham his

victory and who it is, he implies, would similarly aid him in the future.

It is not really, if we are honest, a pretty scene, and it can only have strengthened the triumphalist thoughts the audience were already thinking. The incident is referred to again in Ps. 110:4 where God is said to have sworn an oath to David and his successors, "You are a priest forever after the order of Melchizedek". That Psalm promises the Davidic prince God's help in making his enemies his footstool (verse 1), appoints him to rule in the midst of his foes (verse 2), and invites him to stand at God's right hand while he scatters kings on the day of his wrath and fills the nations with corpses (verses 5-6). The name *El Elyon* or "God Most High" is known from the Ras Shamra tablets as a title of El, the head of the Canaanite pantheon (Baal was his son). Apparently El was the favourite deity of Canaanite Jerusalem and this title of his was transferred to the God of Israel after the city had been captured by David. It is used of him, for instance, in Ps. 57:2. But in the time of the Patriarchs, of course, as the audience must have realized, it could only refer to the Canaanite El.

The story in Gen. 14 is pretending, therefore, that Melchizedek, though a pagan, worshipped under a different name the same Creator God as Abraham, and it sees him standing here for his Hebrew successors, David, Solomon, and the other kings of Israel, and (he is a priest too) for the High Priest of the Jerusalem Temple. In the person of their predecessor Melchizedek these bless the forefather of the race, and in giving Melchizedek a tenth of the booty Abraham in his turn foreshadows the loyal Israelites who in later times would bring tithes of all they possessed to the sanctuary.

(iv)

The Epistle to the Hebrews goes even further than this, and with its well known love of symbolism suggests (in chapter 7) that Abraham was in effect paying homage from afar to Jesus Christ, who was the only true king of Israel and the only true priest of his people, and therefore the only true successor of the mysterious Melchizedek. This most imaginative of all the New Testament books makes great play with many verses and passages in the Old Testament in its attempt to explain to the early Christians how Jesus fulfilled it.

In this instance, however, I think we would do well to admit that it has not made the happiest choice of passage. Gen. 14 shows us the Old Testament at its worst, glorying in Israel's and Jerusalem's special position in God's esteem and savouring the earthly victories over all the other nations which he would give his people. It takes an old legend of a rare success of arms on Abraham's part and a consequent meeting between him and the king of the then still pagan Jerusalem, and blows it up out of all proportion in the interests of what can only be described as Jewish propaganda.

If this is what the promise of "blessing" means, I for one want no part of it. It is not a whit better than the triumphalist and materialist Christian hymns we were criticizing some pages ago, and I suspect that both it and they owe more to the sinful Adam in God's people than to the inspiration of his Spirit. The story-tellers of Genesis do not spare the Patriarchs when they fall from grace. We should be prepared to acknowledge that they themselves can sometimes also fall from grace—and with quite a thud!

(v)

Thankfully, the meeting between Abraham and the king of Sodom is a more realistic one. The defeated ruler makes what he thinks is a generous offer, asking only for his people back but allowing Abraham to keep the booty. But he is in no position to be making any offers, and Abraham with supreme contempt reminds him of this. What right had he to suppose that he could put Abraham in his debt? He would take only what would cover, as we might say, his and his men's expenses.

Abraham comes out of this stirring exploit rather well, ready to take up arms on his nephew's behalf while at the same time clearly despising the kind of life he had chosen to make down in Sodom and the kind of people among whom he had settled. It tells us quite a lot about him and the things he held dear. It is a pity that the story was not content to leave it at that.

A Note on the Title "Hebrews"

When Abraham is given the title Hebrew in Gen. 14, it is the first time it is used in the Bible. Indeed, apart from a few isolated occurrences, it appears only here and in two other distinct contexts, namely as a designation of the clans in Egypt (e.g. Gen 39:14; 40:15; 41:12; 43:32; Exod. 2:6, 11, 13; 3:18; 5:3) and of early Israel during its wars with the Philistines (e.g. 1 Sam. 4:6, 9; 13:3, 19; 14:11, 21; 29:3). It is not nearly so common, for instance, as "Israelites" or, as we should more accurately translate, "sons" or "children of Israel".

This frugal usage was once thought puzzling, but archaeological discovery has shown that the Biblical tradition is in this, as in many other respects, remarkably reliable. For "Hebrews" is in fact the same word as the Mesopotamian *Khabiru* and the Egyptian *Apiru*, terms found frequently in external sources of the second millennium B.C. to describe the various migrating or nomadic peoples of the age. The term is not racial, for the people called *Khabiru* or *Apiru* included not only Semites in their ranks but the members of several ethnic groups. It is rather a sociological designation, the nearest modern equivalent being perhaps "refugees" or "displaced persons". It probably means "those who pass or cross (frontiers)".

Though in later Biblical times the title was assumed to be a racial one describing only Israelites (and their language), it seems from their restricted use of it that the old story-tellers of the tribes had been aware of its original non-ethnic application. Thus Gen. 14 calls Abraham a "Hebrew" because with his raid on the army of the four emperors he was acting like a typical nomadic "malcontent" taking advantage of the unsettled conditions of his time. Similarly, the Israelites in Egypt were called "Hebrews" because they were foreigners temporarily resident in the land, something akin to the so-called "guest workers" from Turkey or Algeria in present-day Germany and France. And finally, the invading clans in the period of the Judges were called "Hebrews" because to other more firmly established powers like the Philistines they may well have appeared as a passing nuisance from outside, who would soon be gone.

"Arameans" (Deut. 26:5) by race, the Patriarchs then were "Hebrews" in their way of life. As to "sons of Israel", it is properly

speaking a tribal designation, referring to the group or confederation of clans who considered themselves descended from Jacob or
Israel, though it too later became an ethnic and national term. But
this did not happen until after the establishment of a monarchy
when "Israel" replaced the older Canaan as the name for Palestine.

RIGHTEOUSNESS

Genesis 15:1–6

1 After these things the word of the Lord came to Abram in a vision,
  "Fear not, Abram, I am your shield; your reward shall be very
2 great." But Abram said, "O Lord God, what wilt thou give me, for I
  continue childless, and the heir of my house is Eliezer of Damas-
3 cus?" And Abram said, "Behold, thou hast given me no offspring;
4 and a slave born in my house will be my heir." And behold, the word
  of the Lord came to him, "This man shall not be your heir; your own
5 son shall be your heir." And he brought him outside and said, "Look
  toward heaven, and number the stars, if you are able to number
6 them." Then he said to him, "So shall your descendants be." And he
  believed the Lord; and he reckoned it to him as righteousness.

In most of the places in Genesis where God is said to renew his
promises to Abraham a few words of repetition suffice. In this
chapter there is a lot more overt doctrinal interest. We do not
have just a straightforward story, and one suspects that theological hands as well as story-telling hands have been at work
on the tradition. We get the same feeling with the next chapter
but one (17). We are used in Genesis to finding our theology
indirectly, in the same way that, for instance, Jesus gives us
theology in his parables. In these chapters it protrudes rather
more, as it sometimes does in Paul's letters.

(i)

The chapter is loosely linked with the preceding one by the
words "after these things", but it does not seem to have the
events related there specifically in mind. The first six verses
show us Abraham not in the aftermath of success but thoroughly disillusioned with life and not a little apprehensive about the

future. God speaks to him in a vision or dream and tells him not to be afraid, for he will be his shield to protect him and will give him a great reward. Clearly time has moved on and the elation of victory has given way to depression and anxiety. At any rate Abraham's reply is querulous, if not downright satirical. He asks God what in effect will be the use of such a reward seeing that he has no son to succeed him. Presumably still within the vision God takes Abraham outside, points to the stars in the heavens and says, "So shall your descendants be." This is enough for Abraham, and he is reassured. The narrator (for the words are not in inverted commas) then adds the comment that God reckoned this profession of faith to him as righteousness.

(ii)

Abraham's statement that his heir was a slave of his called Eliezer used to perplex the scholars. No rule that a slave could inherit in the absence of children was known among the Hebrews or their neighbours. Evidence from the Hurrian (Biblical Horite) city of Nuzi east of the Tigris in Mesopotamia has remedied this deficiency. Excavations conducted there have unearthed archives of an administrative or legal nature, many of which concern marriage and adoption. A custom that was relatively common was the adoption by a childless couple of a friend or on occasion even a slave, who undertook to tend them in their old age and see to it that they had a proper burial, in return for which he was named as their heir. Clearly Abraham must have entered into an arrangement of this kind with Eliezer.

The Nuzi texts date from the fifteenth century B.C. and supply a welcome confirmation of the reliability of the Biblical tradition in this particular. But more important than that for the meaning of the passage is the real question mark which Abraham's arrangement puts against his faith. In Egypt he had shown his lack of faith by his pretence that Sarah was his sister (12:10ff.). Now, it transpires, he has so little confidence in God that he has just made a deal with one of his own servants in case he should die without a son.

(iii)

It is against this background of despondency and doubt on
Abraham's part that we have to understand the famous sentence, "And he believed the Lord; and he reckoned it to him as
righteousness." We should not too quickly remove it from its
context and make it a proof text for our ideas of what faith and
righteousness are over against someone else's. St. Paul uses it
twice, in Rom. 4:3 and Gal. 3:6, to back up his great doctrine of
justification by faith rather than by works. James also uses it
(2:23) but, while agreeing that faith is vital, he adds that "faith
apart from works is dead" (verse 26). It is a moot point whether
either is in touch with the primary thrust of this passage.

The controversy in which Paul and James were engaged was
one that racked the early Church and that came to prominence
again at the time of the Reformation. In the early Church it
turned on the question whether one had first to become a Jew
and keep the Law of Moses before one could become a
Christian. Undoubtedly Paul was right in asserting that faith in
Christ was enough, but he did rather overstate his case, as if
keeping the Law hardly mattered, and James' commonsense
rejoinder that a faith that did not issue in Christian behaviour
was no real faith was needed to redress the balance. Similarly
Martin Luther was right when he attacked the mediaeval
practice of buying credit with God through indulgences and
opposed it with his cry of "faith alone". But he also tended to
overdo it and to cast aspersions on "works", as when he called
the Epistle of James with its down-to-earth practicality an
"epistle of straw".

The contrast in this passage is not, however, between faith
and works, but between faith and absence of faith. The passage
is commending Abraham's faith in God's promises or, to put it
at its simplest, his conviction that things would turn out God's
way even when all the evidence pointed in the opposite direction. Abraham had been sorely tempted to abandon his faith
and dispose his affairs on the assumption that he would have no
son to follow him. His own and his wife's age told him that this
was the sensible thing to do. But after his visionary experience

he recovered his faith and, we must assume, revoked his deed of will in Eliezer's favour. He retreated just in time from the brink of unbelief and was able to face the future with fresh fortitude.

It is thus not so much Abraham's mere act of faith that attracts the narrator's admiration as his clawing his way back to faith after a long and desperate struggle with himself. He is writing presumably after the establishment of the Mosaic Law and is giving it as his opinion that this struggle and its successful outcome deserved the accolade of "righteousness" every bit as much as would in his day a lifelong devotion to the commandments of God (compare Deut. 6:25). This was a daring thought for any Hebrew, with his race's well-known and deep-seated attachment to the Law as the believer's route to God, to think and, if pressed to its logical conclusion, it can be made to fit in neatly enough with Paul's doctrine of justification. I doubt, however, whether the writer meant it to be taken that way. It is the fight of faith not the nature of faith that is his chief concern.

That God on this occasion does not punish Abraham either for his questioning or for his deal with Eliezer confirms this. For his lapse of faith in Egypt Abraham had been taught a short, sharp lesson. Here he is treated with compassion, for God knows that he was not with his rash talk and even rasher action trying this time to do his work for him but was laying bare the black despair of his soul. When we are able in the midst of our doubts and agonies of spirit to cast all our cares upon God and leave them there entirely, we will have gone through something of what Abraham went through and will have some inkling with the theologian who penned verse 6 of what having faith and being righteous are all about.

COVENANT

Genesis 15:7-21

7 And he said to him, "I am the Lord who brought you from Ur of the
8 Chaldeans, to give you this land to possess." But he said, "O Lord
9 God, how am I to know that I shall possess it?" He said to him,

"Bring me a heifer three years old, a she-goat three years old, a ram
10 three years old, a turtledove, and a young pigeon." And he brought
him all these, cut them in two, and laid each half over against the
11 other; but he did not cut the birds in two. And when birds of prey
came down upon the carcasses, Abram drove them away.

12 As the sun was going down, a deep sleep fell on Abram; and lo, a
13 dread and great darkness fell upon him. Then the Lord said to
Abram, "Know of a surety that your descendants will be sojourners
in a land that is not theirs, and will be slaves there, and they will be
14 oppressed for four hundred years; but I will bring judgment on the
nation which they serve, and afterward they shall come out with
15 great possessions. As for yourself, you shall go to your fathers in
16 peace; you shall be buried in a good old age. And they shall come
back here in the fourth generation; for the iniquity of the Amorites is
not yet complete."

17 When the sun had gone down and it was dark, behold, a smoking
18 fire pot and a flaming torch passed between these pieces. On that day
the Lord made a covenant with Abram, saying, "To your descendants I give this land, from the river of Egypt to the great river, the
19 river Euphrates, the land of the Kenites, the Kenizzites, the Kad-
20 monites, the Hittites, the Perizzites, the Rephaim, the Amorites, the
21 Canaanites, the Girgashites and the Jebusites."

The second part of the chapter relates another visionary
experience which Abraham underwent. It is joined directly to
the first six verses in a manner that makes us assume that it must
have happened on the same occasion. But this is probably not
the case. For one thing, the promise with which it is concerned
is not the immediate one of the birth of a son but that of the land
and of its possession by Abraham's descendants in a more
remote future. For another, the timing of the vision is different.
In verses 1–6 the vision most likely took place in the middle of
the night, since the stars in the heavens play a not unimportant
role in it. In verses 7ff., on the other hand, the sun is just going
down as the "deep sleep" falls on Abraham.

(i)

As in verses 1–6 Abraham seems to be in a sceptical frame of
mind, for after he is told that "he" would possess this land, he

asks for some sign that would indicate to him that this was more than a pious hope. There follows an account of a peculiar religious ceremony in which Abraham is instructed to lay the severed halves of three animals opposite one another, and to set down beside them a turtledove and a young pigeon. Night approaches and—a realistic touch this!—Abraham drives away the vultures who had arrived to feed from the carcasses. A "deep sleep" or trance falls on him (the same word is used of Adam in 2:21) and he hears God rehearsing solemnly and in some detail what was to happen to him and his descendants in years to come and how they would finally take over the land. Then, still in the trance, he witnesses a smoking fire pot and a flaming torch (which presumably represent the deity) passing between the severed animals, and he hears God promising once again that he would give the land to his descendants and adding the information that it would stretch from the river of Egypt (not the Nile but a *wady* or broòk west of Gaza mentioned in 1 Kgs. 8:65) to the Euphrates.

There is no reason to doubt that Abraham had the vivid experience described in these verses and passed on a report of it to his family. We have to remember that Abraham was an oriental and that such ecstatic withdrawals from consciousness are a not uncommon feature of many eastern religions. The little bit about having to drive off the birds of prey particularly has an authentic ring to it. But what was the point of it all?

The ceremony which he partially prepared and partially witnessed in a vision was not a sacrifice but a rite to ratify a solemn agreement. We have another reference to such a rite in Jer. 34:18–20. The Babylonians under Nebuchadnezzar were besieging Jerusalem at the time and the populace was in desperate straits. The king, hoping perhaps to unite the whole city in its own defence, made a proclamation that all slave-owners should release their slaves, and it seems that a calf was cut in two and the burghers passed between it to underline the seriousness of their intent. They were in effect inviting God to cut them in two like the calf if they did not keep the bargain they had struck. But as it turned out, the approach of an Egyptian force caused the Babylonians to lift the siege temporarily, and the citizens grabbed their slaves back. The prophet Jeremiah was moved to announce in God's name that the Egyptians would soon be gone and that the fate they had wished upon themselves in the ceremony would then befall them—and quickly!

Of course the idea of God taking an oath against himself is inconceivable. But that Abraham should in his vision see God—or rather the two mysterious fiery objects which represented him—passing between the separate pieces of the animals he had laid out was clearly to him, as it would be to every Hebrew after him, a highly significant symbolism. It was the sign he had craved. It meant that God was entering into a treaty or, as the Bible usually says, a covenant with him. By his willingness to go through in front of his servant a procedure similar to the one by which men sealed their human bargains, God was letting him know that nothing could stand in the way of the fulfilment of his promises, for his own divine honour was at stake in the matter.

(ii)

It is not nearly so certain, however, that God actually said in the vision what the Bible reports him to have said. That he should revive his servant's drooping faith by appearing to him in so dramatic a fashion is one thing. That he should then go on to sketch out the history of the next two or three centuries in a way that almost removed the need for Abraham to have faith at all is quite another. How could it possibly rebound to the credit of Abraham's faith if he knew beforehand not only about the sojourn of his descendants in Egypt and their enslavement and exodus from there but the extent of Israel's boundaries at their widest ever in the distant reign of Solomon (see 1 Kgs. 4:21)?

It is clear that later hands have considerably expanded the old traditions at this point. The expanded text is not really speaking to Abraham but to a much later Hebrew audience and trying to explain for them the long period that they knew had elapsed between Abraham's time and the actual conquest of

Canaan begun by Joshua. The Amorites (an alternative term for the Canaanites) had to have their little hour upon the world's stage, an opportunity, as it were, to set it beyond dispute how wicked they were. Only then could God allow his own people to dispossess them. There is profound theology about God's rule in the events of history behind this explanation, but it is not for all that a very nice theology. God's interest in the Canaanites is restricted to waiting until they deserved the punishment he had marked down for them.

Nor is the forecast about the extent of the Holy Land any nicer. It is making a claim that the boundaries attained by the state of Israel for only the briefest of periods under Solomon were those which God had fixed long before when he made his promise to the first forefather of the race. It is difficult not to catch the strain of the same nasty triumphalist notes, which we have already on more than one occasion had to deplore, sounding through the text.

(iii)

The two renewals of the promise recorded in this chapter were of vital importance to Abraham. They enabled him to battle on through disbelief towards belief, through scepticism towards trust, through doubt towards the conviction that God and he were inseparably covenanted together. They have both solace and hope to offer all who today fight the good fight of faith against what seem to them to be insuperable odds. But their message has not been improved by the explanations which Israel's scholars, however well meaning, have seen fit to add to them. In the case of the first the comment about righteousness has as often as not been misunderstood by Christian theology. In the case of the second the words put in God's mouth have fanned a "superiority" complex which no believer who understood God's ways with men ought ever to have espoused at all.

JEALOUSY

Genesis 16:1-6

1 Now Sarai, Abram's wife, bore him no children. She had an

2 Egyptian maid whose name was Hagar; and Sarai said to Abram,
"Behold now, the Lord has prevented me from bearing children; go
in to my maid; it may be that I shall obtain children by her." And
3 Abram hearkened to the voice of Sarai. So, after Abram had dwelt
ten years in the land of Canaan, Sarai, Abram's wife, took Hagar the
Egyptian, her maid, and gave her to Abram her husband as a wife.
4 And he went in to Hagar, and she conceived; and when she saw that
5 she had conceived, she looked with contempt on her mistress. And
Sarai said to Abram, "May the wrong done to me be on you! I gave
my maid to your embrace, and when she saw that she had conceived,
she looked on me with contempt. May the Lord judge between you
6 and me!" But Abram said to Sarai, "Behold, your maid is in your
power; do to her as you please." Then Sarai dealt harshly with her,
and she fled from her.

With this chapter the poignancy of Abraham's desire for a son
is brought firmly into the centre of the stage. This desire had
been behind Abraham's despairing pact with his servant Eliezer
related at the beginning of the last chapter. But having then
gently led him to abandon his despair and find his faith again,
God now "hardens his heart" and really begins to "turn the
screw" on his chosen one. His wife suggests to him that he have
a child by her maid. Could this be the answer? Tragic consequences have to ensue and work themselves out over many years
before it becomes plain to all concerned that it was not.

(i)

We must not judge Sarah's action in giving Hagar to Abraham
by our standards of morality. For its time it was a not unusual
thing to do, even if barrenness had not been a factor.

As far as we can tell, monogamy was the most common form
of marriage in ancient Israel, but neither polygamy nor concu-
binage was at any time illegal. Jacob had two wives, Leah and
Rachel, and each of them gave him her maid as a concubine.
Samuel's father also had two wives, one of them barren (1 Sam.
1:2); Esau had three (Gen. 36:2-3); Gideon had "many" wives
and at least one concubine (Judg. 8:30-31); and it is well known
that several of Israel's kings kept large harems. There is even a
small section of the Law (Deut. 21:15-17) which, while not

exactly commending it, recognizes polygamy (or at any rate bigamy) as a legal fact.

The presence of children of more than one mother in a household not surprisingly led to conflicts about the inheritance. The general rule was that the eldest son received a double share (Deut. 21:17). Otherwise the sons of full wives had equal rights. Daughters did not inherit except where there was no male issue. Nor did the sons of concubines. However, in their case the father was entitled to make special provision and in effect adopt them as legal sons, if he so desired. This is what happened with the sons of the slave-women Zilpah and Bilhah, who were given equal rank with those of Leah and Rachel by being summoned with them to Jacob's sick-bed to hear his dying wishes (Gen. 49:1ff.).

It is likely that Sarah meant any sons born to Hagar to be treated in this way, since she says, "It may be that *I* shall obtain children by her". Abraham, too, seems to have looked on the arrangement in that light for, though Sarah changed her mind as soon as Hagar was with child and he let her, he eventually recognized Ishmael as his full son and even after the birth of Isaac apparently intended that Ishmael should share the inheritance with him (see 21:11).

(ii)

These considerations obviously have a bearing on how we should assess the participants' motives and actions in the present story.

Sarah's sorrow, even shame, at her childlessness has to be inferred. But in common with Rachel (Gen. 30:1-2) and Hannah (1 Sam. 1:5) she must have regarded it as a disgrace, both an affront to her husband and a chastisement from heaven. See also 21:6-7. How could she do otherwise when the society to which she belonged so prized the birth of children, and especially sons, that when a young woman left her family to be married she was blessed with these words: "Our sister, be the mother of thousands of ten thousands" (Gen. 24:60)? But why in that case had she waited so long before allowing Abraham

access to her maid, even letting him enter into an agreement
with Eliezer? Was it her own faith in God's promise, now alas
dissipated? Or was it simply pride? It is impossible to say. But
whatever the reason, she now gives her slave-girl to her husband
and settles resignedly for descendants by proxy.

Or so it seems. For when Hagar falls pregnant, she suspects
that her erstwhile slave is crowing over her and uses her so
harshly that the girl is forced to flee. This is much more than
mere envy like Rachel's of Leah and Hannah's of Peninnah,
two childless women who were also provoked by their "rivals"
(1 Sam. 1:6). It is a complete *volte-face,* making a nonsense of
whatever motive she may have had in giving her maid to
Abraham in the first place. She even implicates her husband
("May the Lord judge between you and me!") and suggests that
it was his pressure on her that led her to do it. We would not, I
think, be too severe on her by applying to this desperate and
pathetic woman the lines addressed by Iago to Othello:

> O! beware, my lord, of jealousy;
> It is the green-ey'd monster which doth mock
> The meat it feeds on.

(iii)

But can we be any kinder on Abraham? At first sight it looks as
if we should. He responded to his wife's suggestion with what
might seem to us rather too much alacrity and, knowing the
outcome as we do, we cannot help reading the sentence "And
Abraham hearkened to the voice of Sarah" in an ominous light.
We have to remember, however, that in the society of the time it
was a recognized method of securing issue and that the issue so
obtained could easily be made legitimate. Moreover, if his
wife's words to him later are anything to go by, it was clearly not
the first occasion on which he had entertained the idea. It does
appear that following his experience at the time he had made his
pact with Eliezer, a son by a concubine was how he now saw
God's promise working itself out, and that out of deference to
Sarah's feelings he had simply been waiting for her to accept the
inevitable. From his standpoint there was nothing reprehensi-

ble in what he was doing. There was no question of this being a faithless expedient, for it could not be doubted that any son he had by Hagar would be his own.

However, how does he react when Hagar becomes pregnant and Sarah decides to be rid of her? He had been ready to accept Hagar's child as the child of promise. Yet he stood idly by, a man in a male-dominated society, and let all his hopes for the future crash once again to the ground through his wife's jealousy and vindictiveness. And he allowed this pregnant girl, a stranger in a strange land, whose status and that of her unborn child depended entirely on his whim, whom he had not long since bedded, and whose only fault had been a little pardonable bragging, to be driven from his home. It was a craven display of cowardice far worse than he showed in Egypt, for his adversaries here were but two women, not the Pharaoh and his guards. How could he possibly rest now in his recovered faith?

In these few verses the laconic story-teller does a thorough hatchet-job on the father and mother of God's chosen people. It is worthy of Jane Austen at her most savage, and how can we complain that it was not fully merited? Rather, it should make us think with some trepidation about the kind of people God works his wonders on, and that among others means ourselves.

PROVIDENCE

Genesis 16:7-16

7 The angel of the Lord found her by a spring of water in the
8 wilderness, the spring on the way to Shur. And he said, "Hagar, maid of Sarai, where have you come from and where are you going?"
9 She said, "I am fleeing from my mistress Sarai." The angel of the
10 Lord said to her, "Return to your mistress, and submit to her." The angel of the Lord also said to her, "I will so greatly multiply your
11 descendants that they cannot be numbered for multitude." And the angel of the Lord said to her, "Behold, you are with child, and shall bear a son; you shall call his name Ishmael; because the Lord has
12 given heed to your affliction. He shall be a wild ass of a man, his

hand against every man and every man's hand against him; and he
13 shall dwell over against all his kinsmen." So she called the name of
the Lord who spoke to her, "Thou art a God of seeing"; for she said,
"Have I really seen God and remained alive after seeing him?"
14 Therefore the well was called Beer-lahai-roi; it lies between Kadesh
and Bered.
15 And Hagar bore Abram a son; and Abram called the name of his
16 son, whom Hagar bore, Ishmael. Abram was eighty-six years old
when Hagar bore Ishmael to Abram.

In complete contrast to his savage irony at the expense of
Abraham and Sarah, the writer treats Hagar with compassion
and sympathy. There are several features of his story—the
appearance of an angel, the play on Ishmael's name (which like
most Hebrew names is in fact a little statement of belief), the
attachment of the incident to a sacred site—which regularly
appear in the early tales of the Bible, and which reflect ancient
Semitic interests and customs. These are a little off-putting to a
modern reader but, if we make allowance for them, we cannot
help appreciating the delicacy that marks the second half of the
chapter compared with its opening verses.

(i)

Hagar, too, is implicated in the tragedy to follow. She was not
able to hide from her mistress her feelings of triumph or to
prevent herself provoking her sorely and irritating her as,
according to 1 Sam. 1:6, Peninnah did Hannah "because the
Lord had closed her womb". Most of it may have been only in
Sarah's mind, but it was cruel and foolish of her nonetheless.
But it did not deserve the fearful punishment meted out to her,
to be banished without rights or status in a land that was not her
own and where, if she had not returned to her mistress, she
would surely have died before her infant was born. She was an
Egyptian and was clearly making for home along the "way to
Shur" (see Exod. 15:22), the caravan route from Hebron via
Beersheba to the Nile Delta, but she would have had little
chance of making it across the dry territory of the Negeb.
However, she did return, and it was at God's prompting. A

foreigner by birth, she would have been expected to follow
Abraham's religion when she entered his wife's service, and she
probably already knew something about the high hopes for the
future which Abraham's God had put in her master's heart.
And now in the desert he was speaking to her and using the kind
of words she had many a time heard Abraham repeating to
himself and Sarah! She too would have numberless descendants and the son to be born to her would have a great future,
though he would be a fierce man who would not make friends
easily. The boy's name, Ishmael, meaning "God has heard",
would in time to come recall to her mind this frightening yet
marvellous experience of hers, as would the name she used of
God—*El Roi* or "The God who sees". This is a name of the same
type as *El Shaddai* used in the next chapter (17:1) and indeed as
Melchizedek's *El Elyon* or "God Most High" (14:18), and was
probably already a familiar name to Abraham's family and
clan.

We would very much like to know what transpired when she
returned to Abraham's encampment and had her baby. The
next chapter (see 17:18) suggests that Abraham at least was
ashamed of what he had done and welcomed her, and acknowledged Ishmael when he was born. Presumably she told him
about the angel's message. But did he or did he not conclude
from it that Ishmael was not, as he had hoped, the son of
promise? And if he did how did this affect his celebrated faith?
And what of Sarah? Did she relent and receive her kindly, and
only resume her jealousy and hatred (see 21:9ff.) after Isaac was
born? Was it a happy household again, at any rate for a time?
Could it be a happy household again after such a near tragedy?
Frustratingly, and not for the first time, the Bible does not
inform us. But we would be unwise to ignore in the chapters
ahead the scars which these traumatic happenings must have left
on all who experienced them.

(ii)

Probably the notice about the well of Beer-lahai-roi (the first
word has two syllables) does not belong to the story proper, but

was incorporated into the text later. It is an instance of an age-old practice pursued down the centuries by people in the Holy Land of identifying places where incidents in the Biblical tradition occurred. The *Via Dolorosa* in Jerusalem with its Stations of the Cross, where Our Lord is supposed to have stumbled or where Simon of Cyrene was called upon to relieve him of his burden and so on, is a rather more recent example.

The name means "the well of the living one who sees me", i.e. God, and not, as it has been twisted by the text to mean, "the well of the one who lives and sees", i.e. Hagar herself. Perhaps a small shrine was erected at the well in later Israelite times, thus accounting for the precise information given about its location in the text, which is almost an invitation to the pious to go on pilgrimage to it.

(iii)

But the most remarkable feature of this most reticent of stories is its inclusion of the Ishmaelites or Arabs within the scope of God's providence. The words used in the blessing on Ishmael obviously refer to them as a race as much as to him as their individual "ancestor", the warlike tribesmen of the deserts to the south and southeast of Palestine, for ever raiding the settled lands and living out in their lives the savage code of blood-revenge (see the commentary on 4:17ff. in Volume 1).

Were they really thought of as possessing a special blessing along with Israel in contradistinction to the Canaanites and Amorites and other neighbours of Israel, who only in the last chapter were being roundly cursed for their "wickedness"? Or, as I would like to think, is the hatred of these peoples put in God's mouth there the result of Israel's later dealings with them, in other words of Israel's making and not her God's? Does then this story of Hagar, herself a foreigner and the ancestress of a Bedouin people, preserve the genuine attitude of the earliest Hebrew tradition to non-Hebrews, one which saw God's love and providence watching over them too and which reflects a much worthier understanding of the promise in 12:3 that in

Abraham and his seed all the families of the earth should be blessed?

If it does—and surely it does!—then it behoves us who read the Bible today to be wary before taking at their face value the nastier passages about other peoples in Genesis and in other parts of the Old Testament. These are much more likely to be the word of man than the Word of God.

LAUGHTER I

Genesis 17:1–27

1 When Abram was ninety-nine years old the Lord appeared to Abram, and said to him, "I am God Almighty; walk before me, and
2 be blameless. And I will make my covenant between me and you,
3 and will multiply you exceedingly." Then Abram fell on his face; and
4 God said to him, "Behold, my covenant is with you, and you shall be
5 the father of a multitude of nations. No longer shall your name be Abram, but your name shall be Abraham; for I have made you the
6 father of a multitude of nations. I will make you exceedingly fruitful; and I will make nations of you, and kings shall come forth from you.
7 And I will establish my covenant between me and you and your descendants after you throughout their generations for an everlasting covenant, to be God to you and to your descendants after you.
8 And I will give to you, and to your descendants after you, the land of your sojournings, all the land of Canaan, for an everlasting possession; and I will be their God."
9 And God said to Abraham, "As for you, you shall keep my covenant, you and your descendants after you throughout their
10 generations. This is my covenant, which you shall keep, between me and you and your descendants after you: Every male among you
11 shall be circumcised. You shall be circumcised in the flesh of your foreskins, and it shall be a sign of the covenant between me and you.
12 He that is eight days old among you shall be circumcised; every male throughout your generations, whether born in your house, or bought with your money from any foreigner who is not of your
13 offspring, both he that is born in your house and he that is bought with your money, shall be circumcised. So shall my covenant be in
14 your flesh an everlasting covenant. Any uncircumcised male who is

not circumcised in the flesh of his foreskin shall be cut off from his people; he has broken my covenant."

15 And God said to Abraham, "As for Sarai your wife, you shall not
16 call her name Sarai, but Sarah shall be her name. I will bless her, and moreover I will give you a son by her; I will bless her, and she shall be
17 a mother of nations; kings of peoples shall come from her." Then Abraham fell on his face and laughed, and said to himself, "Shall a child be born to a man who is a hundred years old? Shall Sarah, who
18 is ninety years old, bear a child?" And Abraham said to God, "O that
19 Ishmael might live in thy sight!" God said, "No, but Sarah your wife shall bear you a son, and you shall call his name Isaac. I will establish my covenant with him as an everlasting covenant for his
20 descendants after him. As for Ishmael, I have heard you; behold, I will bless him and make him fruitful and multiply him exceedingly; he shall be the father of twelve princes, and I will make him a great
21 nation. But I will establish my covenant with Isaac, whom Sarah shall bear to you at this season next year."
22 When he had finished talking with him, God went up from
23 Abraham. Then Abraham took Ishmael his son and all the slaves born in his house or bought with his money, every male among the men of Abraham's house, and he circumcised the flesh of their
24 foreskins that very day, as God had said to him. Abraham was ninety-nine years old when he was circumcised in the flesh of his
25 foreskin. And Ishmael his son was thirteen years old when he was
26 circumcised in the flesh of his foreskin. That very day Abraham and
27 his son Ishmael were circumcised; and all the men of his house, those born in the house and those bought with money from a foreigner, were circumcised with him.

After the sparse and frugal style of chapter 16, so typical of most Hebrew stories, we meet again in this chapter the wordy theologian at work. God is made to speak for most of it, and to explain at length what he wants done and why. There is hardly any action beyond a short protest from Abraham and at the end the careful carrying out of God's instructions. Like chapter 15 it probably owes a good deal more to Israel's scholars than to her story-tellers.

(i)

Nevertheless, in terms of the plot of the Abraham cycle some

parts of it are very important. If these had been highlighted in a
shorter text instead of being lost in a welter of detail about the
rite of circumcision, their cumulative force might have been
more easily appreciated.

Whether or not we accept literally that Abraham was now
ninety-nine (see the *Note on Genesis as "History"*), it is clear that
a long time has passed since the birth of Ishmael. God appears
once more to Abraham and promises that he will be the father
of a multitude of nations and, as in chapter 15, he speaks of a
covenant with him. The sign of this covenant is to be the
circumcision of all males in the clan, including Ishmael. But
then he announces that Sarah will soon give birth to a son and
when Abraham laughs at this idea and, as it were, reminds God
that he already had a son, God says that though that son will be
blessed, his covenant will be with Sarah's son.

There is tension here and there is paradox and ambivalence.
What would Abraham think of it all? He must long since have
given up hope of a child by his chief wife. But had he fully
centred his hopes on Ishmael, his son by Hagar? He knew of
Hagar's deliverance from death by God in the wilderness, yet
her report of what God had said to her about Ishmael had been,
to say the least, enigmatic. It had talked of many descendants,
but had made no mention of a land to be possessed. But now
here was God renewing his covenant with him, and this time
both a land and Ishmael were mentioned. But was Ishmael
really within its scope? For God also and suddenly added that
the impossible was about to happen. He would have another
son by Sarah and he would be favoured above Ishmael. What in
heaven's name, the poor man might well have asked, was God
up to?

(ii)

In the larger plot of Genesis these issues are not due to be fully
resolved until after Isaac is born (chapter 21), when it will be
brought home to Abraham with the utmost clarity—and with
not a little harshness—what God's will is. We know what
happened then. Hagar was cast out a second time, and Ishmael

with her. He was excluded irrevocably from promise, if not from blessing, and only Isaac remained as heir. But at this moment, it has to be stressed, Abraham does not know that this is how things will turn out.

Is it to be wondered at, then, that he "fell on his face and laughed" when Isaac's forthcoming birth was announced to him? At the beginning of the chapter as God appeared to him, Abraham also "fell on his face", the appropriate attitude of obeisance in the presence of divinity. But at the moment of the new announcement obeisance is ludicrously juxtaposed with laughter. Presumably his bowing low indicated that he was willing to believe what God had said. But the question he asked silently in his own heart and the laugh he laughed out loud showed that he was quite unable as yet to grasp its significance. Abraham's laugh was therefore a deadly serious laugh. It was the involuntary reaction of a bewildered and indeed angry man faced with the inscrutability of God's providence.

It spoke far more loudly of his true state of mind than his outward acquiescence. For that reason his intercession on Ishmael's behalf, "Oh that Ishmael might live in thy sight!", touching as it sounds, should probably be regarded as a cry of resentment rather than of concern for his son. That he loved Ishmael dearly is not really the point at issue. By making this request at this time it was as if he was saying to God, "When are you going to stop badgering me and leave me in peace with what I have?" He was in short taking refuge in the known and the tangible and in his heart if not with his lips refusing to countenance the idea of God working a miracle.

He was not openly rebuked by God for this, but he was instructed to name Sarah's son Isaac. The name Isaac does not in fact mean "he [Abraham] laughs", as the text wants us to think, but is short for "God has laughed", i.e. has smiled or looked favourably, as a Hebrew audience would know well. And no doubt it was given by Abraham to the boy at his birth in accordance with normal Hebrew custom, as again a Hebrew audience would assume (see also 21:3–7). They were willing to accept the story-teller's "fictional" way of putting it, however,

because it placed the emphasis on God and effectively underscored his displeasure with Abraham. We today would prefer to
think of Abraham choosing the name with the memory of his
own preposterous laughter in mind. In the end it comes to the
same thing. The name would recall to Abraham for as long as
he lived the turmoil and confusion that were his prior to God's
miracle, and how in hindsight he had condemned himself
bitterly for his lack of faith.

(iii)

Greater things were afoot in this confrontation between the
human and the divine than can ever take place in our little lives.
The pincers of God's grace were closing fast on Abraham, and
he did not have a chance. We can sympathize with his protests
and his resistance, for what God was doing was in many ways
terribly unfair. But we would be better advised to heed the
warning of Abraham's laughter, and to beware in our own lives
of that dreadful combination of belief with the lips and unbelief
in the heart which is apt to envelop us all when we try to explain
God's ways with men by bringing him down to our own level
and banishing grace and miracle from our perspective.

Do we recall what Our Lord said after his failure with the
Rich Young Ruler?

And Jesus looked around and said to his disciples, "How hard it will
be for those who have riches to enter the kingdom of God!" And the
disciples were amazed as his words. But Jesus said to them again,
"Children, how hard it is to enter the kingdom of God! It is easier for
a camel to go through the eye of a needle than for a rich man to enter
the kingdom of God". And they were exceedingly astonished, and
said to him, "Then who can be saved?" Jesus looked at them and
said, "With men it is impossible, but not with God; for all things are
possible with God."

(Mark 10:23–27)

CIRCUMCISION

Genesis 17:1–27 *(cont'd)*

(iv)

The rest of the chapter is loquacious and not very profound.

For instance, it makes an attempt to link the covenant with a change in Abraham's and Sarah's names. Up to this point in Genesis the forms Abram and Sarai have been used (though in this commentary I have kept all through the more familiar later forms), and it is suggested here that Abram was changed on God's instructions to Abraham because, meaning "father of a multitude", it accorded better with his status under the promise as forefather of many nations. But the audience would immediately know that this was a false etymology, since there is only a partial and surface resemblance in sound between the second part of the name (*raham*) and the Hebrew word for "multitude" (*hamon*). They enjoyed such word-play, as many other examples of "significant" meanings attached to personal and place names in Genesis show, including the name of Isaac later in this same chapter (see the last section) and that of Beer-lahai-Roi in the previous chapter (see on 16:7–16). But it was no more than a game to them. They must have been well aware that Abram and Abraham were in reality but alternative forms, a shorter and a longer, of the same name, and that it properly meant "the father (i.e. God) is exalted". Similarly Sarai and Sarah were the same name (meaning "princess") with only a slight difference in the final syllable. We would be very foolish not to take the naming and re-naming ceremonies retailed every few chapters in Genesis with a good pinch of salt.

It is noteworthy also that the favourite name used by the Patriarchs for God appears for the first time in this chapter, in verse 3, "I am God Almighty" (see also 28:3; 35:11; 43:14; 48:3; 49:25). It was this name that was replaced in Moses' time by the well known *Yahweh* or "The Lord" (see Exod. 6:3). The Hebrew is *El Shaddai,* which is a name of the same type as *El*

Roi ("God who sees") in 16:13 and indeed as the pagan *El Elyon* ("God Most High") in 14:18. The form is difficult, and the scholars are dubious about whether it in fact means "God Almighty", suspecting this to be another instance of an "invented" translation But their own suggestions (e.g. the Rabbinical "God the All-sufficient" or the more modern "God the Mountain-one") are linguistically no more convincing. We have to admit that the name is so archaic that its meaning is lost in the mists of time.

(v)

Again, we should probably be rather sceptical about the prominent position given to circumcision in this chapter. We may well have here yet another example of reading back a later situation into Patriarchal times.

Circumcision has been important down the ages to the Jewish people mainly because it served along with their distinctive dietary customs to mark them out from the other nations among whom they lived. But this can hardly have been the case in the early Biblical period. The Semitic peoples of Mesopotamia did not practise circumcision, but it seems to have been nearly universal among the Semitic peoples of the Levant and Arabia, including not only the Ishmaelites or Arabs who are in this part of the Bible brought into close relation with the Hebrews, but the Moabites and Ammonites whom the Hebrews did not much like (see 19:30–38) and, of course, the Canaanites whom they were continually anathematizing. When therefore the Mosaic Law told them to keep themselves pure from Canaanite ways (as in Deut. 7:1–5; 9:4–5; 20:16–18, etc.), it cannot have had circumcision over against non-circumcision in view.

There is little doubt that the writer of this chapter was aware of this situation, which is one of the reasons why it is so ambivalent. He brings Ishmael as Abraham's son within the covenant as far as circumcision is concerned, yet in almost the same instant he speaks of the covenant applying only to Isaac and his descendants. My impression, however, is that he *wants* us to think only of Israel as the people of circumcision, just as only they were the people of promise and covenant, and is more or less inviting his audience to ignore the fact that other peoples also knew of the practice.

Once more we catch the distasteful whiff of Hebrew arrogance and exclusivism. Fortunately, however, his attempt to obscure the issue does not quite come off. The Ishmaelites or Arabs cannot altogether be left out of the reckoning, since their "ancestor" is present in the tradition, and therefore the other Semitic peoples of early Biblical times cannot altogether be left out of the reckoning either. Indeed, we could almost say that by making so much of the rite of circumcision the chapter achieves the exact opposite effect to the one it intended. Far from excluding other peoples from God's providence it compels us to make room for them. We will have to remember this when we consider what happens in chapter 21 after Isaac is born.

WARNING

Genesis 18:1–19:29

Abraham's hospitality and Sarah's laughter (18:1–15)

1 And the Lord appeared to him by the oaks of Mamre, as he sat at the
2 door of his tent in the heat of the day. He lifted up his eyes and looked, and behold, three men stood in front of him. When he saw them, he ran from the tent door to meet them, and bowed himself to
3 the earth, and said, "My lord, if I have found favour in your sight, do
4 not pass by your servant. Let a little water be brought, and wash
5 your feet, and rest yourselves under the tree, while I fetch a morsel of bread, that you may refresh yourselves, and after that you may pass on—since you have come to your servant." So they said, "Do as you
6 have said." And Abraham hastened into the tent to Sarah, and said, "Make ready quickly three measures of fine meal, knead it, and
7 make cakes." And Abraham ran to the herd, and took a calf, tender and good, and gave it to the servant who hastened to prepare it.
8 Then he took curds, and milk, and the calf which he had prepared, and set it before them; and he stood by them under the tree while they ate.

9   They said to him, "Where is Sarah your wife?" And he said, "She
10 is in the tent." The Lord said, "I will surely return to you in the
spring, and Sarah your wife shall have a son." And Sarah was
11 listening at the tent door behind him. Now Abraham and Sarah
were old, advanced in age; it had ceased to be with Sarah after the
12 manner of women. So Sarah laughed to herself, saying, "After I
13 have grown old, and my husband is old, shall I have pleasure?" The
Lord said to Abraham, "Why did Sarah laugh, and say, 'Shall I
14 indeed bear a child, now that I am old?' Is anything too hard for the
Lord? At the appointed time I will return to you, in the spring, and
15 Sarah shall have a son." But Sarah denied, saying, "I did not laugh";
for she was afraid. He said, "No, but you did laugh."

The Lord's soliloquy and Abraham's intercession (18:16–33)

16 Then the men set out from there, and they looked toward Sodom;
17 and Abraham went with them to set them on their way. The Lord
18 said, "Shall I hide from Abraham what I am about to do, seeing that
Abraham shall become a great and mighty nation, and all the
19 nations of the earth shall bless themselves by him? No, for I have
chosen him, that he may charge his children and his household after
him to keep the way of the Lord by doing righteousness and justice;
so that the Lord may bring to Abraham what he has promised him."
20 Then the Lord said, "Because the outcry against Sodom and
21 Gomorrah is great and their sin is very grave, I will go down to see
whether they have done altogether according to the outcry which
has come to me; and if not, I will know."
22   So the men turned from there, and went toward Sodom; but
23 Abraham still stood before the Lord. Then Abraham drew near, and
said, "Wilt thou indeed destroy the righteous with the wicked?
24 Suppose there are fifty righteous within the city; wilt thou then
destroy the place and not spare it for the fifty righteous who are in it?
25 Far be it from thee to do such a thing, to slay the righteous with the
wicked, so that the righteous fare as the wicked! Far be that from
26 thee! Shall not the Judge of all the earth do right?" And the Lord
said, "If I find at Sodom fifty righteous in the city, I will spare the
27 whole place for their sake." Abraham answered, "Behold, I have
taken upon myself to speak to the Lord, I who am but dust and
28 ashes. Suppose five of the fifty righteous are lacking? Wilt thou
destroy the whole city for lack of five?" And he said, "I will not
29 destroy it if I find forty-five there." Again he spoke to him, and said,

"Suppose forty are found there." He answered, "For the sake of
30 forty I will not do it." Then he said, "Oh let not the Lord be angry,
and I will speak. Suppose thirty are found there." He answered, "I
31 will not do it, if I find thirty there." He said, "Behold, I have taken
upon myself to speak to the Lord. Suppose twenty are found there."
32 He answered, "For the sake of twenty I will not destroy it." Then he
said, "Oh let not the Lord be angry, and I will speak again but this
once. Suppose ten are found there." He answered, "For the sake of
33 ten I will not destroy it." And the Lord went his way, when he had
finished speaking to Abraham; and Abraham returned to his place.

Lot's hospitality and Sodom's sin (19:1–11)

1 The two angels came to Sodom in the evening; and Lot was sitting in
the gate of Sodom. When Lot saw them, he rose to meet them, and
2 bowed himself with his face to the earth, and said, "My lords, turn
aside, I pray you, to your servant's house and spend the night, and
wash your feet; then you may rise up early and go on your way."
3 They said, "No; we will spend the night in the street." But he urged
them strongly; so they turned aside to him and entered his house;
and he made them a feast, and baked unleavened bread, and they
4 ate. But before they lay down, the men of the city, the men of
Sodom, both young and old, all the people to the last man,
5 surrounded the house; and they called to Lot, "Where are the men
who came to you tonight? Bring them out to us, that we may know
6 them." Lot went out of the door to the men, shut the door after him,
7, 8 and said, "I beg you, my brothers, do not act so wickedly. Behold, I
have two daughters who have not known man; let me bring them out
to you, and do to them as you please; only do nothing to these men,
9 for they have come under the shelter of my roof." But they said,
"Stand back!" And they said, "This fellow came to sojourn, and he
would play the judge! Now we will deal worse with you than with
them." Then they pressed hard against the man Lot, and drew near
10 to break the door. But the men put forth their hands and brought
11 Lot into the house to them, and shut the door. And they struck with
blindness the men who were at the door of the house, both small and
great, so that they wearied themselves groping for the door.

Lot's prevarication (19:12–23)

12 Then the men said to Lot, "Have you any one else here? Sons-in-law,

sons, daughters, or any one you have in the city, bring them out of
13 the place; for we are about to destroy this place, because the outcry against its people has become great before the Lord, and the Lord
14 has sent us to destroy it." So Lot went out and said to his sons-in-law, who were to marry his daughters, "Up, get out of this place; for the Lord is about to destroy the city." But he seemed to his sons-in-law to be jesting.
15 When morning dawned, the angels urged Lot, saying, "Arise, take your wife and your two daughters who are here, lest you be
16 consumed in the punishment of the city." But he lingered; so the men seized him and his wife and his two daughters by the hand, the Lord being merciful to him, and they brought him forth and set him
17 outside the city. And when they had brought them forth, they said, "Flee for your life; do not look back or stop anywhere in the valley;
18 flee to the hills, lest you be consumed." And Lot said to them, "Oh,
19 no, my lords; behold, your servant has found favour in your sight, and you have shown me great kindness in saving my life; but I cannot flee to the hills, lest the disaster overtake me, and I die.
20 Behold, yonder city is near enough to flee to, and it is a little one. Let me escape there—is it not a little one?—and my life will be saved!"
21 He said to him, "Behold, I grant you this favour also, that I will not
22 overthrow the city of which you have spoken. Make haste, escape there; for I can do nothing till you arrive there." Therefore the name
23 of the city was called Zoar. The sun had risen on the earth when Lot came to Zoar.

Lot's wife and the destruction of Sodom and Gomorrah (19:24–29)

24 Then the Lord rained on Sodom and Gomorrah brimstone and fire
25 from the Lord out of heaven; and he overthrew those cities, and all the valley, and all the inhabitants of the cities, and what grew on the
26 ground. But Lot's wife behind him looked back, and she became a
27 pillar of salt. And Abraham went early in the morning to the place
28 where he had stood before the Lord; and he looked down toward Sodom and Gomorrah and toward all the land of the valley, and beheld, and lo, the smoke of the land went up like the smoke of a furnace.
29 So it was that, when God destroyed the cities of the valley, God remembered Abraham, and sent Lot out of the midst of the overthrow, when he overthrew the cities in which Lot dwelt.

The story in these two chapters is not quite the longest (that in chapter 24 contains a few more lines) but it is the most complicated in the Abraham epic. In terms of plot it is held together by the activities of the three men—or so they are called—who at its start appear to the patriarch at Mamre and announce once again that Sarah will have a son. It suddenly and amazingly transpires that one of them is the Lord, and he severely chides Sarah (who had been listening nearby) for laughing at the news. Thereafter the "men" set out with Abraham in the direction of Sodom. Two of them go on ahead, while the third (the Lord) stops and tells Abraham how concerned he has become about that wicked city. Abraham tries to intercede on its behalf, but without success. At that point, we are told, "the Lord went his way" and Abraham returned to Hebron. The other two "men" (now revealed as angels) proceed to Sodom where they are welcomed by Lot and, after a bout of trouble with the inhabitants, pronounce doom in God's name upon the city. They have some trouble with Lot also, but manage to rescue him and his family—though not his wife!—just before the disaster engulfs Sodom and its neighbours.

The story is a powerful and compelling one, jagged and staccato, cryptic and mysterious, with sometimes no obvious connection between its parts. It sounds many notes, mostly of warning—hence the heading to this section—but there is also, if we listen hard enough for it, a note of hope. Let us see what we can make of it.

LAUGHTER II

Genesis 18:1–15 *(cont'd)*

(i)

The opening paragraph of the story shows us a typical scene of eastern hospitality.

In the east hospitality has always meant much more than holding a supper party or giving a bed to a friend for the night—

our usual understanding of the term. It means literally taking strangers into one's home, and is a highly esteemed virtue, particularly in a nomadic society like that to which Abraham belonged. In the eyes of such a society the guest is almost sacred, and *any* passing traveller, even a member of a hostile tribe, is entitled to become one. The honour of entertaining him is as often as not claimed by the sheikh or chief of the clan himself and the reception is as lavish as it can be made.

When, therefore, in this story Abraham bows low before the three men and "hastens" to supervise the preparation of a meal and stands respectfully by while they eat, he is not doing it because he suspected that they were specially important. Not till one of them spoke of Sarah having a child could he have had the slightest inkling that they were more than chance visitors. No, the whole point is that he did not at first know who they were.

On the other hand, we are probably not intended to praise him too much for what he does. The Epistle to the Hebrews has his example in mind when it talks of "entertaining angels unawares" (13:2). But later in the same story Lot is every bit as assiduous as Abraham in giving hospitality to "angels", and it is unlikely that the story-teller wishes to single him out for commendation. It seems that he is simply presenting Abraham behaving as a clan chief of his day would have been expected to behave, and is not thinking of pointing a moral.

(ii)

The main lessons which he wants to get over in this part of the story are to be found, first, in the peculiar manner of God's appearance and, second, in Sarah's doing what not long since her husband had done, laughing at God's promise.

The way the "arrival" of God is reported goes well beyond the normally accepted means in ancient Israel of describing communication between the divine and the human. Often God could be "seen" doing things in a vision or a dream (as by Abraham in Gen. 15); often his "spirit" took hold of men (as of Saul in 1 Sam. 10:10); or his "word" came to them (as to the prophet in Jer. 1:4) or he even "spoke" to them directly (as to Abraham in Gen. 12:1); and often he sent his "angels", who could at times be pictured as though they were almost human (e.g. 2 Sam. 24:15–17; 1 Kgs. 19:5–8; also Luke 1:11–13, 26ff.). But hardly at all in the Old Testament (if we discount God's walking in the garden to look for Adam or putting a mark on Cain's brow or doing the other earthy things he does in the origin stories earlier in Genesis, stories which are not "true" in the sense that this story is "true) do we have God, as it were, mixing with human beings as if he were one of them, washing his feet and eating a meal prepared for him. His two companions, later called angels, do this too, but this would not have worried a Hebrew audience so much. But they must have raised a very surprised eyebrow when the story-teller, having begun his story in the usual manner with the phrase "The Lord appeared", then went on to speak of three men and all but identify one of the three with God. It must have seemed to them dangerously near contravening in words the second of their ten commandments ("You shall not make for yourself a graven image, or any likeness...").

But on second thoughts they would realize that a good Hebrew like the story-teller of Genesis could not fairly be accused of any such impropriety, but must have had some other purpose in portraying God so daringly and so concretely. And being themselves Hebrews, they would soon have guessed what it was. It can only have been to emphasize the crucial significance of the drama that was being played out in this portion of Genesis. Or to phrase if differently, the author wanted God to be seen to be present in these events in a very special way. Abraham's life was fast approaching its climax, and in the truest of senses the world's future hung on what was now happening.

We miss his point completely if with some of the Fathers of the Church we are tempted to equate the three visitors with the three Persons of the Christian Trinity. That would account nicely enough for the exceptional nature of the appearance. But this story is a real drama, describing real events that mattered vitally to the people who experienced them, and that ought to matter vitally to us precisely because they mattered to them. It is not a secret code to intrigue Christians living long after the events with hidden allusions to issues which could not possibly have concerned a Hebrew audience. The story-teller makes God choose an extraordinary means of revealing himself on this occasion because it matched the extraordinary importance of the occasion, and for no other reason.

(iii)

We are given no hint of Abraham's reaction to this strangest of all Genesis' renewals of the promise, but we do get Sarah's. Waiting in the background like a dutiful oriental wife, ready to be summoned should she be required, she overhears what the men say to her husband, and she laughs. There is poignancy and grim humour and a touch of indelicacy in what she says to herself. She was well past the childbearing age and sexual pleasure was for herself and her husband now only a distant memory! How could she have a child?

But her laughter is if anything even more blameworthy than Abraham's a short while previously (17:17). It is difficult to believe that he had not told her what God had said to him then, though, being human, he may well not have let her know of his own querulous response. But if that is so, then Sarah was not expressing a new and genuine astonishment, but was reiterating a disbelief that had been gnawing at her from at least that moment onwards. Her own rather crude thoughts confirm this, suggesting as they do that she had not allowed sexual relations to be resumed. So does God's statement (both of them must have realized by now who was behind this visit!) to Abraham with its classical "Is anything too hard for the Lord?", and so does his even abrupter reply when Sarah came out from the shadows protesting—"No, but you did laugh!"

The Epistle to the Hebrews seems to me once again to get this passage wrong when in 11:11 it praises Sarah's faith. Like her husband before her she had to be dragged into the realm of grace, resisting all the way. God had to fight a very hard battle to convince them that he was on the point of working a miracle and to get them to accept their part in bringing it about.

INTERCESSION

Genesis 18:16–33 *(cont'd)*

(iv)

In its cryptic way the story has so far left us to make our own inferences about Abraham's state of mind, but now it suggests strongly that at last he was beginning to close with his destiny and to glimpse something of what it meant. God is pictured deciding within himself to take Abraham into his confidence and tell him of his horror at the "outcry" against Sodom and Gomorrah which had reached his ears. By so doing he would give his servant an insight into his character, and he would then be able to charge the "great and mighty nation" which was to descend from him to "do righteousness and justice" and be a chosen people worthy of the name. God then announces to Abraham that he was about to "go down" to Sodom and Gomorrah to see if what he had heard was true.

There are far-reaching nuances attaching in Hebrew to the words "cry" (or, as the RSV renders it, "outcry") and "go down". The former would recall to the audience Abel's blood "crying" for revenge from the ground (Gen. 4:10) and from a later time the enslaved Hebrews in Egypt groaning under their bondage and "crying out" to God for help (Exod. 2:23). The latter would remind them how once before the Lord had "come down to see" Babel's city and tower (Gen. 11:5–7) and how in the future he was again to "come down" in answer to his people's "cry because of their taskmasters" and deliver them "out of the hand of the Egyptians" (Exod. 3:7–8). The cry, then, that God was responding to was the cry of Sodom and Gomorrah's victims, those who suffered sorely because the sin of these cities was "very grave". It meant that he would—and does—hear the cry of the world's ill-used, corrupted, and enslaved millions pleading in their agony· and lostness for justice and redress.

Abraham was being told that such was the world that God was intent on saving. We are back with a vengeance in the time and atmosphere of the Flood and the Tower of Babel. Like the inhabitants of Babel, Sodom and Gomorrah are *in effect* the unredeemed mass of mankind in microcosm. God could not stay silent and unfeeling in heaven as they sinned and suffered. He had to "come down" to see, and then he would know what to do. Only now he had a people of his own to aid him. God is therefore letting Abraham know that he and they after him had a role to play in saving the world too. Almost in the same breath as he guarantees their future by announcing the miracle of Isaac, he forcibly turns them in the person of their ancestor away from their own concerns and makes them think of the godless humanity for whose sakes ultimately, indeed for whose sakes solely, they existed.

When we put it this way, it ceases to be something to puzzle over that in this story Isaac's coming birth is so closely linked with the fate of Sodom and Gomorrah. On the contrary, if truth were to be served, they had to be brought together. They were the two sides of the same coin, the problem and its solution, the crying sin and need of men and the miraculous Gospel of God. Not by celebrating chapter 14's grossly overrated victory nor by exulting in chapter 17's triumphant forecast of far-flung empire but in working in humble faith with God to save a world undone would Abraham and his seed become a blessing to all the families of the earth. With a few swift and simple strokes of his story-telling brush the author of this chapter vividly expresses fundamental truths about God and his purposes which it would take a modern theologian yards of turgid print to put into words.

(v)

To Abraham's eternal credit he immediately sensed something of what was going on. For before the Lord's two companions were out of sight he launched into his sturdy intercession on Sodom's behalf with its famous catch-phrase, "Shall not the Judge of all the earth do right?" No doubt his motives were not entirely disinterested, for his nephew Lot lived in Sodom. But it was Sodom's fate he concentrated on. Would, he asked, the presence in it of fifty, forty-five, forty, thirty, twenty, even ten righteous people save it from its just deserts? Each time God's answer was that it would. For the sake of such a number, even ten, "I will not destroy it".

The passage with its repetitiveness may sound rather naive and simplistic to us, but we have to think of it from a Hebrew audience's point of view. They rather liked this kind of thing in their stories, as a look back at an even better known chapter (Gen. 1) with its successive panels each with almost the same wording should remind us. In this they were more like our children than ourselves (see the commentary on 1:6–25, *A story for children?*). The repetitions do not in this case add very much to the content of the message, but surely even we can recognize how they increase the *tension?* Could Sodom be saved? Would Abraham move God to relent?

Remarkably the requests stop short at ten. Why not five or even one? But Abraham was satisfied. He knew that nothing he could do could now prevent God's retribution descending on Sodom and its wicked neighbours.

We should not judge him too harshly for giving up. Abhorrent as the "civilized" ways of Sodom and Gomorrah must have been to him as nomadic wanderer, he went a lot further in his attempt to save them than most of his descendants would have done, showing nothing of that intense vindictiveness and hatred which they were later to show when with God's name on their lips they put the Canaanites to the sword. He was learning fast and he can hardly be blamed, living when he did, for not seeing further.

We, however, *can* see further. For this passage says more than it knows about God's ways with sinful men. It makes it painfully clear that God is not mocked. But it is not at the deepest level about a particularly wicked group of cities and the judgment pronounced on them from above. Rather, like the Flood story and the Tower of Babel story it convicts us all, for all of us even now live with Lot in Sodom, and all of us even now deserve destruction. "None is righteous, no, not one" (Rom. 3:10, loosely quoting Ps. 14:1–3 or 53:1–3). But no! One is, the Son of God himself! And in the Incarnation he "came down" to see and to know, and because of his Cross we can all escape. This is the Gospel which as God's people today we have to preach, this the ground of the intercession which as Abraham's successors we have to make, this the "blessing" which we have to offer to all earth's families.

Our passage does not end with good news. In fact it leads on to a bitter doom that even after three or four millennia makes us shudder when we think of it. But in a strange way its very refusal to argue things out to their logical conclusion makes room for good news, and we are entitled to glimpse it behind the destruction which at this moment occupies its foreground. At the least we are entitled to give thanks that God's servant as the miracle of Isaac's birth drew near saw that it concerned more than the happiness of his own little clan.

VICE

Genesis 19:1–11 *(cont'd)*

(vi)

It is very important that we be precise and circumspect in what we say about the opening scene of chapter 19. It is too easy to assume that it is speaking only about unnatural vice and the punishment that awaits any society that permits it.

This passage has given our language the word "sodomy" to denote homosexual acts between individual males. But we do not need to read far into it to find that it is not single acts of that kind that it is describing so much as a concerted sexual attack by the whole male population of Sodom on two innocent strangers. Old and young alike they surround Lot's house and demand, "Bring them out to us, that we may know them", "know" plainly being used with its sexual connotation (see Gen. 4:1, 17; 38:26 (AV) etc.). No doubt we are meant to think of the "angels" as young men in their prime whose handsome demeanour arouses the lust of a citizenry already deeply stained by the practice. But there is as much condemnation of the Sodomites' savage inhospitality as there is of the means by which they expressed it.

It would appear that the story-teller has chosen "sodomy" as but one example of Sodom's general wickedness and is not intending to set it forth as the sole or even the chief cause of its consequent destruction. There was much more to the "outcry" against it and its neighbours than a single sin. This is confirmed if we look at other allusions to the Genesis story in Scripture. Only Jude (verse 7) highlights Sodom's "unnatural lust". Our Lord, on the contrary, concentrates on the other main feature of this scene, Sodom's inhospitality: "And if anyone will not receive you . . . truly, I say to you, it shall be more tolerable on the day of judgment for the land of Sodom and Gomorrah than for that town" (Matt. 10:14–15). Ezekiel (thinking perhaps of Lot's choice of the "best" territory in chapter 13, a choice which took him to Sodom) broadens the picture even further. "She and her daughters (i.e. Gomorrah and the other cities of the plain) had pride, surfeit of food, and prosperous ease, but did not aid the poor and needy. They were haughty and did abominable things before me; therefore I removed them, when I saw it" (Ezek. 16:49–50).

(vii)

I would like therefore, to suggest that we miss the full force of God's judgment on the cities of the plain if we merely moralize about their vicious sexual behaviour and lose sight of their wider wickedness. Especially is this so if we make our moralizing the starting point of an onslaught on "Gay Lib" and other homosexual lobbyists in our own time.

The Old Testament is in no doubt that homosexuality was an "abomination" and roundly condemns it along with incest, adultery, child-sacrifice, and bestiality as deserving of the death penalty. See Leviticus chapters 18 and 20. The second of these chapters even adds resorting to mediums and wizards and cursing one's father and mother to the list. By "all these things" the nations round about "defiled themselves" (Lev. 18:24). They were practices quite unworthy of a people that claimed to be "holy to the Lord" (Lev. 20:26).

As Christians, however, we ought to follow the New Testament rather than the Old in ethical matters. It has to be honestly admitted that in such matters (as in the not unrelated matter of its opinion of other races and peoples) the Old Testament is far too often exclusivist and brutal in a way that cannot possibly be called Christian; and this verdict stands, however evil and distasteful the practice that it is laying down the law about. In particular, as Christians we ought to take with the utmost seriousness Jesus' words to the Pharisees when they dragged before him the woman taken in adultery (also, remember, a capital offence according to Leviticus): "Let him who is without sin among you be the first to throw a stone at her" (John 8:7). This does not in the least mean that Jesus condoned adultery, not even when he said to the woman, "Neither do I condemn you". Rather it means that he abhorred censoriousness just as much, if not more. He is in effect doing what Ezekiel did in the chapter we have just quoted. Ezekiel is not gentle with Sodom, but his main purpose in the oracle in chapter 16 is to upbraid Jerusalem for her apostasy, which was to him worse than anything Sodom had done. So in John 8 does Jesus widen the circle of sin to take in the seemingly good as well as the obviously bad. Only he does this consistently and unerringly and all the time, whereas the Old Testament, in spite of passages like Ezek. 16, can never quite bring itself to abandon its superior and hectoring tone.

There is a time and a place for arguments about moral issues like homosexuality or, for that matter, adultery. No society can avoid making up its mind on such issues, and Christians are as entitled as anyone else to demand a hearing for their views. I for one am certain that they should be countering the creeping permissiveness of this modern age more insistently than they are doing, and I am not afraid to say so out loud, though I would hope that they would employ New Testament rather than Old Testament weapons.

But the time is not now and the place is not here as we study Genesis chapter 19. Its theme is human sin in general and God's reaction to it, not the health of society in this or that particular. And its thrust is towards making us judge ourselves, not judge others. Sodom and Gomorrah are not just two more of the world's thoroughly wicked cities. They are in the last analysis ourselves and all "civilized" men as even now we brazenly flout *all* God's laws and bring down on our heads his deserved retribution. Unless we see that and see that chiefly as this story's inexorable corollary, we will never be able to see beyond it (as, you will recall, Abraham's open-ended intercession in the last chapter fleetingly invited us to do) to God's mercy and God's love.

PREVARICATION

Genesis 19:12–23 *(cont'd)*

(viii)

Gen. 19, however, is not only about Sodom and Gomorrah. It is about Lot, the man who had heard God's call with Abraham and had then spurned it, and had come to Sodom seeking an easier way of life, the man too who, even after his rescue by Abraham when he was captured by the army of the four great kings, elected to return there. He had by now settled down to city life and become a property owner, married and fathered two daughters who were old enough to be planning marriage.

The portrait we are given in this chapter of the last stages in the disintegration of his personality is devastating. He is not presented as a bad man. Indeed at the start of the story he is still capable of bravery and kindness. But by the end of it, though he escapes the cataclysm, he is revealed for the pathetic and broken figure he is.

The story opens with him sitting at the gate of Sodom as the two strangers arrive. His nomadic upbringing asserts itself and he invites them into his house for the night. No more than Abraham at Hebron does he know who they are. But he knows the Sodomites and when the strangers politely decline his invitation and say they will spend the night in the open, he is horrified and insists that they come home with him. His fears for their safety are fully justified, for within a short time a lustful mob is clamouring at his door. Lot courageously if somewhat rashly tries to protect his guests. He goes out to the mob and offers them his daughters if only they will leave the two young men along. This cannot but seem to us excessively zealous, if not unforgivably cruel, but a Hebrew audience would not have seen it that way. Having taken upon himself the responsibilities of hospitality, Lot was duty bound to carry them through, oblivious of the risk to himself and his. As he himself said, they had come under the shelter of his roof. The audience would have approved.

The reaction of the mob to Lot's brave gesture is also revealing. What right had this alien whom we were generous enough to allow to stay among us to judge us and offer us girls instead of boys? As an immigrant he should be adopting our ways, not flaunting his in our faces. He needed to be taught a sharp lesson.

Just as in this passage the story-teller brilliantly encapsulates the degradation of Sodom, so he obviously wishes to engage our sympathies on Lot's side. He had chosen to live in Sodom, but he was unhappy there and unwelcome. He was still at heart Abraham's nephew and he had a nomad's conscience. There was still hope for him.

(ix)

The two angels, whose chief purpose in visiting Sodom was to see if the "outcry" against it was merited (see 18:21), are by now thoroughly convinced that it deserved destruction, and as a foretaste of what was coming to it, they struck the mob around Lot's house with blindness. This should not be thought of as permanent blindness but as something akin to what happened to St. Paul on the Damascus road (Acts 9:3–9), a paralysis in the presence of the divine majesty, though in this case, of course, the sufferers were a very different sort of people.

But the angels' action marks also a turning point for Lot. As they performed it, he must have been wondering hard who they might be, as well as greatly relieved that they had saved him from the consequences of his own foolhardiness. Is the author perhaps suggesting that there was something absurd about him hurrying to their defence when in fact they had to defend him, something of Alexander Pope's "fool" who rushes in "where angels fear to tread"?

At any rate the two now openly declare why they have come and earnestly advise Lot to flee with his family while there is still time. But once again Lot is unable to carry through what he had begun. Remorselessly he is being revealed in his true colours. He is both frightened and impressed by what the angels tell him, for by this time he is aware that they come from the God he had once worshipped, and he urges immediate flight on his relatives. But his resolution vanishes when his intended sons-in-law laugh at him and accuse him of joking, and he does nothing more that night. When the cards are down he still prefers Sodom to God. It was there that he had made his new home, his family were there and, it is implied if not exactly stated, there he possessed what Ezekiel called "surfeit of food and prosperous ease". His future sons-in-law must be right. There was no need to get alarmed.

The next morning came and with it his last chance. But as the writer so succinctly puts it, he still "lingered". The angels in fact had to manhandle him and his wife and daughters out of the city. And even then Lot prevaricated. He pleaded with the angels that "yonder little city" should be spared and he be allowed to settle there rather than have to flee into the hill-country where he had lived in his nomadic days. Like Bunyan's man with the muckrake, even as safety beckoned, "he could look no way but downwards".

There must be some "writing up" in the story at this point. Zoar, as Gen. 14:2 makes clear, was the later name of the town called Bela in Abraham's time, and it is in shape and sound not unlike the Hebrew word for "little". It was the only one of the cities of the plain to survive, and it is therefore not impossible that Lot made for it after the disaster was past. But that it survived because of his selfish request and, though a pagan city, took itself a new name from his description of it as "little" is pushing credulity too far. The play on the word "little" would seem, then, to be an addition of the story-teller's. But it is nonetheless a very effective addition, ironically contrasting Lot's wheedling intercession with Abraham's noble one in the previous chapter and putting the final touch of sombre colour on his cameo sketch of this well-intentioned but utterly self-centred and hopelessly indecisive "little" man.

Once more we have to accuse the New Testament of failing to catch the Old Testament's drift. The Letter to the Hebrews praised Sarah for her faith (11:11), quite forgetting her awful silent laughter. Now we find Peter in his second Epistle (2:7) talking of God rescuing "righteous Lot, greatly distressed by licentiousness of the wicked". There is some truth in this assessment, but it is quite unbalanced for all that. Lot did not like some of the things around him, but other things he did like, and their hold on him was by far the stronger. Peter would have been better advised to heed Genesis' own verdict on what happened: "God remembered Abraham and sent Lot out of the midst of the overthrow" (19:29). It was for Abraham's sake, not his own, that he was delivered.

Lot is not an example to us. No less than his notorious wife, he is a warning. She "looked back" and was slain for it. He "lingered" even as he was being saved. As human beings we all belong in Sodom and Gomorrah. As Christians are we "lingerers" and prevaricators like Lot? See Matt. 6:21; 6:24; 8:19–22.

JUDGMENT

Genesis 19:24–29 *(cont'd)*

(x)

The destruction of Sodom and Gomorrah is set forth in the usual Old Testament manner as having been brought about by the direct intervention of God. But it was not a "miracle" in the sense that the other event with which this story is concerned—the birth of a son to a woman in her old age—was a "miracle". The Hebrews may have seen God as the prime mover in both cases, but they were perfectly capable of distinguishing between extraordinary but *repeatable* events in nature or in history—events like famine or earthquakes or victories or defeats in war—and extraordinary events which took place *only once* because God so willed it and had a special purpose to fulfil through them.

We in our different way make this same distinction. We can still as believers talk—and talk meaningfully—of God being in or behind both kinds of event. But only in the case of the second kind do we tend to insist on God being able to "break his own rules" and perform a "miracle". We avoid the word "miracle" with the first kind, and certainly we do not normally say things like "The Lord rained brimstone and fire". This is because, living in an "enlightened" age, we know that such happenings also have natural causes and scientific explanations.

The story-teller does not dwell on the details of how the cities of the plain met their end, but he gives us enough information to make his account consonant with what a modern geologist would term seismic or volcanic activity in an area of high mineral density. The Dead (in Hebrew, Salt) Sea lies well below sea level and has no natural outlet to the south. This has resulted in a salt content too rich to allow any sort of marine life and in the presence in its waters and in the surrounding territory of large quantities of other minerals like bitumen and sulphur. The sea is divided into two parts by the *Lisan* or "tongue", a peninsula extending from the eastern shore. Above this promontory the water is extremely deep, reaching in places 1,200 ft., but below it it is very shallow. At the present day it is around 30ft. deep, but geologists inform us that at one time it was even shallower, and that indeed the southern section of the Dead Sea was formed in the relatively recent past.

We must have in this chapter a reminiscence of how that came about. The allusions in 13:10 and 14:3 suggest that the valley of Jordan merged into the valley of Siddim and that the two together extended as far as Zoar, in other words that the Dead Sea did not yet exist. This is inaccurate. What is true is that the shallow lower portion of the Dead Sea did not yet exist, and that it was in this region, called at the time the valley of Siddim, that the "cities of the plain" were situated (see Map 1). It was, it seems, very fertile, though it was also "full of bitumen pits" (14:10). At some stage in the early or mid-second millennium B.C. an earth tremor or similar seismic irregularity ignited the minerals and gases in these pits, causing an immense explosion and conflagration which engulfed four of the five cities, leaving only the most southerly, Bela or Zoar, untouched. As the area returned to its former state, the ground slowly sank and the waters of the Dead Sea gradually moved south to cover most of it.

It is even possible to account naturalistically for the death of Lot's wife. Caught in the open by the falling debris, she was incinerated on the spot, and it was this that led to the fantastic tale of her being turned into a pillar of salt. There is a mountainous ridge at the southwest corner of the present Sea called *Jebel Usdum* (Arabic for "Mount Sodom") which is in fact composed largely of rocksalt and which is constantly crumbling and re-forming itself. It seems that one of the temporary projections or pinnacles on this ridge—it can hardly in the circumstances still be standing—bore some resemblance to a female figure and became linked in popular imagination with the present story.

(xi)

But of course the lesson of the story for us has to do not with geological science but with the God whose hand, as we believe no less than the ancient Hebrews, though metaphorically rather than literally, was behind these dreadful events. In the final analysis the corrupt civilization of the plain disappeared from the scene not through an unusual if explainable concatenation of natural circumstances but because its wickedness stank in his nostrils. The warning is there as clear as a pikestaff for all to ponder. If they continue as they are doing, today's equally corrupt civilizations will go the same way—for all we know through the horrifying nuclear weapons they have themselves created. This time God need only stand aside for an instant and it will happen.

The warning is there too for God's own people today. They can escape the catastrophe, even though like Lot they delay and prevaricate to the last moment. But if like his wife they go beyond this, if they "look back" when that last moment has passed, they will perish with the rest of mankind. She was remembered for her action by Our Lord himself (Luke 17:32) when he chose her to be the type of those who at his coming will seek to gain their life, but will lose it. He surely also had her example in mind when he said, "No one who puts his hand to the plough and looks back is fit for the kingdom of God" (Luke 9:62).

(xii)

The story of Sodom and Gomorrah ends appropriately and dramatically with Abraham returning to the place where earlier God had left him (18:33) and looking down from the heights there as the smoke rose "like the smoke of a furnace" from the valley in which his nephew had so tragically made his home. What were his thoughts as he surveyed the awful vista? The story-teller does not say, but he adds his own conclusion that it was because God remembered Abraham that Lot escaped, a veritable "brand plucked from the fire" (Zech. 3:2). To that extent at least his intercession had been worthwhile. We, praying Abraham's prayer today for a world in peril, may not save it from its doom—that is for God to decide—but we may just possibly rescue a few. And if we "remember Lot's wife"—and, one could add, Lot himself—we ourselves may just possibly be among those few.

INCEST

Genesis 19:30–38

30 Now Lot went up out of Zoar, and dwelt in the hills with his two

daughters, for he was afraid to dwell in Zoar; so he dwelt in a cave
31 with his two daughters. And the first-born said to the younger, "Our
father is old, and there is not a man on earth to come in to us after the
32 manner of all the earth. Come, let us make our father drink wine,
and we will lie with him, that we may preserve offspring through our
33 father." So they made their father drink wine that night; and the
first-born went in, and lay with her father; he did not know when she
34 lay down or when she arose. And on the next day, the first-born said
to the younger, "Behold, I lay last night with my father; let us make
him drink wine tonight also; then you go in and lie with him, that we
35 may preserve offspring through our father." So they made their
father drink wine that night also; and the younger arose, and lay
with him; and he did not know when she lay down or when she arose.
36, 37 Thus both the daughters of Lot were with child by their father. The
first-born bore a son, and called his name Moab; he is the father of
38 the Moabites to this day. The younger also bore a son, and called his
name Ben-ammi; he is the father of the Ammonites to this day.

This appalling little passage is reminiscent of the equally
appalling passage in 9:20–27, which showed us Noah, the
erstwhile hero of the Flood, sprawling naked in his tent in a
drunken stupor. For not being modest enough to avert his gaze
Ham was cursed and, though he had not been present, his son
Canaan was cursed along with him. Here Lot is made drunk by
his daughters, who then lie with him in turn. The offspring of
these incestuous liaisons are named as the ancestors of Israel's
eastern neighbours, Moab and Ammon (see Map 2).

(i)

The story is loosely linked with the end of the story of Sodom
and Gomorrah. Lot had pled with the angels to spare Zoar for
him, but he is now afraid to stay there and flees to the very hills
he had then been so anxious to avoid. Perhaps the people of
"little" Zoar had driven him out. Anyway, he who had abandoned his tent for a fine town house (19:3) has to seek refuge in a
miserable cave on the plateau east of the Dead Sea where the
Moabites and Ammonites were later to settle. The implication
is that no one else lived there at the time. His daughters, having
lost their husbands-to-be and despairing of finding others,

inveigle him into incest so that they may "preserve offspring" by him. It is a suitably squalid and ironic setting for our last glimpse of this tragic figure before he disappears for ever from the pages of Genesis and of history.

(ii)

One gets the feeling, however, that the narrator has already lost interest in Lot and is more concerned in these verses to cast aspersions on the Moabites and Ammonites than on him. We have no means of ascertaining whether Lot was from the beginning of Hebrew tradition connected with Moab and Ammon (it is not a name like Ishmael with obvious ethnic associations) or whether it was the fact that the previous story ended with him in Zoar on the east shore of the Dead Sea which led to the connection being made. I suspect the second.

But if that is the case, then we probably ought not to regard this episode as an integral part of the epic of Abraham. It supplies, as we have seen, a not inappropriate denouement to the sub-division of that epic which traces Abraham's deteriorating relations with his deviant and devious nephew. But its main purpose seems to be to say something nasty about the origin of two nations whom in later centuries the Hebrews had little cause to like (see, for example, Num. 25:1–5). We should treat it with the same suspicion we treated the "curse" on Canaan in Volume 1 (see the commentary on the passage). The author clearly intended his readers to class the Moabites and Ammonites, born in incest, along with the cities of the plain, sunk in "sodomy". This does not mean that God did, or that we should.

"EXPERIENCE"

Genesis 20:1–18

1 From there Abraham journeyed toward the territory of the Negeb, and dwelt between Kadesh and Shur; and he sojourned in Gerar.
2 And Abraham said of Sarah his wife, "She is my sister." And
3 Abimelech king of Gerar sent and took Sarah. But God came to

Abimelech in a dream by night, and said to him, "Behold, you are a dead man, because of the woman whom you have taken; for she is a
4 man's wife." Now Abimelech had not approached her; so he said,
5 "Lord, wilt thou slay an innocent people? Did he not himself say to me, 'She is my sister'? And she herself said, 'He is my brother.' In the integrity of my heart and the innocence of my hands I have done
6 this." Then God said to him in the dream, "Yes, I know that you have done this in the integrity of your heart, and it was I who kept you from sinning against me; therefore I did not let you touch her.
7 Now then restore the man's wife; for he is a prophet, and he will pray for you, and you shall live. But if you do not restore her, know that you shall surely die, you, and all that are yours."
8   So Abimelech rose early in the morning, and called all his servants, and told them all these things; and the men were very much
9 afraid. Then Abimelech called Abraham, and said to him, "What have you done to us? And how have I sinned against you, that you have brought on me and my kingdom a great sin? You have done to
10 me things that ought not to be done." And Abimelech said to Abraham, "What were you thinking of, that you did this thing?"
11 Abraham said, "I did it because I thought, There is no fear of God at
12 all in this place, and they will kill me because of my wife. Besides she is indeed my sister, the daughter of my father but not the daughter of
13 my mother; and she became my wife. And when God caused me to wander from my father's house, I said to her, 'This is the kindness you must do me: at every place to which we come, say of me, He is
14 my brother.'" Then Abimelech took sheep and oxen, and male and female slaves, and gave them to Abraham, and restored Sarah his
15 wife to him. And Abimelech said, "Behold, my land is before you;
16 dwell where it pleases you." To Sarah he said, "Behold, I have given your brother a thousand pieces of silver; it is your vindication in the eyes of all who are with you; and before every one you are righted."
17 Then Abraham prayed to God; and God healed Abimelech, and also
18 healed his wife and female slaves so that they bore children. For the Lord had closed all the wombs of the house of Abimelech because of Sarah, Abraham's wife.

After the destruction of Sodom and Gomorrah Abraham, still the wanderer, leaves the open hill-country of Judah, where he had been relatively unharassed, and "sojourns" for a time near the Canaanite state of Gerar on the coastal plain. It was while he was living in this vicinity that Isaac was born (21:2), but before that we have this story of trouble arising between him and Abimelech, the king of Gerar. This had to be amicably settled if conditions were to be right for Sarah's confinement. But the story is not a short one, so there must be more behind it than that.

(i)

It begins similarly to the story of Abraham in Egypt in chapter 12, with Abraham pretending that Sarah is his sister and the ruler of the place taking her into his harem. It probably contains, therefore, as that story did, a considerable element of "writing up". But let us set that problem aside and enquire rather why the story should appear at this particular juncture. It seems to me that the story-teller is intentionally contrasting Abraham's behaviour in Gerar with his behaviour in Egypt, and is this time commending it. He is giving it as his opinion that Abraham has learned with experience.

The scene is quickly set with nothing being said that might draw attention either to Abraham's cowardice or to Sarah's "beauty", both of which were highlighted in chapter 12. Abimelech is immediately warned by God in a dream who she really is, and his plea of innocence is accepted first by God and then by Abraham, whom he upbraids for his deceit, but in an apologetic or at any rate an aggrieved tone. Contrast this with Pharaoh guessing the truth on his own and peremptorily confronting Abraham with it before expelling him from Egypt in no uncertain manner (12:18–19). In Egypt, too, it will be remembered, Abraham made no reply to Pharaoh, but here in Gerar he launches into a lengthy justification of his deception which he claims had more to do with there being "no fear of God at all in this place" than with any fearfulness on his part. He also stresses that Sarah was not only his wife but his half-sister, as if to say that he had not in fact been lying (incidentally, this is the only time we are given this interesting piece of information). Finally Abimelech, far from driving Abraham out, allows him to settle where he likes in his kingdom, and Abraham prays to

God to remove the curse of barrenness which he had brought on Abimelech's wife and concubines.

(ii)

But though the author may wish to commend Abraham, can we? There are a number of things about the story which in all honesty we can hardly assent to or even understand. Apart from the idea of Abimelech being attracted by an old woman—and we must suppose by this time a pregnant old woman!—there is Abimelech's dream in which he as a pagan is not only addressed by but himself acknowledges and answers the God of Israel. There is his deference as a powerful monarch to a passing stranger who was merely a minor clan chief, and there are Abraham's not very convincing and rather hypocritical excuses. Perhaps worst of all, there is the report at the end that God had in fact punished Abimelech and his house, although earlier he had admitted to him, "I know that you have done this in the integrity of your heart".

It is unlikely that a Hebrew audience would have been so bothered by these things as we are. For instance, they would have distinguished between God's forgiveness of Abimelech and Abimelech's sin which, though committed in ignorance, had still been committed and so still merited punishment. And they would have seen a certain poetic justice in the punishment: Abimelech had taken another man's wife, so it was his wives who suffered.

(iii)

But we are not able easily to regard the episode in that light. It is tempting, therefore, to look for the same irony in this story that we detected in 12:10–20. Might it not, in spite of what it seems to be saying on the surface, have been intended in an oblique sort of way to castigate Abraham for resorting once again to expedience, and for resorting to it moreover on the very eve of the greatest event in his life? If that is so, then its real purpose will be to serve as a stern reminder to us all that the fulfilment of God's promises, in our lives as in Abraham's, owes nothing to human deserving and everything to his grace.

But this lesson, as we have seen a number of times and will see again, is by no means neglected in the Abraham stories. It is my judgment that this story was not meant by the author to be taken negatively like the parallel story in chapter 12, but to be a contrary image of that story. It does not exempt Abraham from criticism—the Old Testament rarely does this with its heroes—but the emphasis is on him regretting his stratagem almost at once, making a clean breast of things, and graciously interceding for the man he had wronged. The author is, I feel, suggesting that though it had been woefully weak in the past, Abraham's faith was now strong enough to enable him to face the stirring but also traumatic events that lay ahead. He wants us to understand his actions as confirming, if not exactly matching, his noble and generous demeanour throughout the story of Sodom and Gomorrah.

But I do not make this judgment at all confidently. If the reader prefers to look at the story negatively and find in it not a fillip to Abraham's faith but a criticism of it and a warning to his own, he is free to do so, and I will not say that he may not be right.

(iv)

There is one other feature of this rather poorly written story which is very important for the development of the plot of the whole epic and which a Hebrew audience would not have failed to notice, though they may not have greatly liked it. This is that for once relations between God's people and their pagan neighbours are friendly and peaceable. We will be considering this further in the commentary to 21:22–34 ("Fulfilment" II).

"FULFILMENT" I: A SON

Genesis 21:1–21

1 The Lord visited Sarah as he had said, and the Lord did to Sarah as
2 he had promised. And Sarah conceived, and bore Abraham a son in
3 his old age at the time of which God had spoken to him. Abraham
called the name of his son who was born to him, whom Sarah bore

4 him, Isaac. And Abraham circumcised his son Isaac when he was
5 eight days old, as God had commanded him. Abraham was a
6 hundred years old when his son Isaac was born to him. And Sarah
said, "God has made laughter for me; every one who hears will laugh
7 over me." And she said, "Who would have said to Abraham that
Sarah would suckle children? Yet I have borne him a son in his old
age."

8 And the child grew, and was weaned; and Abraham made a great
9 feast on the day that Isaac was weaned. But Sarah saw the son of
Hagar the Egyptian, whom she had borne to Abraham, playing with
10 her son Isaac. So she said to Abraham, "Cast out this slave woman
with her son; for the son of this slave woman shall not be heir with
11 my son Isaac." And the thing was very displeasing to Abraham on
12 account of his son. But God said to Abraham, "Be not displeased
because of the lad and because of your slave woman; whatever
Sarah says to you, do as she tells you, for through Isaac shall your
13 descendants be named. And I will make a nation of the son of the
14 slave woman also, because he is your offspring." So Abraham rose
early in the morning, and took bread and a skin of water, and gave it
to Hagar, putting it on her shoulder, along with the child, and sent
her away. And she departed, and wandered in the wilderness of
Beer-sheba.

15 When the water in the skin was gone, she cast the child under one
16 of the bushes. Then she went, and sat down over against him a good
way off, about the distance of a bowshot; for she said, "Let me not
look upon the death of the child." And as she sat over against him,
17 the child lifted up his voice and wept. And God heard the voice of the
lad; and the angel of God called to Hagar from heaven, and said to
her, "What troubles you, Hagar? Fear not; for God has heard the
18 voice of the lad where he is. Arise, lift up the lad, and hold him fast
19 with your hand; for I will make him a great nation." Then God
opened her eyes, and she saw a well of water; and she went, and filled
20 the skin with water, and gave the lad a drink. And God was with the
lad, and he grew up; he lived in the wilderness, and became an expert
21 with the bow. He lived in the wilderness of Paran; and his mother
took a wife for him from the land of Egypt.

This beautifully composed story, a jewel of simple Hebrew
narrative compared with the tortuous tale that precedes it,
fittingly marks the high point of the epic that began with God's

call to Abraham at the beginning of chapter 12. In so far as the promises given to the patriarch in Harran could be fulfilled in his own lifetime, they were now being fulfilled. The second of these promises was of descendants who would become a great nation, and the first step towards its realization was the birth of a son. The Lord visited Sarah "as he had said", and the birth took place at the time of which he "had spoken" to Abraham.

(i)

It is a story of the highest artistry. But this does not mean that it is an enjoyable story or even a nice one. It is in fact neither of these. It opens with laughter, but very quickly it moves on to tears, and there it ends with seemingly only a little belated kindness on God's part to alleviate its overwhelming sadness.

Abraham and Sarah rejoice when she is safely delivered of a boy. Abraham, who has now reached his century of years (!), circumcises Isaac when he is eight days old, as was the Hebrew custom at a later date; it is probably being suggested that he established the custom. Sarah sums up their happiness with the words: "God has made laughter for me", another play on the infant's name. There is irony in these words, for both she and Abraham must have been thinking of the two previous occasions on which they had laughed (17:17; 18:12). But there is also a genuine recognition that a miracle had taken place, for this laughter is set forth as God's doing.

The euphoria lasted for quite a time, for laughter did not give way to tears until the child was weaned, which in the ancient East took place much later than is usual nowadays. According to 2 Maccabees 7:27, in the period just before Christ it was normal for a mother to suckle her child for three years. We have probably to assume a similar lapse of time here. A feast was held to celebrate Isaac's weaning, and it was then that Sarah saw Ishmael, a lad of fifteen or sixteen now (see 17:25), playing with her own little boy, and all her latent jealousy and resentment rose to the surface. Not even God's miracle in giving her a son in her old age could remove the bitterness in her soul, and she demanded that Abraham cast him and his mother out. "The son of this slave woman shall not be heir with my son Isaac."

(ii)

It was an act of heinous cruelty, made all the more so by the fact that it was the second time she had adopted this course of action. On this occasion, however, Abraham did not stand shamefacedly by, but asserted his authority. He had obviously decided to share his inheritance between his two sons, as he was entitled to do (see the commentary on 16:1–6). Equally obviously he had concluded that God's reply to him when he had laughed, a reply which had favoured Isaac (see 17:15–21), did not extend to rejecting Ishmael, and certainly not to doing what his wife had asked.

But just at this point God intervened and told him that this was exactly what he must do. The promise would work itself out through Isaac alone, and though Ishmael as his son would have a great future, he had as of this moment to be excluded. The compromise which with the best of motives Abraham had attempted to weave was blown sky-high by a piece of divine savagery that can hardly be equalled in any other part of Scripture. Abraham could only obey, but it must have been with a heart near to breaking that the next morning he gave some bread and water to Hagar and sent her and Ishmael out into the desert.

The "tears" follow, and strangely they are Ishmael's tears. It is impossible to avoid the impression that in this part of the story Ishmael is still a young child. He had been "put" on Hagar's shoulder by Abraham and now, in despair as their provisions run out, his mother "casts" him down under a bush. Later, too, she is told by God to "lift up the lad and hold him fast". Not easy things to do with a youth of sixteen or so! But perhaps the story-teller was simply carried away by the intolerable pathos of the incident and like many a story-teller before and after him is indulging in a little dishonesty for the sake of effect. Be that as it may, God hears the lad weeping and guides

Hagar to a well of water, repeating his promise at Beer-lahai-roi (16:10-12) that he would "make him a great nation".

The story concludes by giving us a little information about what happened in the future. With God watching over him, Ishmael grows up in the desert and becomes an expert bowman and his mother procures a wife for him from her own home country of Egypt.

God's solicitude at the end of the story is tenderly portrayed and mitigates the savagery of his earlier sentence of exclusion, but it can hardly be said to cancel it out.

(iii)

In human terms the story of Abraham's relations with Sarah and Hagar, no less than that of his relations with Lot, has ended in disaster. An innocent woman and her boy were expelled for good from Abraham's encampment, where they had lived for many years and had been given to understand, even after Isaac's birth, that he would be treated as Abraham's full son. There is no suggestion that Ishmael had been acting superior to little Isaac. Rather the picture is a touching one of an older boy helping a younger at his play. And, of course, now that Sarah had her own child, there could no longer be any question of Hagar crowing over her. It looks as if on a human level the sole reason for their sudden expulsion was the unassuageable envy and jealousy of a bitter old woman with no forgiveness or even kindliness in her heart. At this level, too, Abraham's conduct was scarcely less culpable. He protested, but nevertheless he obeyed God—how noble of him! No, most of us would rather say, at what cost in human misery and suffering!

Yet this is the whole point of the story. Abraham did obey God, and he obeyed him because he was convinced that this was God's will. It was the cruel demand that faith made on him. And the story-teller is in no doubt that he was right. There may be a hint of prejudice in his final remark that Ishmael married an Egyptian woman, but since Abraham himself had taken an Egyptian woman to wife, probably not. On the contrary, the thrust of the story on any unbiased reading of it is to enlist our sympathies on the side of Hagar and her son.

The story-teller's skill here is quite breathtaking. By that very emphasis he removes the incident from the sphere of human explanation and places responsibility for it squarely upon God. In our human judgment Hagar and Ishmael did not deserve their fate. The story-teller agrees, but he insists that it was still God's will. So was the miracle, every bit as undeserved, which he had wrought in the lives of a vacillating Abraham and his thoroughly ill-natured wife. There is no way we can in this chapter blame the prejudice on the author. The prejudice is plainly God's. The Bible's word for it is grace.

GRACE

Genesis 21:1-21 *(cont'd)*

It is the consistent message of the Bible that the workings of God's grace are not only marvellous but can be very perturbing, quite beyond our ability to understand. We can never hope to explain or account for them by rational means and in the end of the day have, like Abraham, simply to accept them. However, there are some things which can be said to make the thought of them a little more endurable to our ways of thinking. Most of these things may be illustrated from this story of Isaac's birth or the stories that lead up to it in Genesis.

First, however, a Christian perspective, namely that Jesus himself, the gentlest and most loving of men, believed in grace implicitly. It was he who said, "The last will be first, and the first last" (Matt. 20:16), and he who also said, "There will be two men in one bed; one will be taken and the other left. There will be two women grinding together; one will be taken and the other left" (Luke 17:34–35). In this as in most of the other great problems of theology it is a serious mistake to try to set a "Christian" New Testament over against a "Jewish" Old Testament. We may wish to do this sometimes in matters of human behaviour or "ethics", but theology is a different thing altogether.

Second—and here we return to Genesis—those who are the recipients of grace have every reason to rejoice but none at all to boast. All of them know in their hearts that they are in the same case as Abraham and Sarah, who resisted God nearly all the way and refused until the very last moment to believe that he could really work a miracle in their lives.

Third, to complain when someone seems to be "outside" is to take God's prerogative away from him and to put his behaviour under the slide-rule of our standards of judgment. This is what Cain did on his own behalf when he could not stomach God's preference for Abel's offering (see the commentary in Volume 1 on 4:3-7, *I will be gracious to whom I will be gracious*). And it is what Abraham did on behalf of Hagar and Ishmael when he was "displeased" at Sarah's vicious suggestion. We would tend to conclude that Cain, from the way he disported himself later, deserved his fate and that, by the same token, Hagar and Ishmael did not deserve theirs. But in such a fundamental matter it is not our place to decide.

Fourth, to be glad when someone is "outside" is worse, and quite inexcusable. By his genuine sympathy with Hagar the story-teller of Gen. 21 makes this plain. It is a pity that St. Paul has muddied the waters here by his careless and unfeeling comparison in Gal. 4:21ff. between Hagar, "bearing children for slavery", and the Jewish Law which enslaves men. He comes dangerously near justifying Sarah's intolerance, whereas the author of this chapter seems to me to be making almost the opposite point. That in one exceptional case human vindictiveness happened to coincide with the divine will is no warranty for us to confuse our prejudices with that will. Rather does it hint that in the vast majority of other cases what God's people want and what God wants are likely to be poles apart.

Fifth, those "outside" are not abandoned by God. If human pride and evil overreach themselves as they did at Babel and as they did in Sodom and Gomorrah, he may have to act in retribution. But most of the time his providence overshadows those whom he has excluded from his grace. As Cain stalked arrogantly from his presence, God put a protecting mark on his forehead. As Hagar and Ishmael wandered weeping in the desert, God's mercy found and provided for them.

Sixth, those "inside" are free, if they so choose, to fling God's grace back in his face and so exclude themselves. Sarah does not quite seem to have done this, but even as he was being rescued, Lot did, and so did his wife.

Seventh, and perhaps most important of all to grasp, those who are singled out for God's favour are not singled out for their own sakes but for the sake of the rest of mankind. This was in essence the lesson learned by Abraham in the intercession scene in chapter 19. It is also the main point of Paul's great argument in Romans chapters 9–11. We are worried that in Genesis Israel's election should have meant Ishmael's exclusion. In Romans Paul is trying to explain why the Church's election should in its turn have left Israel out in the cold. The answer in both cases is that election was for service, not privilege. Israel was first chosen and then set aside by God so that the Gentile races might come to know him. With Israel's example as a warning, the Church dare not now act exclusively. She has to make a place for all God's erring children of whatever race—and of course that includes Israel too. "If their rejection means the reconciliation of the world, what will their acceptance mean but life from the dead?" (Rom. 11:15). One day those "outside" must find their way "inside", otherwise it is all a sick joke. In the final analysis, therefore, the "blessing" to all the families of the earth is far more important than the "promise" to the elect, which is simply the means by which the "blessing" will be realized.

As I am only too well aware, these seven points which I have listed do not even begin to solve the problem of God's grace. There remain irreconcilable contradictions between, for instance, God's sovereign will and man's freedom. But taken together they may move us an inch or two closer to fathoming God's ways with men. If we must "know" more, I can only suggest humbly that we fasten our gaze upon the Cross. There all the contradictions we can think of are at their most glaring, but they are mysteriously held in unity in the person of Jesus Christ who, as at once God and man, experienced them from both sides of the divide and, our faith tells us, resolved them.

"FULFILMENT" II: THE BLESSING

Genesis 21:22-34

22 At that time Abimelech and Phicol the commander of his army said
23 to Abraham, "God is with you in all that you do; now therefore swear to me here by God that you will not deal falsely with me or with my offspring or with my posterity, but as I have dealt loyally with you, you will deal with me and with the land where you have
24 sojourned." And Abraham said, "I will swear."
25   When Abraham complained to Abimelech about a well of water
26 which Abimelech's servants had seized, Abimelech said, "I do not know who has done this thing; you did not tell me, and I have not
27 heard of it until today." So Abraham took sheep and oxen and gave
28 them to Abimelech, and the two men made a covenant. Abraham set
29 seven ewe lambs of the flock apart. And Abimelech said to Abraham, "What is the meaning of these seven ewe lambs which you have
30 set apart?" He said, "These seven ewe lambs you will take from my hand, that you may be a witness for me that I dug this well."
31 Therefore that place was called Beer-sheba; because there both of
32 them swore an oath. So they made a covenant at Beer-sheba. Then Abimelech and Phicol the commander of his army rose up and
33 returned to the land of the Philistines. Abraham planted a tamarisk tree in Beer-sheba, and called there on the name of the Lord, the
34 Everlasting God. And Abraham sojourned many days in the land of the Philistines.

Set between the high drama of the birth scene and the famous sacrifice scene in chapter 22, the simple little episode recorded in these verses in one sense relieves the almost unbearable tension that envelops the climax of the Abraham epic. But in another sense it itself has a not unimportant role to play in that climax. Just as the story of Isaac's birth relates to the second promise given in 12:1-3, that of progeny, and the story of the purchase of a field coming in chapter 23 relates to the first promise given there, that of a land, so this short report can be considered a fulfilment in foretaste of the final promise made to Abraham, that he and his seed should become a "blessing" to all the families of the earth. Almost as if he were afraid his Hebrew audience would have missed the point of Ishmael's exclusion, the story-teller spells out what in his view the "blessing" was really about.

(i)

The passage contains yet another of the explanations of place-names of which Genesis is so fond and brings in yet another title of God used by the Patriarchs.

Beersheba in the Negeb of Judah was apparently at this time within Gerar's sphere of influence. According to this story it received its name from a treaty or agreement entered into by Abimelech and Abraham after the king's servants had inter-fered with Abraham's access to a well there. The name consists of two words, *beer* (to be pronounced with two syllables) meaning "well", and *sheba* meaning both "seven" (the number of the ewe lambs employed in the ceremony) and "oath". We in this historically-minded age are not likely to be as impressed by such artificial plays on words as the ancient Hebrews seem to have been (see also the commentary on the name Beer-lahai-roi in chapter 16).

The divine title is *El Olam*. We note again the element *El*, as in *El Roi* in 16:13 and *El Shaddai* in 17:1. The title means "the God of eternity" or, since "eternity" is hardly a Hebraic concept, more accurately "the God of time past and time to come".

(ii)

In the present context, however, it is not these antiquarian features but the friendly dealing between Abraham and a pagan king that emerge as the story's leading point of interest. Judging by the snide remarks made elsewhere in Genesis about the other races who lived in the area of Palestine, we can take it that Hebrew audiences would not much relish the thought of this.

They would prefer the vituperation implied in the account of the origin of Moab and Ammon at the end of chapter 19 or even the ambivalence that runs through the story of Ishmael's fate earlier in this chapter. But here the message was straightforward, and it was not possible for them—nor is it for us—to twist it.

The story-teller indeed rubs in the lesson by reminding his audience that Gerar was situated in the territory later to be occupied by the hated Philistines. It was in the "land of the Philistines" that the son of promise had been born and weaned, and while he was there Abraham had successfully lived in peace and amity with his pagan neighbours and their ruler. He had been invited to settle there (20:15) and, as the last words of this story have it, he had still "many days" to sojourn there. There can surely be little doubt that the author is setting forth this episode at the well, when resentment quickly gave way to co-operation, as the ideal of how God's people should get on with unbelievers or, as we could even say, with God's enemies.

Not only God's ancient people but his people today can learn much from it. Far too frequently in the past the Church has turned to the wrong passages in the Old Testament—several of them, as we have seen, in Genesis—to justify its own all too human hatreds and prejudices, and has not noticed stories like this one. As a result it has thrown up far too many Sarahs from its ranks and has as often as not been a "blessing" to nobody.

SACRIFICE I: MAN'S SACRIFICE

Genesis 22:1–19

1 After these things God tested Abraham, and said to him, "Abra-
2 ham!" And he said, "Here am I." He said, "Take your son, your only son Isaac, whom you love, and go to the land of Moriah, and offer him there as a burnt offering upon one of the mountains of which I
3 shall tell you." So Abraham rose early in the morning, saddled his ass, and took two of his young men with him, and his son Isaac; and he cut the wood for the burnt offering, and arose and went to the

4 place of which God had told him. On the third day Abraham lifted
5 up his eyes and saw the place afar off. Then Abraham said to his
   young men, "Stay here with the ass; I and the lad will go yonder and
6 worship, and come again to you." And Abraham took the wood of
   the burnt offering, and laid it on Isaac his son; and he took in his
7 hand the fire and the knife. So they went both of them together. And
   Isaac said to his father Abraham, "My father!" And he said, "Here
   am I, my son." He said, "Behold, the fire and the wood; but where is
8 the lamb for a burnt offering?" Abraham said, "God will provide
   himself the lamb for a burnt offering, my son." So they went both of
   them together.
9   When they came to the place of which God had told him,
   Abraham built an altar there, and laid the wood in order, and bound
10 Isaac his son, and laid him on the altar, upon the wood. Then
11 Abraham put forth his hand, and took the knife to slay his son. But
   the angel of the Lord called to him from heaven, and said, "Abra-
12 ham, Abraham!" And he said, "Here am I." He said, "Do not lay
   your hand on the lad or do anything to him; for now I know that you
   fear God, seeing you have not withheld your son, your only son,
13 from me." And Abraham lifted up his eyes and looked, and behold,
   behind him was a ram, caught in a thicket by his horns; and
   Abraham went and took the ram, and offered it up as a burnt
14 offering instead of his son. So Abraham called the name of that
   place The Lord will provide; as it is said to this day, "On the mount
   of the Lord it shall be provided."
15   And the angel of the Lord called to Abraham a second time from
16 heaven, and said, "By myself I have sworn, says the Lord, because
17 you have done this, and have not withheld your son, your only son, I
   will indeed bless you, and I will multiply your descendants as the
   stars of heaven and as the sand which is on the seashore. And your
18 descendants shall possess the gate of their enemies, and by your
   descendants shall all the nations of the earth bless themselves,
19 because you have obeyed my voice." So Abraham returned to his
   young men, and they arose and went together to Beer-sheba; and
   Abraham dwelt at Beer-sheba.

Before he could finally be sure that he had found the right man,
God had one more test for Abraham to pass. Abraham had
acquiesced in the expulsion of his older son, Ishmael, but he
had protested perhaps just a little too much. How would he

react if he were commanded to get rid of his second son, Isaac, especially since he had been revealed as God's favourite, the one through whom the promises would move on towards fruition after he was dead? In being presented with this command Abraham was in effect being forced to choose between God's promises and God himself. Was his devotion to God's person stronger than his devotion to God's cause?

There can be no more fundamental question addressed by God to men than this, and it is because Abraham gave the right answer that his faith will be celebrated, and justly celebrated, as long as time shall last. It took him many years to win through to a faith like this, but he made it in the end.

(i)

In spite of the protests of her prophets and psalmists, Israel hesitated long before dispensing altogether with the Temple sacrifices, and indeed might not have done so at all had not the Romans in A.D. 70 destroyed her central shrine and effectively removed the means of performing them. We find this difficult to understand, and much prefer nowadays to listen to an Amos condemning them:

> I hate, I despise your feasts
>> and I take no delight in your solemn assemblies.
> Even though you offer me your burnt offerings and cereal offerings,
>> I will not accept them,
> and the peace offerings of your fatted beasts
>> I will not look upon.
> Take away from me the noise of your songs:
>> to the melody of your harps I will not listen.
> But let justice roll down like waters,
>> and righteousness like an ever-flowing stream.

> (Amos 5:21–24)

See also Mic. 6:6–8 and Ps. 40:6–8. Obviously Israel did not take these passages in the way we take them. We are inclined to see in them proof that God never did, nor does he now want sacrifice from his worshippers, but just-dealing and humility and faithfulness to the basic precepts of morality. The Hebrews must have regarded them as rhetorical exaggerations, not prohibiting sacrifice as such but drawing attention to God's ethical demands as equally important.

In this reluctance to do what in our view they ought to have done long before, they may have seen further than we do, and further than perhaps they themselves knew. God does *not* simply ask good behaviour and brotherly love from us, though he does ask these things and we neglect them at our peril. He asks also a willingness to forget self completely, to surrender ourselves and ours and all we possess to him, for only when we stand before him naked and helpless, dependent solely on his grace, and not even daring to take that for granted, can he get through to us. This even more than a belief in God's providence and promises is what faith is about. And in its dim and broken way the institution of sacrifice witnessed to it, this supreme demand of God to possess a man or a woman's whole being.

(ii)

There are some scholars who argue that Gen. 22 is an antiquarian tale put around to account for a change at the dawn of Israel's history from human sacrifice to animal substitute. This seems to me to be reading the story with blinkers on. This story is not interested in sacrifice as a cultic rite and how it should be properly and fittingly observed. It is the basic demand of God enshrined in the practice that it is concerned with.

This is the sacrifice which in its crudest ancient form Abraham was now enjoined to make. Everything else in his life that seemed important was shown to be secondary to that—his personal happiness, his hopes for the future, and not least the very promises of God, the nature of which he had with such difficulty and only lately won through to understanding. If he would not give up his only son to God—note the savagery of the word "only", as if Ishmael had ceased to exist—then there was something that was more precious to him than God. He was being compelled to relive that existential moment in Harran when God's call had first come to him. Then all that had happened to him previously had been put remorselessly into perspective. Now all that had happened to him since was given the same treatment. God's will had to be obeyed, because he was God. That came first, and beside it nothing else mattered.

No more than we can encompass the workings of his grace can we with our human minds grasp this outrageous demand of God's that in the moment it is issued turns all our righteousness into "filthy rags" (Isa. 64:6, AV). We can only recognize that he makes it by right of all men, give thanks that Abraham so long ago met it fair and square with the answer "I will", and bitterly regret that none of the rest of us has been able to come within a million miles of matching his response.

SACRIFICE II: GOD'S SACRIFICE

Genesis 22:1-19 *(cont'd)*

This scarifying chapter, which bestrides the world of the Old Testament like a colossus, is also a magnificent piece of literature. It beautifully exemplifies three fundamental marks of Hebrew narrative as we meet it in the epic stories of the Patriarchs. It is worth while thinking some more about these marks because we will find that they lead us on naturally to this story's ultimate meaning, which is deeper even than the meaning we uncovered in the last section.

(i)

The first of these marks is *frugality and reserve.* In this tale as in many another in Gen. 12ff. we are given the barest essential facts and no more. It is almost completely devoid of the kind of circumstantial detail a modern author would delight in. There is no description of the location beyond a statement that it was a mountain in a district called Moriah three days' journey from Beersheba (obviously therefore not the Moriah associated with the Temple in 2 Chron. 3:1). Nor is there any description of what Abraham or Isaac looked like, of the clothes they wore, of what the weather was like, of what kind of wood was used, of the asses or the servants.

Even more remarkable is the absence of psychological observation. God gives no reason for his command, but simply makes it. We are told nothing of Abraham's reaction, of his amazement, his anger perhaps, his bitterness, his grief. And only one small question gives us a hint of Isaac's bewilderment at what is going on. Likewise, after it is all over and the ram has been slaughtered instead of Isaac, there are no tears of relief and joy, no words even exchanged between father and son. We get only the expected play on the place's name (which is if anything more than usually irrelevant because the author has not bothered to inform us where it was) and another renewal of the promise of descendants which includes some laconic words approving of Abraham's response (and in addition some nasty ones about these descendants possessing "the gate of their enemies").

It is almost as if the author were trying his best to empty his story of drama, and for good measure to rob it at the end of its climax. Yet how dramatic it is! How strongly God's imperial claims come across! How vivid is the progress of father and son through the vacant landscape! How unbearable is the suspense as Isaac asks his question, how taut the tension as Abraham raises his knife, how immense the relief when he catches sight of a ram caught in a bush! This is Hebrew story-telling at its masterly best. It is not the kind of story-telling we are used to from modern writers, but even across the centuries and in English translation it can grip us so that the knuckles of our clenched hands show white, and move us to the most intense of emotions.

(ii)

The frugality and reserve of the Genesis stories ask a lot of the reader. Time and again we have to make inferences from the scantiest of evidence about scenery and character and motive, and to think hard about what the stories mean and what they have to teach us. It very soon becomes apparent that, enjoyable as they are, they are not there primarily to entertain us but to challenge us. It is this ability to challenge all sorts and conditions of men across the centuries about the significance of life that is their second main characteristic. If I were asked to define it further, I would call it *an obsession with truth.*

By this I do not mean that they are historically accurate, for often they are not. Their very terseness makes it plain that they are not concerned with reporting carefully what happened. The authors are not historians but story-tellers, and the truth they serve is not historical truth but, as we might phrase it, life's truth. By asking so much of the reader, they haul him in his imagination back into their own ancient world. We almost hear God's call being issued to Abraham, see his visions and receive his promises. We descend with Lot to Sodom, plead with him for mercy, are tempted with his wife to look back. With Sarah we see Isaac and Ishmael playing together, with Abraham sadly consent as Hagar is banished with her son. We argue with God as Abraham did and come up against the same blank wall of divine grace and the divine will. And nowhere more so perhaps than in this story in chapter 22, where we too sense the totalitarian demands of God and feel the agony and confusion of the human beings who encountered them.

All this happened many centuries ago, indeed several millennia ago, and in a society in so many ways strange and alien to us, but it is as if it were happening in front of our eyes. We are involved in what is taking place, and as we read we are uplifted and brought low, comforted and convicted, driven to despair and made to grasp desperately for faith along with God's people of old. This is what I mean by the ability of the stories to confront us with the truth, not with the historian's facts nor the scientist's formulas but with the story-teller's apprehension of reality, that truth about God and about ourselves which is perceived in the hurly-burly of life as men go about their daily business.

(ii)

A third mark of Hebrew narrative, met with in many of Genesis' stories but not in them all, is what I would term *a long perspective.* Their foreground is Palestine in the Patriarchal age but their background is eternity. We cannot but be aware that what is happening has a future reference.

I am not referring here to the later additions which link the Patriarchs too precisely for our liking with the future history of Israel. As we have seen, a good number of these are selfish and exclusivist, drawing attention to Jerusalem's coming glory (end of chapter 14) or justifying Israel's conquest of the Canaanites (chapter 15) or saying offensive things about neighbouring nations with whom she was to quarrel (end of chapter 19). They spoil rather than clarify the original message of the stories.

But I am not referring either to the habit of many Christians of reading back prophecies of Christ or the Church into the Old Testament which could not possibly have meant anything to the Hebrews for whom it was first composed. That mechanical method of making the Old Testament a slave of Christian doctrine is just as counterfeit, and it is rightly frowned upon nowadays, for it in effect regards the Old Testament's first audiences as irrelevant.

I mean the way in which for the Christian reader the things of Christ every now and again leap mysteriously from the pages of this book to remind us with some force that the God of the Old Testament and the God of Jesus of Nazareth are one and the same. We can see that what is said or done had real significance for the Hebrews. The original meaning is not ignored or replaced but it takes on, as it were, a new life in the light of the Gospel.

We noticed this particularly in Genesis in Abraham's intercession for Sodom in chapter 18, where he began speaking about fifty righteous persons and gradually got it down to ten, but then stopped. The story itself almost invites us as Christians to reduce the number to one. If the presence of such a number of the righteous would have been enough to save that one city, we now know that one righteous man has in fact by what he did saved a whole world. It is as if the writer had left the gap for our imaginations to fill.

The story in Gen. 22 similarly arouses our antennae with its magical phrase, "God will provide himself the lamb for a burnt offering, my son." Here, I believe, is to be found the deepest meaning of the story, and it is a Christian meaning. I also believe that in finding it we are not reading in what is not there.

Abraham was commanded to surrender his dearest possession to God as a sign that he was ready to sacrifice himself to him. He was willing to do so, so strong was his faith, but in the end he was not in fact required to go through with it. Jesus was also willing to make this supreme sacrifice of himself, and he had to go through with it. With this chapter to guide us we can see him *as man* offering his whole self utterly to God, going into death's darkness alone with that awful cry of dereliction on his lips, all his human hopes—and as a man he had these as we have them—in ruins, with only his faith in God to sustain him. His Cross was more than a way for him to carry the punishment of our sin. It was at last one man making the sacrifice which as God's creatures we all owe to our Creator, but which none of us, not even Abraham, has ever been able to make.

But there is more to it even than that. For Jesus was also God, and in the Cross he *as God* also offered himself wholly to men. That is the other side of God's command to us to sacrifice our all to him. He in love is ready to give his all to us. This too takes us beyond the cancelling of human sin, important as that may be. It is the vision of God's self-giving in his Son that Abraham's reply to Isaac ultimately conjures up before our eyes.

"FULFILMENT" III: THE LAND

Genesis 22:20–23:20

20 Now after these things it was told Abraham, "Behold, Milcah also
21 has borne children to your brother Nahor: Uz the first-born, Buz his
22 brother, Kemuel the father of Aram, Chesed, Hazo, Pildash,
23 Jidlaph, and Bethuel." Bethuel became the father of Rebekah. These
24 eight Milcah bore to Nahor, Abraham's brother. Moreover, his
concubine, whose name was Reumah, bore Tebah, Gaham, Tahash, and Maacah.

1 Sarah lived a hundred and twenty-seven years; these were the
2 years of the life of Sarah. And Sarah died at Kiriath-arba (that is,

Hebron) in the land of Canaan; and Abraham went in to mourn for
3 Sarah and to weep for her. And Abraham rose up from before his
4 dead, and said to the Hittites, "I am a stranger and a sojourner
among you; give me property among you for a burying place, that I
5 may bury my dead out of my sight." The Hittites answered Abraham,
6 "Hear us, my lord; you are a mighty prince among us. Bury your
dead in the choicest of our sepulchres; none of us will withhold from
7 you his sepulchre, or hinder you from burying your dead." Abraham
8 rose and bowed to the Hittites, the people of the land. And he said to
them, "If you are willing that I should bury my dead out of my sight,
9 hear me, and entreat for me Ephron the son of Zohar, that he may
give me the cave of Mach-pelah, which he owns; it is at the end of his
field. For the full price let him give it to me in your presence as a
10 possession for a burying place." Now Ephron was sitting among the
Hittites; and Ephron the Hittite answered Abraham in the hearing
11 of the Hittites, of all who went in at the gate of his city, "No, my lord,
hear me; I give you the field, and I give you the cave that is in it; in the
presence of the sons of my people I give it to you; bury your dead."
12, 13 Then Abraham bowed down before the people of the land. And he
said to Ephron in the hearing of the people of the land, "But if you
will, hear me; I will give the price of the field; accept it from me, that
14, 15 I may bury my dead there." Ephron answered Abraham, "My lord,
listen to me; a piece of land worth four hundred shekels of silver,
16 what is that between you and me? Bury your dead." Abraham
agreed with Ephron; and Abraham weighed out for Ephron the
silver which he had named in the hearing of the Hittites, four
hundred shekels of silver, according to the weights current among
the merchants.
17 So the field of Ephron in Mach-pelah, which was to the east of
Mamre, the field with the cave which was in it and all the trees that
18 were in the field, throughout its whole area, was made over to
Abraham as a possession in the presence of the Hittites, before all
19 who went in at the gate of his city. After this, Abraham buried Sarah
his wife in the cave of the field of Mach-pelah east of Mamre (that is,
20 Hebron) in the land of Canaan. The field and the cave that is in it
were made over to Abraham as a possession for a burying place by
the Hittites.

The crisis of faith past, the epic of Abraham moves calmly
towards its resolution. It is mainly now concerned with the

winding up of family and clan affairs. We have first a genealogical notice catching up on how things were going back in Abraham's homeland in Upper Mesopotamia (22:20–24). Then there are Sarah's death and burial (chapter 23), arrangements for Isaac's marriage (chapter 24) and finally, together with further genealogical notices, a short report of Abraham's own death (25:1–18). These stories and notices would be lovingly cherished among the tribes of Israel, for they illumined their own beginnings and touched on matters dear to their hearts. But they do not raise, as the previous chapters have done, issues of tremendous theological or spiritual import, and we shouldn't scour them too earnestly in search of sermons for our modern age. It is enough that we note some things that need to be explained for today's readers and for the rest savour the tranquillity of the chapters before, with the opening of the Jacob cycle of stories, we are plunged once again into conflict and tension.

(i)

Following the shattering events of chapter 22 Abraham continued to stay in Beersheba, but after a time he must have returned to Hebron, for it was there that Sarah died. Living in Hebron (which, rather strangely, is only here given its more ancient name of Kiriath-arba) were a group of Hittites, who had probably come from Asia Minor to Palestine for purposes of trade. After a rather complicated process of bargaining, which reminds us of how eastern merchants even today often conduct their business, Abraham purchased from one of them a field with a cave in it, and there he buried his wife.

Sarah does not come out of the stories in Genesis as at all a nice person, and her jealousy and vindictiveness are rather mercilessly exposed in them. But it is only fair to emphasize that she must have attracted much love and loyalty from her husband for, as this story shows, he went to a lot of trouble to have her decently buried. Perhaps at the close of her life she too won through to a clearer faith, one that could not but be shot through with sharp remorse but that nevertheless found solace in the thought of God's forgiveness and grace. The Bible is silent on the matter, but it would be less than charitable of us to suppose otherwise.

(ii)

There is some evidence from sources discovered at Boghazköy, the site of the capital of the old Hittite kingdom, that the transaction between Abraham and Ephron was in one particular at least in accord with Hittite legal practice. Abraham clearly wished only to acquire a cave to bury his wife, but he was persuaded by Ephron to buy the field in which it was situated as well. Ephron even offered to give the lot to him for nothing. It appears from our new sources that in Hittite law feudal obligations were attached to the ownership of property. We may suppose then that the wily Hittite was trying to be quit of these obligations—whatever they were—by off-loading them upon Abraham. The fact that the two men had to conclude the deal "in the hearing" of the other members of the community lends credence to this supposition.

If we accept it, it would supply yet another indication of the faithfulness of the tradition behind the Patriarchal stories. But we hardly need it in order to get the real point of this story, which is that Abraham succumbed gracefully to Ephron's machinations, insisting on paying in cash and making no objection to purchasing the field along with the cave. There is gentle humour in it, for Abraham must have known he was being "done". But the upshot was that a Hebrew now owned for the first time an actual piece of what was later to become the Holy Land. It was only a tiny foothold and, as Abraham himself reminds us, he was still a "stranger and a sojourner" in the land, but it was a harbinger of things to come.

In the larger context of the uncertain pilgrimage of God's people towards a heavenly home this scarcely seems of much consequence, and Stephen may have been right to ignore the incident (rather pointedly, I think) when he said in his speech in Acts 7:5 of God bringing Abraham to Canaan, "Yet he gave him no inheritance in it, not even a foot's length". But perhaps we should again be charitable. Knowing of Israel's intense devotion down through the centuries to this particular corner of Western Asia we would be mean to begrudge her her little thrill of pride. But, one wonders, did the Hebrews relish with quite the same pleasure the story's ironic corollary that this plot of sacred soil was bought at full market price, if not above it, from a foreigner, and was not seized by force of arms? Or that it was not intended to house the living, but the dead?

MATCHMAKING I

Genesis 24:1-67

Abraham's servant is given his commission (verses 1-9)

1 Now Abraham was old, well advanced in years; and the Lord had
2 blessed Abraham in all things. And Abraham said to his servant, the oldest of his house, who had charge of all that he had, "Put your
3 hand under my thigh, and I will make you swear by the Lord, the God of heaven and of the earth, that you will not take a wife for my
4 son from the daughters of the Canaanites, among whom I dwell, but will go to my country and to my kindred, and take a wife for my son
5 Isaac." The servant said to him, "Perhaps the woman may not be willing to follow me to this land; must I then take your son back to
6 the land from which you came?" Abraham said to him, "See to it
7 that you do not take my son back there. The Lord, the God of heaven, who took me from my father's house and from the land of my birth, and who spoke to me and swore to me, 'To your descendants I will give this land,' he will send his angel before you,
8 and you shall take a wife for my son from there. But if the woman is not willing to follow you, then you will be free from this oath of
9 mine; only you must not take my son back there." So the servant put his hand under the thigh of Abraham his master, and swore to him concerning this matter.

The servant reaches the well (verses 10-14)

10 Then the servant took ten of his master's camels and departed, taking all sorts of choice gifts from his master; and he arose, and
11 went to Mesopotamia, to the city of Nahor. And he made the camels

kneel down outside the city by the well of water at the time of
12 evening, the time when women go out to draw water. And he said,
"O Lord, God of my master Abraham, grant me success today, I
13 pray thee, and show steadfast love to my master Abraham. Behold, I
am standing by the spring of water, and the daughters of the men of
14 the city are coming out to draw water. Let the maiden to whom I
shall say, 'Pray let down your jar that I may drink,' and who shall
say, 'Drink, and I will water your camels'—let her be the one whom
thou hast appointed for thy servant Isaac. By this I shall know that
thou hast shown steadfast love to my master."

The servant and Rebekah (verses 15–27)

15 Before he had done speaking, behold, Rebekah, who was born to
Bethuel the son of Milcah, the wife of Nahor, Abraham's brother,
16 came out with her water jar upon her shoulder. The maiden was very
fair to look upon, a virgin, whom no man had known. She went
17 down to the spring, and filled her jar, and came up. Then the servant
ran to meet her, and said, "Pray give me a little water to drink from
18 your jar." She said, "Drink, my lord"; and she quickly let down her
19 jar upon her hand, and gave him a drink. When she had finished
giving him a drink, she said, "I will draw for your camels also, until
20 they have done drinking." So she quickly emptied her jar into the
trough and ran again to the well to draw, and she drew for all his
21 camels. The man gazed at her in silence to learn whether the Lord
had prospered his journey or not.
22 　When the camels had done drinking, the man took a gold ring
weighing a half shekel, and two bracelets for her arms weighing ten
23 gold shekels, and said, "Tell me whose daughter you are. Is there
24 room in your father's house for us to lodge in?" She said to him, "I
am the daughter of Bethuel the son of Milcah, whom she bore to
25 Nahor." She added, "We have both straw and provender enough,
26 and room to lodge in." The man bowed his head and worshipped the
27 Lord, and said, "Blessed be the Lord, the God of my master
Abraham, who has not forsaken his steadfast love and his faithfulness toward my master. As for me, the Lord has led me in the way to
the house of my master's kinsmen."

Laban's welcome (verses 28–33)

28 Then the maiden ran and told her mother's household about these

29 things. Rebekah had a brother whose name was Laban; and Laban
30 ran out to the man, to the spring. When he saw the ring, and the
bracelets on his sister's arms, and when he heard the words of
Rebekah his sister, "Thus the man spoke to me," he went to the man;
31 and behold, he was standing by the camels at the spring. He said,
"Come in, O blessed of the Lord; why do you stand outside? For I
32 have prepared the house and a place for the camels." So the man
came into the house; and Laban ungirded the camels, and gave him
straw and provender for the camels, and water to wash his feet and
33 the feet of the men who were with him. Then food was set before him
to eat; but he said, "I will not eat until I have told my errand." He
said, "Speak on."

The servant's story (verses 34–49)

34, 35 So he said, "I am Abraham's servant. The Lord has greatly blessed
my master, and he has become great; he has given him flocks and
herds, silver and gold, menservants and maidservants, camels and
36 asses. And Sarah my master's wife bore a son to my master when she
37 was old; and to him he has given all that he has. My master made me
swear, saying, 'You shall not take a wife for my son from the
38 daughters of the Canaanites, in whose land I dwell; but you shall go
to my father's house and to my kindred, and take a wife for my son.'
39, 40 I said to my master, 'Perhaps the woman will not follow me.' But he
said to me, 'The Lord, before whom I walk, will send his angel with
you and prosper your way; and you shall take a wife for my son from
41 my kindred and from my father's house; then you will be free from
my oath, when you come to my kindred; and if they will not give her
to you, you will be free from my oath.'
42 "I came today to the spring, and said, 'O Lord, the God of my
master Abraham, if now thou wilt prosper the way which I go,
43 behold, I am standing by the spring of water; let the young woman
who comes out to draw, to whom I shall say, "Pray give me a little
44 water from your jar to drink," and who will say to me, "Drink, and I
will draw for your camels also," let her be the woman whom the
Lord has appointed for my master's son.'
45 "Before I had done speaking in my heart, behold, Rebekah came
out with her water jar on her shoulder; and she went down to the
46 spring, and drew. I said to her, 'Pray let me drink.' She quickly let
down her jar from her shoulder, and said, 'Drink, and I will give
your camels drink also.' So I drank, and she gave the camels drink

47 also. Then I asked her, 'Whose daughter are you?' She said, 'The
   daughter of Bethuel, Nahor's son, whom Milcah bore to him.' So I
48 put the ring on her nose, and the bracelets on her arms. Then I
   bowed my head and worshipped the Lord, and blessed the Lord, the
   God of my master Abraham, who had led me by the right way to
49 take the daughter of my master's kinsman for his son. Now then, if
   you will deal loyally and truly with my master, tell me; and if not, tell
   me; that I may turn to the right hand or to the left."

Rebekah departs with her family's blessings (verses 50–61)

50 Then Laban and Bethuel answered, "The thing comes from the
51 Lord; we cannot speak to you bad or good. Behold, Rebekah is
   before you, take her and go, and let her be the wife of your master's
   son, as the Lord has spoken."
52   When Abraham's servant heard their words, he bowed himself to
53 the earth before the Lord. And the servant brought forth jewelry of
   silver and of gold, and raiment, and gave them to Rebekah; he also
54 gave to her brother and to her mother costly ornaments. And he and
   the men who were with him ate and drank, and they spent the night
   there. When they arose in the morning, he said, "Send me back to
55 my master." Her brother and her mother said, "Let the maiden
56 remain with us a while, at least ten days; after that she may go." But
   he said to them, "Do not delay me, since the Lord has prospered my
57 way; let me go that I may go to my master." They said, "We will call
58 the maiden, and ask her." And they called Rebekah, and said to her,
59 "Will you go with this man?" She said, "I will go." So they sent away
   Rebekah their sister and her nurse, and Abraham's servant and his
60 men. And they blessed Rebekah, and said to her, "Our sister, be the
   mother of thousands of ten thousands; and may your descendants
61 possess the gate of those who hate them!" Then Rebekah and her
   maids arose, and rode upon the camels and followed the man; thus
   the servant took Rebekah, and went his way.

Rebekah meets her future husband (verses 62–67)

62 Now Isaac had come from Beer-lahai-roi, and was dwelling in the
63 Negeb. And Isaac went out to meditate in the field in the evening;
   and he lifted up his eyes and looked, and behold there were camels
64 coming. And Rebekah lifted up her eyes, and when she saw Isaac,
65 she alighted from the camel, and said to the servant, "Who is the
   man yonder, walking in the field to meet us?" The servant said, "It is

66 my master." So she took her veil and covered herself. And the
67 servant told Isaac all the things that he had done. Then Isaac
brought her into the tent, and took Rebekah, and she became his
wife; and he loved her. So Isaac was comforted after his mother's
death.

This story of how a wife was obtained for Isaac is slightly longer
than the story of the events leading up to the destruction of
Sodom and Gomorrah in chapters 18 and 19, but compared
with its bewildering shifts of scene and character it is simplicity
itself. It is expansive where that story was cryptic, and has more
of the idyllic atmosphere of romance as found, for example, in
the book of Ruth than of the clash of epic. But it should not on
that score be thought of as coming from a different background
of story-telling. Events are still frugally related and hard
information is still as scarce. What we do get is a richer use of
dialogue, probably because God is not directly present in the
action and the human participants are, as it were, freed to adopt
with each other the rather extravagant habits of speech which
have always been typical of formal conversations in the East.
There is also a good deal of repetition, especially in the long
address by Abraham's servant to Laban, which recapitulates
much of what had happened previously, but that too, as we
have seen, is a feature that appears in quite a few Hebrew
stories. But chiefly this is a happy story, and for that reason if
for no other we should not expect to be confronted with the
tension and challenge and anxiety which so pervaded chapters
18 and 19 or the pulsating sacrifice story in chapter 22. It is that
rare thing in the Bible, a pleasant straightforward story which is
not getting at us. We can relax as we read it—and how often can
we do that in Genesis?

MATCHMAKING II

Genesis 24:1-67 *(cont'd)*

(i)

There are a couple of difficulties in the narrative, neither very
serious.

The first concerns the mention of Rebekah's father Bethuel in verse 50. The marriage between Isaac and Rebekah was an arranged one as most marriages in antiquity were and he, as the father of the intended bride, ought to have been conducting the negotiations with Abraham's servant. But in fact it was her brother Laban who welcomed the servant and it was he and the girl's mother who received the bride-price and who asked her, "Will you go with this man?" The easiest way out of this difficulty is to assume that Bethuel was already dead and that his name has slipped into the text at this point through a careless error. This would also nicely explain the unusual circumstance of Rebekah being asked for her consent. Isaac was not asked for his before the servant set out. It seems, however, from the evidence of certain marriage documents discovered by the archaeologists, that in the Mesopotamia of the time the girl's agreement had to be sought if her father was dead and it was some other male relative who was negotiating on her behalf.

The second difficulty arises from sentiments being put into Laban's mouth that could be taken to suggest that he worshipped Abraham's God; thus "Come in, O blessed of the Lord" in verse 31 and "The thing comes from the Lord" in verse 50. This, of course, could not have been the case. Probably the story-teller found it convenient to "forget" that Abraham's Aramean relatives were still pagan because he was keen to emphasize that God was behind Isaac's marriage. He is pretending that the reason God approved of Abraham's decision to seek a wife for his son among his own kinsmen was that they unlike the Canaanites belonged to the chosen people, whereas the truth of the matter was that both peoples were equally pagan and that Abraham was only doing what most fathers in a tribal society would have done, insisting that his son marry "within the tribe". We catch a whisper here of that hatred and suspicion of other nations which we have noticed several times before being foisted onto the Genesis narrative, but it is no more than a whisper and it can hardly be said to spoil the gentle and peaceful atmosphere of the story. The stories of Jacob's dealings with Laban are rather more careful in this regard; see for example 31:29–30.

(ii)

If there are lessons in this amiable story they are to be sought in the wry little sketches of the main characters.

The picture of *Abraham,* bowed down with years, settling his affairs before he died does not lack an overlay of pathos. He makes his servant swear a solemn oath by God not to take a wife for his son from the Canaanites but to look for one for him in the "old country". This, as we have seen, was in accordance with tribal custom, but it can scarcely be called a sturdy demonstration of a faith resolutely breaking with the past. He wholly accepts God's will that his family's future lies in Canaan, but he cannot help in his declining years glancing back at the happy times he had in Mesopotamia as a young man. Also, there must be a touch of irony, probably unconscious, in the story-teller having Abraham call God "the God of heaven and earth". Even if we allow that the real Abraham could have used such a high-sounding title, would he have used it to back up what was after all a rather selfish undertaking? But what comes through most strongly in the story is the old exile's fear for his son's safety and for the fulfilment of the promise. Knowing that he would die soon, he urgently impresses upon his servant that he must not now or at any later stage in the negotiations take Isaac to Mesopotamia. Perhaps the memory of that frightening scene in the land of Moriah was still vividly with him. His son must not be exposed to any more danger. It is a touching picture of an old man's worries and apprehension. It is not meant too unkindly and I don't think it really detracts from his great victory of faith, but it reminds us that life's close, even for an Abraham, is not necessarily or always a time of peace and serenity.

Abraham's servant comes out of the story rather better than his master. There can be no doubting this man's intense loyalty both to Abraham and to Abraham's God. When he reaches the well he does not rush things, but waits patiently for God's guidance. But when he is sure that he has found the right girl he acts with determination even at the risk of offending his hosts. Is there a hint of his growing confidence in the way the author introduces his three acts of worship in the story? At the well we have simply "And he said" (verse 12). As he accepts Rebekah's invitation to lodge in the family home, we have "The man bowed his head and worshipped" (verse 26). And when Laban agrees to the marriage, we have "He bowed himself to the earth before the Lord" (verse 52). It would be nice to think that this was the same servant as the Eliezer who had been promised the inheritance in chapter 15 before either Ishmael or Isaac were born. That would add a generous and unselfish spirit to the qualities of faithfulness and sense of duty he so attractively reveals in this story.

In this story we make the acquaintance for the first time of *Rebekah* and *Laban,* both of whom are to figure so prominently later on in the stories about Jacob. The girl is carefree as she comes out with the women to draw water; she responds generously to the servant's request for a drink, nor does she forget about his camels; she is sure that there will be room for him—and for them—in the encampment; she runs home excitedly to tell of the stranger who had brought rich presents; she obviously pleases Abraham's servant; she says "Yes" with alacrity when asked if she will go with him to be Isaac's bride; and she shows both curiosity and, by drawing up her veil, an engaging modesty when after the journey she sees her future husband approaching. A vivacious and pleasant girl—but is there not just a suggestion of impetuousness in some of her actions, an impetuousness which prepares us for the brazen prejudice on Jacob's behalf she was to show in the famous scene in chapter 27, when Esau's blessing was filched from him? Similarly there is Laban's openhearted hospitality and his obvious concern for Rebekah's welfare. But there is also something slightly ominous in the words "When he saw the ring, and the bracelets on his sister's arms" (verse 30), something of that greed and deviousness which was to make him such a formidable opponent of Jacob when he in his turn came to Mesopotamia in search of a wife.

Finally we have *Isaac* "meditating" as he waits at home—no man of action this!—and catching sight of the caravan in the distance and leading Rebekah solicitously to his tent and, it seems, genuinely falling in love with her. But, as we will remember, he had not been consulted by Abraham about the marriage, though he was (see 25:20) nearly forty years old at the time. We need not take that figure quite literally, but he was clearly no youngster. Would it be unfair to take from this that he was essentially a retiring and timid man, or with the story's last sentence in mind—"So Isaac was comforted after his mother's death"—even a bit of a "mammy's boy"?

The story-teller is not straining at high drama or deep significance in this chapter. He has a quiet faith that God was in the events he records, but he does not labour the point too much. There are no great confrontations between God and man here. In the same way he wants us to be sympathetic towards his characters, but he has no intention of idealizing them. He balances sweetness with just the right measure of acerbity and bite. We know that these are real human beings he is telling us about, not all that different from ourselves. It is impossible not to admire his cool mastery of his craft.

GENEALOGY

Genesis 25:1–18

1,2 Abraham took another wife, whose name was Keturah. She bore
3 him Zimran, Jokshan, Medan, Midian, Ishbak, and Shuah. Jokshan was the father of Sheba and Dedan. The sons of Dedan were
4 Asshurim, Letushim, and Le-ummim. The sons of Midian were Ephah, Epher, Hanoch, Abida, and Eldaah. All these were the
5,6 children of Keturah. Abraham gave all he had to Isaac. But to the sons of his concubines Abraham gave gifts, and while he was still living he sent them away from his son Isaac, eastward to the east country.
7 These are the days of the years of Abraham's life, a hundred and
8 seventy-five years. Abraham breathed his last and died in a good old age, an old man and full of years, and was gathered to his people.

9 Isaac and Ishmael his sons buried him in the cave of Machpelah, in
10 the field of Ephron the son of Zohar the Hittite, east of Mamre, the
field which Abraham purchased from the Hittites. There Abraham
11 was buried, with Sarah his wife. After the death of Abraham God
blessed Isaac his son. And Isaac dwelt at Beer-lahai-roi.
12 These are the descendants of Ishmael, Abraham's son, whom
13 Hagar the Egyptian, Sarah's maid, bore to Abraham. These are the
names of the sons of Ishmael, named in the order of their birth:
14 Nebaioth, the first-born of Ishmael, and Kedar, Adbeel, Mibsam,
15 Mishma, Dumah, Massa, Hadad, Tema, Jetur, Naphish, and
16 Kedemah. These are the sons of Ishmael and these are their names,
by their villages and by their encampments, twelve princes accord-
17 ing to their tribes. (These are the years of the life of Ishmael, a
hundred and thirty-seven years; he breathed his last and died, and
18 was gathered to his kindred.) They dwelt from Havilah to Shur,
which is opposite Egypt in the direction of Assyria; he settled over
against all his people.

The two genealogies in this chapter continue those at the end of
chapter 9 and in chapters 10 and 11, which were discussed in
Volume 1. Like them they should be regarded as giving valuable
information about how the Hebrews saw their relationships
with surrounding peoples, but not as telling us anything about
real historical individuals. It is worth repeating in this regard
Bruce Vawter's helpful analogy, which I quoted in Volume 1. It
is as if, he suggests, we were to record our own history in the
following fashion: "The descendants of Europe: Britain,
France, Spain ... Britain became the father of America,
Canada ... To Spain also children were born: California,
Mexico ... The descendants of America: Virginia, Georgia,
Carolina ... Georgia became the father of Atlanta, Augusta,
Savannah ..." and so on. Just as in chapter 10 we had a
geographical lesson in the form of a fictitious family tree of
distant peoples in Africa and Asia, which narrowed down in
chapter 11 to the Aramean tribes of Mesopotamia with whom
the Hebrews had the closest blood ties, so these lists in chapter
25 concentrate on the Semitic peoples of Arabia with whom
they also felt a kinship, though not quite so close.

(i)

What then are we to say about the marriage of Abraham to Keturah? It is not impossible that Abraham after Hagar's departure and Sarah's death took another wife, though we are nowhere told anything else about her. What is impossible is that she bore him the children mentioned in the opening verses of this chapter. The names which can be identified (e.g. Dedan, Midian) are not those of individuals but of places or areas in north Arabia. In exactly the same way the names of Ishmael's descendants given later in the chapter point to areas or places (e.g. Kedar, Dumah, Tema) further east in the north Arabian and Syrian deserts.

A moment's thought should be enough to tell us that nations and tribes do not come into being in this manner, that is, by direct descent from single progenitors. When, therefore, these genealogies imply that the founders or forefathers of the Arab tribes were sons or grandsons of Abraham, who were born in Palestine and moved from there to the areas which these tribes later inhabited, they cannot be recording accurate history. They are saying something that was important to the Hebrews, but it is not history in our sense of the term. The same will be true in the case of the peoples of Moab and Ammon to the immediate east of Canaan, who according to the end of chapter 19 were descendants of sons born incestuously to Lot, and of the peoples of Edom to its southeast, who according to the genealogy to come in chapter 36 had sons of Esau as their ancestors.

I give on Map 2 a rough sketch of the localities in the vicinity of Palestine with which these various peoples were associated. It will be seen that from both a geographical and a racial standpoint the Canaanites ought to have been among them, but it will be remembered that as a result of Hebrew prejudice they were classified in chapters 9 and 10 as a Hamitic or African people. This should remind us that the information preserved in these lists is not only valuable, but sometimes biased as well. See the commentary on 9:20–29 in Volume 1.

(ii)

There are some sceptical scholars who argue that not only the genealogies but the Patriarchal stories as a whole are about ethnic groups and not about individuals—in other words, that all the Patriarchs are personifications of peoples or tribes or clans. But this cannot be so for the very simple reason that the names of most of the Patriarchs and their wives—Abraham, Lot, Sarah, Hagar, even Esau and Jacob—have no direct ethnic associations. They are not generally used as ethnic titles and in fact they stick out like sore thumbs in the genealogies.

It follows from this that we have to recognize the presence in Genesis 12ff. of two distinct kinds of tribal tradition:

(a) stories about the Patriarchs as individuals, that is, about real heroes and heroines of Israel's distant past, the memory of whose exploits was treasured and passed on from generation to generation among their descendants

(b) genealogical lists in which most of the names are of peoples or tribes or of the places associated with them. The Patriarchs are introduced into these from time to time as fathers or grandfathers to highlight a particularly close kinship, but they do not strictly speaking belong in them.

For the most part the two kinds of tradition are kept apart. But sometimes we have to admit that they overlap. Ishmael, for instance, is an ethnic name as well as an individual one. And both Esau and Jacob have second names—Seir or Edom and Israel—which are ethnic. This means that traditions about peoples do now and again intrude into stories about individuals, and we have to be careful to distinguish them as far as we are able.

The disentangling can be a tricky business, affording many opportunities for disagreement among the scholars, but for our purpose in this commentary commonsense should serve as a reasonably satisfactory guide most of the time. We do not need an expert to tell us, for example, that several aspects of Esau's appearance as described in the latter part of chapter 25 have more to do with the people of Edom than with him as an individual. Nor, on the contrary, do we require expert guidance to see that the story of Esau's reconciliation with Jacob in chapter 33 has few, if any, ethnic corollaries, since in historical times Edom and Israel were usually bitter enemies. Contrast the savage treatment of Moab and Ammon in 19:30ff.

(iii)

Readers who are interested in pursuing these antiquarian matters further may consult a Bible Dictionary or one of the larger technical Commentaries. The reason I have spent time on them is the same reason as prompted me to write the *Note on Genesis as "History"* following our discussion of the story of Abraham in Egypt. It is vital that we learn to detect where extraneous material has got mixed up with the stories in Gen. 12ff., whether it is genealogical material as in this chapter or later additions as in chapter 12. Only by isolating such material and setting it aside will we be able to confront the real Abraham and Isaac and Jacob and profit fully from their experience.

It is the stories that carry the chief message of Genesis. They are not "history" in our sense of the term either, but we shouldn't be put off by that (see the discussion in the section called *"Sacrifice"* II). They are something much better, an avenue into the life of God's people of old. In them far more immediately than in the most painstaking and detailed historical account do we make the confrontation I have spoken of and know for sure that we have made it.

DEATH

Genesis 25:1-18 *(cont'd)*

When at the end of chapter 24 Rebekah caught sight of Isaac approaching and asked who he was, the servant answered, "It is my master". This suggests that Abraham had died while his servant was in Mesopotamia. After his burial Isaac seems to have moved from Hebron, first to Beer-lahai-roi (where Hagar had had her vision) and then to the area around Beersheba (where he had spent his own earlier years). Presumably the servant on returning to Hebron and learning of Abraham's death and Isaac's departure carried on till he caught up with his new master. In its characteristic Hebrew way the story leaves us to infer all this, concentrating its attention at the close on the dramatic meeting between Isaac and Rebekah. It mentions Sarah's earlier death because in a sense Rebekah was taking her place, but does not think it necessary to say a thing about Abraham's more recent death.

(i)

And when in this chapter we are at last told that the great man had died and been buried beside his wife in the cave of Machpelah, how laconic the report is! It is set between two genealogical lists which we find it difficult to imagine even the Hebrews thinking anything like as important. The patriarch's great age is mentioned, but little more. We can hardly help turning back in our minds to chapter 5, where the even longer lives of the antediluvian heroes like Methuselah were meticulously recorded before litany-like the list repeated that they all "died". Abraham was not even given the consolation of seeing his future daughter-in-law before he passed on. The continuance of the promises was left in the hands of the God who made them and the demise of the human being to whom they were first addressed rates only a few brief lines of Scripture. There is a nice and tender touch in the notice that Ishmael was present at the funeral, but nothing is made of it either, as we are not told that it led to any further meetings between the brothers.

The quaint phrase "gathered to his people" is used also of Ishmael in verse 17, and later of Isaac in 35:29, of Jacob in 49:33, and of Moses and Aaron in Deut. 32:50. It is more fully explained in 2 Kgs. 22:20, which speaks in the same context of God gathering King Josiah to his fathers and of him being gathered to his grave in peace. Compare the equally quaint phrase "slept with his fathers" used of David, Solomon and the other kings of Israel (1 Kgs. 2:10; 11:43; 14:20 etc.). Nothing should be read into these phrases of a belief in a life beyond the grave. The Hebrews looked forward to a peaceful death in old age, when their bodies would be buried beside those of their forbears while their "shades" joined all the other "shades" and lingered on for a time, in a condition of extreme weakness, in the subterranean world of Sheol (see Job 3:13–19; Isa. 14:9–11). When the body had mouldered into dust, this ghostly form also disappeared. Not until the very close of the Old Testament period was there any conception of a meaningful life after death. Death was to all intents and purposes the end. The Old Testament makes no bones about this. Death comes to all men and, as it is here peremptorily emphasized, it came to Abraham too.

To us who do have a belief in life beyond the grave and in spite of that usually make such a fuss about dying, the terse and sober descriptions of death in the Old Testament are not very welcome. Perhaps we ought to feel rebuked by them. The Hebrews did not have our Christian hope, yet they were able to face death bravely and accept it with realism and dignity. To them this short paragraph would appear not at all sad, but a fitting commentary on life as it was, even an Abraham's life, a brief and passing episode during which human beings could have a glimpse of eternity, but only as they related themselves to him who alone was eternal, who was there before they came on the scene and who would be there when they were gone.

> My days are like an evening shadow;
>   I wither away like grass.
> But thou, O Lord, art enthroned for ever;
>   thy name endures to all generations.

> (Ps. 102:11–12)

There is a precious insight here into faith's priorities which is not cancelled out even by Our Lord's resurrection from the dead and the hope it gives us that we can follow on his coat-tails into everlasting life.

(ii)

So concludes what has indeed been an epic tale, a tale of a faith tempered in the fires of life's experience to emerge at last as purest steel. Abraham believed God's promises enthusiastically and on the strength of them he set out on an uncertain journey towards an even more uncertain future. At no time did God make it easy for him. He had to learn the hard way that faith and expediency did not mix. He laughed at the thought of his wife having a son in her old age and protested bitterly when his other son Ishmael was excluded from the promises, but he had to recognize that accepting such instances of God's peculiar providence was a large part of what faith was about. He did his best for his wayward nephew but had to admit failure. He came to see, as few of his descendants after him saw, that God's purpose included more than the safety and prosperity of his own small clan, interceding manfully for Sodom and Gomorrah, but there too he failed. Finally, he heard God's command to give up what was dearest above all to him, to sacrifice the very son whom God himself had miraculously given him—and he obeyed, though he could see no reason in it and his heart was breaking.

Did this man know happiness? Probably now and again, as when Ishmael and Isaac were born or as when God stayed his hand in the land of Moriah. But that was not what mattered. His destiny—his cross, if you like—was to show faith, to lift himself time after time from the floor of disappointment and despair and return to the fight of life, to hear tremendous promises and yet be content with the flimsiest of fulfilments before he died, to follow desperately God's retreating shadow because he knew there was nothing else worth following, to lay down his pilgrim's staff while still in the valley of deep darkness, seeing only the faintest rays of the sun's rising on the distant hills. What an example is there for us whose faith is fitful and fleeting and cold and selfish, hardly deserving the name! Abraham was not perfect, and Genesis does not pretend that he was. No more than we do did he merit or earn the grace shown to him. But he did merit and he did earn the accolade given him by future generations of Jews—and by Christians and Muslims as well—"the father of the faithful".

As he died Abraham, as a good Hebrew, would have had no notion of his own survival after death. But with a little Christian licence we can surely put into his mouth the words which John Bunyan put into the mouth of Mr. Valiant-for-Truth in his *Pilgrim's Progress,* as that intrepid soul received his summons to enter the Celestial City. I can think of no better epitaph.

> "Though with great difficulty I am got hither, yet now I do not repent me of all the trouble I have been at to arrive where I am. My sword I give to him that shall succeed me in my pilgrimage, and my courage to him that can get it. My marks and scars I carry with me, to be a witness for me, that I have fought his battles, who will now be my rewarder. . . ." So he passed over, and all the trumpets sounded for him on the other side.

JACOB: AN EPIC OF CONFLICT

CONFLICT

Genesis 25:19-34

19 These are the descendants of Isaac, Abraham's son: Abraham was
20 the father of Isaac, and Isaac was forty years old when he took to
wife Rebekah, the daughter of Bethuel the Aramean of Paddan-
21 aram, the sister of Laban the Aramean. And Isaac prayed to the
Lord for his wife, because she was barren; and the Lord granted his
22 prayer, and Rebekah his wife conceived. The children struggled
together within her; and she said, "If it is thus, why do I live?" So she
23 went to inquire of the Lord. And the Lord said to her,
"Two nations are in your womb,
and two peoples, born of you, shall be divided;
the one shall be stronger than the other,
the elder shall serve the younger."
24 When her days to be delivered were fulfilled, behold, there were
25 twins in her womb. The first came forth red, all his body like a hairy
26 mantle; so they called his name Esau. Afterward his brother came
forth, and his hand had taken hold of Esau's heel; so his name was
called Jacob. Isaac was sixty years old when she bore them.
27 When the boys grew up, Esau was a skilful hunter, a man of the
28 field, while Jacob was a quiet man, dwelling in tents. Isaac loved
Esau, because he ate of his game; but Rebekah loved Jacob.
29 Once when Jacob was boiling pottage, Esau came in from the
30 field, and he was famished. And Esau said to Jacob, "Let me eat
some of that red pottage, for I am famished!" (Therefore his name
31, 32 was called Edom.) Jacob said, "First sell me your birthright." Esau
33 said, "I am about to die; of what use is a birthright to me?" Jacob
said, "Swear to me first." So he swore to him, and sold his birthright
34 to Jacob. Then Jacob gave Esau bread and pottage of lentils, and he
ate and drank, and rose and went his way. Thus Esau despised his
birthright.

Genesis' second Patriarchal epic begins with two brief stories, that of the birth of Jacob and Esau and that of the bartered birthright. They establish its mood right away as one of family conflict and intrigue. We are given no more than an outline sketch of events, but how penetrating it is in the implicit judgments it passes on the human beings involved! It is scarcely less so in its assessment of the strange and seemingly cruel will of God which it sees operating in the background.

(i)

Like the wife in many another Biblical birth story, Rebekah was barren. Isaac prayed to God for children and his prayer was answered with twins. It is a nice pious scene, but even before Rebekah was delivered of them, there are portents of trouble to come. She interpreted the kicking inside her as her babies quarrelling with each other and had her interpretation confirmed by a private divine oracle. This spoke rather enigmatically about two nations in her womb, but the part which she would have fastened upon was the forecast that the younger son would be the stronger of the two and the elder would serve him. When the children were born and the second came out grasping the heel of the first, Rebekah must have concluded that God had given her a secret insight into the future.

The scene then shifts quickly to when the boys were grown, and we are told that the elder, called Esau, was a man of the open country, skilled in hunting, while the younger, called Jacob, was a quiet man who preferred the orderly round of a shepherd's life closer to the encampment. Nothing is yet made of this difference, and it is probable that they had been assigned their respective tasks by their father because they were suited to them. But the seeds are there of the classic clash of many of the world's great stories, that between the man of action and the man of thought, the practical man and the brooder, the bold and the careful, the doer and the schemer.

And when we discover that not only are the personalities of the brothers so contrary but that the devout parents are both showing partiality, we know that it is only a matter of time before this family is split wide open. A reason is given for Isaac's favouring of Esau—he brought him meat while (we can almost hear him saying) Jacob sat around all day doing nothing. No reason is given for Rebekah's favouring of Jacob, but presumably we are meant to connect it with the oracle she received during her pregnancy. But in case it be thought that this implies that her favouritism was better placed, it should be pointed out that she cannot have told Isaac what God had said to her, for it is evident that he knows nothing about it, nor does he later when he calls Esau to bless him. A wife who was less than honest with her husband and a husband whose first thought was for his creature comforts. It can hardly be said to be a recipe for domestic harmony!

(ii)

Conflict all round. There in miniature in its first brief episode is the constituent plot of the whole Jacob cycle.

Let us attempt a short summary. There is the conflict, just underlined, between Isaac and Rebekah. There is the central conflict between Jacob and Esau which breaks out openly in chapter 27. There is the festering conflict between Jacob and his uncle Laban which takes up the bulk of chapters 29-31, with within it a conflict of jealousy between Jacob's wives Rachel and Leah.

We have to wait till the end of chapter 31 before a hopeful note is sounded with the rather grudging treaty between Jacob and Laban, to be followed in chapter 33 by the more generous reconciliation between Jacob and Esau, though it should be noted that the generosity was mainly on Esau's side. But even after that the family was anything but united. Chapter 34 contains a horrible story of lust and revenge which shows Jacob's sons unrepentantly vindictive and greatly distresses their father. And almost the last recorded incident in the lengthy epic is a report (35:22) of Reuben, Jacob's oldest son, lying with Bilhah, his father's concubine. The last is the departure of Esau (36:6) as "he went into a land away from his brother". No one could pretend that we have in all this a story with a happy ending.

But there is more to it than that. Perhaps the most perturbing events of all in the epic are the intermittent appearances of God to Jacob. Each of them—at Bethel (28:10–22), at Mahanaim (32:1), at Peniel (32:24–32) and again at Bethel (35:9–15)— takes place at a moment of crisis in his life, and each of them seems—at least on the surface—to have as its purpose to comfort and strengthen him and assure him that God was on his side. It is even suggested at Peniel—where Jacob was renamed Israel—that, having won his contest with Laban and being on the point of winning his contest with Esau, Jacob was able to wrestle with God and defeat him too.

So to the human conflicts which fill this pulsating epic we have to add a conflict between Jacob and God. And he wins them all!

(iii)

It is clearly not going to be easy to find spiritual lessons in this rumbustious and disquieting set of stories. True, Jacob tri- umphs. But his triumph is of a very different sort from Abraham's. The epic ends as it began, in an atmosphere of suspicion and strife which seems to have been little improved by the temporary patching up of quarrels, and all through it God is as partisan as any of the human characters. There is almost no evidence that I can see of lives being improved, except in the case of Esau, and he is the one who receives the least reward.

Yet I am sure that there are lessons in it. They are patently not moralizing lessons about the sweetening influence of religion in family relationships. Those who want that kind of thing would be better advised to turn to the Joseph cycle which comes next. Here the issues are far more elemental. There is desperation in the air as he who is at once the most devious and the most heroic character in the epic fights for a place in the sun—and fights dirty—and fights too to retain his hold on the God who had promised to be his champion. The lessons we find will have to match that scenario.

A Note on the Names Jacob and Esau

We ought, from a historical standpoint, to be rather distrustful of the explanations attached to the names of Esau and Jacob. They tell us more about the fondness of Hebrew audiences for plays on the meanings of words—a fondness we have noticed more than once before—than about what was in the mind of Isaac and Rebekah when the boys were born.

The verb in Jacob's name means "to follow at the heel", and the name is in fact a little prayer by his parents that God who had protected their boy at birth would continue to protect him throughout his life. It can only therefore have been later, when Jacob's character was known, that it was linked sarcastically with the fact that his hand had been holding his brother's heel when he was born. In a similar vein Esau in 27:36 comments with bitter irony that his brother was well called Jacob, since he had "supplanted" or "overtaken" him twice, previously in the matter of his birthright and now in the matter of his blessing.

The case with Esau's name is rather different. Its real meaning is unknown, though presumably the Hebrews were aware of it. But whereas the invented meanings of Jacob's name arise out of the stories about him, the plays on Esau's name have more to do with the Edomites as a people than with him as an individual. He came out of the womb "red" (Hebrew *admoni*) and "hairy" (Hebrew *se'ar*) and because of the latter was called Esau (Hebrew *'esaw*). He might as easily have been called Edom (Hebrew *edom*) because of his redness, but nothing is said about this in the birth report because an explanation of that name had become associated with the "red" pottage (Hebrew *adom*) which in the next story he pleads with Jacob to give him. Even an English reader can see that there is a distinctly closer phonetic resemblance between Edom and the two adjectives for "red" than between Esau and the word for "hairy". It is only when we realize that the land of Edom had another name, Seir (Hebrew *se'ir*) (see 32:3; 36:9), that things begin to fall into place. The etymology applied primarily to this name and was at some unknown point in Hebrew tradition transferred secondarily to Esau.

It would seem then that Esau originally had no more connection with the land of Edom than Lot had with Moab and Ammon (see commentary on 19:30ff.). He would from his occupation be a rougher man than Jacob, but the redness and hairiness are really describing not him but the sunburnt natives of the territory of Edom or Seir to the south and southeast of Palestine with their garments of animal hide. It is yet another instance of ethnic or national traditions getting mixed up with stories about the Patriarchs. There was, as we have seen, a similar confusion between "nations" and individuals in the oracle granted to Rebekah during her pregnancy.

BIRTHRIGHT

Genesis 25:19–34 *(cont'd)*

The story of how Jacob defrauded Esau of his birthright fairly crackles with venom and venality. The venom is Jacob's, the venality Esau's.

(i)

There is evidence from texts discovered at Nuzi (we have already referred to these to illumine Abraham's transaction with his servant Eliezer in chapter 15) that selling a birthright was not unknown in the Near East of the Patriarchal period. One such text records a purchase price of three sheep! But presumably that was a deal between poor men and the birthright may not have been worth much more. In the present case it involved the headship of a sizeable clan and what was for the time a not inconsiderable inheritance, of which the first-born was entitled to a double share (see Deut. 21:17).

Nor can we leave out of account the divine promises with their prospect of a glorious future which were so much a part of the life of this particular clan and which the chief would be expected to cherish and hold in trust for future generations. Esau's birthright as the first-born of Isaac was not at all an ordinary one, and when he parted with it, there was a lot more at stake than prestige and wealth.

(ii)

It is tempting to detect behind Jacob's unseemly haste in taking advantage of Esau's hunger his mother's influence. It is not at all unlikely that, being Rebekah's favourite, he was already privy to her secret confidence that he would one day outdo his brother. If, as is also likely, she had told him that her confidence was based on an oracle from the ancestral God, and had talked with him about that God's great promises to Abraham, his grandfather, then Jacob must have had a very good idea of what his older brother's inheritance meant. We can picture him and his mother having many a "quiet" discussion about how they might wrest it from him.

And now Esau was at his mercy! He knew his brother well and shamelessly he demanded his birthright in exchange for a bowl of the "red pottage" he was boiling. And when Esau agreed, he did not forget to make him swear an oath to make the agreement binding. Without such a solemn undertaking Esau could easily have reneged on the bargain later.

It is the Jacob of the later stories in a nutshell, a cool customer indeed, selfish and cunning, who waits his chance patiently and when it comes strikes mercilessly. But there is another side to it too. Jacob was aware of what hung on this birthright and having got it he was never going to let it go. That will have to be remembered to his credit when we make our final assessment of his character.

(iii)

We can hardly help feeling sorry for Esau as, exhausted and starving, he burst into the encampment. If a hunter caught nothing, he went hungry, and if his hunt were a long one, he could well be in a pitiable state when he returned. Esau's desire for food was not like his father's. Isaac had plenty to eat normally and only wanted game for a change. Esau's hunger was the hunter's hunger after long and empty days in the field, temporary perhaps, but on occasions—and this was one— almost a matter of life and death.

Probably, if he thought about it at all, Esau thought he was merely selling his double share of his father's property, not his right to the headship of the clan. In that case, he might well have argued, what was a little more wealth when his father died against the meeting of his present urgent need? It has also been suggested that he expected the "red" mixture to be a rich blood soup and not, as it turned out, a weak lentil broth.

But we need not look so far for reasons to explain his action. His birthright was simply irrelevant to his situation, and so was what was on the menu. If Jacob had asked for the moon, he would have given him that, if he could. And he would have given it though he were only offered a stale crust in return. He felt himself to be dying of hunger and here in front of him was the means of satisfying it. Nothing else mattered. It did not even occur to him that if he had waited a few moments more he could have had all the food he wanted.

(iv)

It is probable that the story-teller was as sorry for Esau as we are. When, therefore, we read his comment, "Thus Esau despised his birthright", we should not rush to moralize.

We do scant justice to the realism of this scene if we take from it merely a warning as we go about our daily business not to put the desires of the flesh before the demands of God. That lesson is there, just as Jacob's example of tenacity in the cause of the promise is there—but only if we are willing to ignore the ruthlessness and poisonous hatred which motivated him. Esau in the heat of the moment does show a venality and crass materialism that would be hard to equal. And to that extent he reaped what he sowed. But we have to remember to his credit that later on he took the lead in seeking reconciliation with his brother. No more than in the case of Jacob can we yet draw up his final balance sheet.

I feel myself that the story-teller's comment is chiefly a sad and ironic admission of the tragic results that would inevitably flow from this incident. It does not bring God's will directly into it. Nevertheless we can hardly help going back to God's answer to Rebekah of only a few verses previous when during her pregnancy she had gone to "inquire of the Lord". Her boys were hardly men and God's partisan decree was already beginning to work itself out. And there was nothing Esau—or for that matter Jacob—could do to prevent it.

The writer of the Epistle to the Hebrews draws his own moral from this scene, pleading with his readers to let no "root of bitterness" spring up among them. None of them was to be "immoral or irreligious like Esau, who sold his birthright for a single meal" (12:16). I don't think that his adjectives are quite suitable for the Esau of Genesis, but he does catch finely the poignant tragedy of Esau's action in his next verse: "For you know that afterwards, when he desired to inherit the blessing, he was rejected, for he found no chance to repent, though he sought it with tears." He also, at the end of the chapter (verses 25-29), lifts his moralizing to a much higher level when he speaks of not rejecting him who warns from heaven, of the shaking of the whole universe and of receiving a kingdom that cannot be shaken, and of offering to God acceptable worship, with reverence and awe; "for our God is a consuming fire". That is the kind of level which with his final cryptic and devastating comment I believe the story-teller is here inviting us to aim at in our interpretation.

TIMIDITY

Genesis 26:1-33

1 Now there was a famine in the land, besides the former famine that was in the days of Abraham. And Isaac went to Gerar, to Abimelech
2 king of the Philistines. And the Lord appeared to him, and said, "Do not go down to Egypt; dwell in the land of which I shall tell you.
3 Sojourn in this land, and I will be with you, and will bless you; for to you and to your descendants I will give all these lands, and I will
4 fulfil the oath which I swore to Abraham your father. I will multiply your descendants as the stars of heaven, and will give to your descendants all these lands; and by your descendants all the nations
5 of the earth shall bless themselves: because Abraham obeyed my voice and kept my charge, my commandments, my statutes, and my laws."
6,7 So Isaac dwelt in Gerar. When the men of the place asked him

about his wife, he said, "She is my sister"; for he feared to say, "My wife," thinking, "lest the men of the place should kill me for the sake
8 of Rebekah"; because she was fair to look upon. When he had been there a long time, Abimelech king of the Philistines looked out of a
9 window and saw Isaac fondling Rebekah his wife. So Abimelech called Isaac, and said, "Behold, she is your wife; how then could you say, 'She is my sister'?" Isaac said to him, "Because I thought, 'Lest I
10 die because of her.'" Abimelech said, "What is this you have done to us? One of the people might easily have lain with your wife, and you
11 would have brought guilt upon us." So Abimelech warned all the people, saying, "Whoever touches this man or his wife shall be put to death."

12 And Isaac sowed in that land, and reaped in the same year a
13 hundredfold. The Lord blessed him, and the man became rich, and
14 gained more and more until he became very wealthy. He had possessions of flocks and herds, and a great household, so that the
15 Philistines envied him. (Now the Philistines had stopped and filled with earth all the wells which his father's servants had dug in the
16 days of Abraham his father.) And Abimelech said to Isaac, "Go away from us; for you are much mightier than we."

17 So Isaac departed from there, and encamped in the valley of
18 Gerar and dwelt there. And Isaac dug again the wells of water which had been dug in the days of Abraham his father; for the Philistines had stopped them after the death of Abraham; and he gave them the
19 names which his father had given them. But when Isaac's servants
20 dug in the valley and found there a well of springing water, the herdsmen of Gerar quarrelled with Isaac's herdsmen, saying, "The water is ours." So he called the name of the well Esek, because they
21 contended with him. Then they dug another well, and they quar-
22 relled over that also; so he called its name Sitnah. And he moved from there and dug another well, and over that they did not quarrel; so he called its name Rehoboth, saying, "For now the Lord has made room for us, and we shall be fruitful in the land."

23, 24 From there he went up to Beer-sheba. And the Lord appeared to him the same night and said, "I am the God of Abraham your father; fear not, for I am with you and will bless you and multiply your
25 descendants for my servant Abraham's sake." So he built an altar there and called upon the name of the Lord, and pitched his tent there. And there Isaac's servants dug a well.

26 Then Abimelech went to him from Gerar with Ahuzzath his
27 adviser and Phicol the commander of his army. Isaac said to them,

"Why have you come to me, seeing that you hate me and have sent
28 me away from you?" They said, "We see plainly that the Lord is with
you; so we say, let there be an oath between you and us, and let us
29 make a covenant with you, that you will do us no harm, just as we
have not touched you and have done to you nothing but good and
have sent you away in peace. You are now the blessed of the Lord."
30, 31 So he made them a feast, and they ate and drank. In the morning
they rose early and took oath with one another; and Isaac set them
32 on their way, and they departed from him in peace. That same day
Isaac's servants came and told him about the well which they had
33 dug, and said to him, "We have found water." He called it Shibah;
therefore the name of the city is Beer-sheba to this day.

This chapter gathers together some stories that had Isaac as
their chief character. They concern a journey he made to Gerar
in a time of famine and his relations with its king and people.
The king is called Abimelech and the commander of his army is
called Phicol (verse 26). These are the same names as appear in
chapters 20 and 21, which relate to the time when Abraham had
also lived near Gerar. This can hardly be right. Perhaps the
Abimelech of the present chapter was the son of the one who
had dealings with Abraham and the name of his father's general
has been carelessly transferred to it from the Abraham story.
Only Ahuzzath, the king's adviser, who is mentioned along with
Phicol, will then properly belong here.

(i)
However, when we examine the stories more closely we find
that not only do they share the names of Abimelech and Phicol
with chapters 20 and 21 but that the incidents they describe are
more or less replicas of the ones contained in these chapters.
Like Abraham before him, Isaac pretends that his wife was his
sister and lands himself in bother with the king. His herdsmen
dispute with Abimelech's about access to water as Abraham's
had done. And the chapter concludes with a treaty of friendship
between Isaac and Abimelech which like the one in chapter 21
involves a play between the Hebrew words for "well" and
"oath" and the name of the town of Beersheba.

There are also differences. This Abimelech does not take Rebekah into his harem but suspects the truth when he looks out of a window and sees Isaac "fondling" her. Isaac is not rewarded with silver nor is he allowed to settle where he pleased as Abraham had been, but is driven away to the borders of Gerar's territory because by his successful husbandry he was getting too rich and powerful for Abimelech's liking. The two groups of herdsmen quarrel over two wells, not one, and these are then given appropriate names—Esek meaning "contention" and Sitnah meaning "enmity". Also Isaac's servants dig a well which is not attacked, which is then named Rehoboth meaning "room", i.e. room to make camp unmolested. None of these names appears in the earlier stories. Finally, the treaty with Abimelech is not this time over a well, though one had been found by Isaac's men just before and they came to tell him of it when the king had departed.

Most scholars conclude that these differences do not quite cancel out the similarities betwen the two sets of stories or quite prevent the impression being formed that Isaac is here intentionally being recreated in his father's image. I am inclined to agree with them and to find therefore in this chapter a more than usual amount of "writing up". The fact that it calls the inhabitants of Gerar Philistines whereas chapter 21 had been careful to speak only of the "land of the Philistines", meaning the land later occupied by them, is an indication of this. I am particularly dubious about the first half of the chapter where for the third time no less in Genesis a wife-sister scene is presented to us.

The second half of the chapter rings more true, however. We need not lay too much stress on the place-naming ceremonies it records, but it is a fact that disputes over wells were common occurrences in Patriarchal times. There is no reason to doubt that Abraham and Isaac both experienced them on many occasions. It is not therefore at all impossible that a famine forced Isaac to move from Beer-lahai-roi in the Negeb desert, where he had been staying since Abraham's death, into the region of Gerar, and that while he was there his clansmen quarrelled frequently with the indigenous inhabitants about watering rights. It would be to organize some kind of *modus vivendi* with the incomers that the king and his adviser came out from Gerar.

(ii)

For our purposes the significant feature about these quarrels is that each time Isaac quit and moved elsewhere. The conflicts in this part of the epic are resolved by the "hero" abandoning the field. It is not difficult to guess the reason for Isaac's cowardice. The memory of that awful moment in his boyhood when the father he loved had bound him with ropes and stood over him with a knife in his upraised hand must have haunted him ever after. It was that which made him so timid and fearful. That and having had to live for so long in the shadow of a great father.

The other glimpses we have been given of Isaac can now be seen in perspective—the grown man of chapter 24 forbidden at any cost to leave Canaan, the "meditator" in the field of the same chapter, the favourer of Esau in chapter 25 because his elder son was the man of action he could never be. And still to come is the aged Isaac of chapter 27, suspicious at what is going on but in the end giving in to the impostor. Isaac was the man who ran away from trouble. He was not big enough to be the chief of a clan. It is not really surprising that so few authentic stories about him were handed down among his descendants and that those which were had to be doctored to make them a little more impressive.

(iii)

Yet, as this chapter also reminds us, God appeared to timid Isaac more than once to renew to him the promises of land and progeny and blessing which he had made to his father. "Fear not", he said, "for I am with you." There is comfort here for us ordinary folks, who like Isaac are so often fearful amid life's trials and like him can never aspire to the stature of an Abraham. God was the God of Isaac as well as the God of Abraham.

BLESSING

Genesis 26:34–27:40

34 When Esau was forty years old, he took to wife Judith the daughter of Be-eri the Hittite, and Basemath the daughter of Elon the Hittite;
35 and they made life bitter for Isaac and Rebekah.

1 When Isaac was old and his eyes were dim so that he could not see, he called Esau his older son, and said to him, "My son"; and he
2 answered, "Here I am." He said, "Behold, I am old; I do not know
3 the day of my death. Now then, take your weapons, your quiver and
4 your bow, and go out to the field, and hunt game for me, and prepare for me savoury food, such as I love, and bring it to me that I may eat; that I may bless you before I die."

5 Now Rebekah was listening when Isaac spoke to his son Esau. So
6 when Esau went to the field to hunt for game and bring it, Rebekah said to her son Jacob, "I heard your father speak to your brother
7 Esau, 'Bring me game, and prepare for me savoury food, that I may
8 eat it, and bless you before the Lord before I die.' Now therefore, my
9 son, obey my word as I command you. Go to the flock and fetch me two good kids, that I may prepare from them savoury food for your
10 father, such as he loves; and you shall bring it to your father to eat,
11 so that he may bless you before he dies." But Jacob said to Rebekah his mother, "Behold, my brother Esau is a hairy man, and I am a
12 smooth man. Perhaps my father will feel me, and I shall seem to be
13 mocking him, and bring a curse upon myself and not a blessing." His mother said to him, "Upon me be your curse, my son; only obey my
14 word, and go, fetch them to me." So he went and took them and brought them to his mother; and his mother prepared savoury food,
15 such as his father loved. Then Rebekah took the best garments of Esau her older son, which were with her in the house, and put them
16 on Jacob her younger son; and the skins of the kids she put upon his
17 hands and upon the smooth part of his neck; and she gave the savoury food and the bread, which she had prepared, into the hand of her son Jacob.

18 So he went in to his father, and said, "My father"; and he said,
19 "Here I am; who are you, my son?" Jacob said to his father, "I am Esau your first-born. I have done as you told me; now sit up and eat
20 of my game, that you may bless me." But Isaac said to his son, "How

is it that you have found it so quickly, my son?" He answered,
21 "Because the Lord your God granted me success." Then Isaac said to
Jacob, "Come near, that I may feel you, my son, to know whether
22 you are really my son Esau or not." So Jacob went near to Isaac his
father, who felt him and said, "The voice is Jacob's voice, but the
23 hands are the hands of Esau." And he did not recognise him, because
his hands were hairy like his brother Esau's hands; so he blessed him.
24, 25 He said, "Are you really my son Esau?" He answered, "I am." Then
he said, "Bring it to me, that I may eat of my son's game and bless
you." So he brought it to him, and he ate; and he brought him wine,
26 and he drank. Then his father Isaac said to him, "Come near and kiss
27 me, my son." So he came near and kissed him; and he smelled the
smell of his garments, and blessed him, and said,

"See, the smell of my son
  is as the smell of a field which the Lord has blessed!
28 May God give you of the dew of heaven,
  and of the fatness of the earth,
  and plenty of grain and wine.
29 Let peoples serve you,
  and nations bow down to you.
  Be lord over your brothers,
  and may your mother's sons bow down to you.
  Cursed be every one who curses you,
  and blessed be every one who blesses you!"

30 As soon as Isaac had finished blessing Jacob, when Jacob had
scarcely gone out from the presence of Isaac his father, Esau his
31 brother came in from his hunting. He also prepared savoury food,
and brought it to his father. And he said to his father, "Let my father
32 arise, and eat of his son's game, that you may bless me." His father
Isaac said to him, "Who are you?" He answered, "I am your son,
33 your first-born, Esau." Then Isaac trembled violently, and said,
"Who was it then that hunted game and brought it to me, and I ate it
all before you came, and I have blessed him?—yes, and he shall be
34 blessed." When Esau heard the words of his father, he cried out with
an exceedingly great and bitter cry, and said to his father, "Bless me,
35 even me also, O my father!" But he said, "Your brother came with
36 guile, and he has taken away your blessing." Esau said, "Is he not
rightly named Jacob? For he has supplanted me these two times. He

took away my birthright; and behold, now he has taken away my blessing." Then he said, "Have you not reserved a blessing for me?"

37 Isaac answered Esau, "Behold, I have made him your lord, and all his brothers I have given to him for servants, and with grain and wine I have sustained him. What then can I do for you, my son?"

38 Esau said to his father, "Have you but one blessing, my father? Bless me, even me also, O my father." And Esau lifted up his voice and wept.

39 Then Isaac his father answered him:

"Behold, away from the fatness of the earth shall your dwelling be,
and away from the dew of heaven on high.

40 By your sword you shall live,
and you shall serve your brother;
but when you break loose
you shall break his yoke from your neck."

The story of the filching of Esau's blessing is one of Genesis' best known and is another masterpiece of Hebrew narrative art. It makes public what had hitherto been a private feud and forces an open rift between the two brothers. The story begins in an atmosphere of whispering and intrigue. There is suspense in its middle section, and dramatic irony in that we, the audience, know what Isaac does not know. And at the end there is a terrifying juxtaposition of divine purpose and human perplexity which in its emotional intensity is every bit the equal of the scene in chapter 21 where Abraham had on God's command to send Hagar and Ishmael out into the desert.

(i)

There are a couple of features of the story which require some explanation.

First, it is common sense to conclude that Isaac was on his deathbed when he called Esau to give him his blessing. That is the place from which blessings are usually pronounced; Isaac is described as old and blind; and he himself speaks as though he had not long to live. Presumably therefore he died shortly after this scene. This, however, is contradicted by the notice in 35:29, according to which his death took place a good while after Jacob's return from Mesopotamia. We must assume that the report of his death was delayed till that point because of the tradition that he lived till he was a hundred and eighty years. At the time of the blessing he was according to the last verse of chapter 26 only (!) a little past a hundred (compare 25:20, 26). In the same way, it will be remembered, we concluded that Abraham died while his servant was in Mesopotamia seeking a wife for Isaac, that is, if we follow 21:5, when he was about one hundred and forty and Isaac about forty. Yet 25:7 tells us that he was one hundred and seventy-five when he died. It is clear that someone has not done his arithmetic very well and matched up the traditions of the ages of the Patriarchs with the content of the stories.

Second, it would be wise to recognize the intrusion now and then of an ethnic interest, especially in what is said in the blessing pronounced on Esau at the end. The first blessing, meant for him as the elder of the two sons but stolen by Jacob, slips in the information that Isaac and Rebekah had had other children, but is otherwise very much in line with the promises to Abraham. It dwells rather more on the fertility of the land God would give his people and is rather more triumphalist in its forecast of nations serving them. But the second blessing does seem to have the history of Edom specifically in mind. Esau as an individual is never in Genesis subject in a real sense to his brother, nor does he need to break Jacob's yoke from his neck. He simply agrees to go away (36:6). The land of Edom, however, was subdued by David (2 Sam. 8:13–14) and did not regain its independence until the reign of Joram a century and a half later (2 Kgs. 8:20–22). It is likely that these later events are being alluded to in the second part of this blessing and that only the first part of it is original to the story.

It may be that the frequent use in the text of the word "hairy" is also due to a desire to connect Esau with Seir-Edom. In the story there is of course a necessary contrast between Esau's roughness and Jacob's smoothness, but it is perfectly well accounted for by the different styles of life of the two men.

(ii)

The stage for the stealing of the blessing is set by the brief report at the end of the previous chapter that Esau had married two Hittite wives and that they had been making life bitter for Isaac and Rebekah. There is perhaps a suggestion in this that Esau brought what was coming to him upon himself by so blatant a neglect of tribal custom. Certainly later Hebrew audiences with their congenital distrust of foreigners could well have looked at it that way. But it should be noted that Isaac, though distressed by the marriages, did not let them affect his judgment when shortly afterwards he felt the time was near to bless his older son before he died. Nor should we forget that Abraham himself had married outside the clan circle when he took Hagar, his wife's maid, as a second wife.

Rather the marriages effectively point up the continuing dissension in this unhappy family. They highlight Esau's wilfulness. They also demonstrate Isaac's weakness in that he was unable to prevent them. But chiefly perhaps they remind us of an implacable Rebekah in the background bent on her younger son's advancement. The report says the two Hittite women caused difficulties for her. But from what we know of her, they would not exactly have been given a warm welcome!

EFFRONTERY

Genesis 26:34–27:40 *(cont'd)*

(iii)

The story proper begins with whispered conversations not meant for other ears. There is skulduggery afoot and each of the four characters is implicated in it.

By making the request he did of Esau, *Isaac* revealed not only his intention to pass on the headship of the clan to his oldest son in spite of his marriages with foreign women, but to favour him to the very end because of his liking for the tasty meals he caught for him. There is no suggestion that he knew anything about the earlier deal over the birthright between Esau and

Jacob and was therefore going against God's will. Nevertheless this was no way to impart a blessing, to be thinking of his stomach even as he planned his family's future. Jacob and his other sons ought to have been summoned too to receive their lesser share in it. When Jacob himself was in the same position his father was now in, he called all his sons to his bedside and treated the occasion with the dignity it deserved (chapter 49).

Esau, however, did know about the birthright he had sold and the solemn oath he had taken when selling it. By acceding to his father's request and going out to hunt without telling anyone about it, was he hoping that all might yet be well, that once he had received the blessing, it would cancel out his youthful indiscretion and leave the inheritance intact? Or was he calculating that the chieftainship at least would be preserved to him, though he might when his father died still have to keep his bargain with his brother and hand over a double share of the property to him? We can only speculate, but as he left for the fields he must have been painfully aware that he had two quarries to keep in view, and that the blessing might be more difficult to ensnare than any wild animal.

If Isaac showed favouritism it was at least, as it had always been, out in the open. *Rebekah's* hopes for Jacob, on the other hand, must by the nature of the case have been harboured in secret. She would have gained nothing by making a show of her favouritism in front of her husband and their oldest son, and she knew it. Clearly not a word of what God had said to her in his oracle so long before had ever passed her lips in public. She must also have often impressed it upon Jacob never in an unguarded moment to let anything slip about the birthright he had acquired. A formidable woman indeed to have concealed all the prejudice and antipathy in her soul for so many years!

But now when, as she realized on overhearing the conversation between Isaac and Esau, the time to act had come, with what effrontery she acted! It was a terrible risk she was taking, to cook from a couple of kids a tempting meal the equal of those that Esau had over the years so often and lovingly prepared from freshly caught game for Isaac's discerning palate, and then to dress Jacob up in his older brother's clothes and cover his smoother hands and the nape of his neck with skins from these same kids. Would the old man be so easily deceived? His eyes were dim, but were his other senses so atrophied? But something had to be done and done quickly, if all were not to be lost. Peremptorily she squashed Jacob's cautious protests, and infused her steel into him. Martin Luther catches the scene to perfection when, describing her approach to her son as he stood outside Isaac's tent, he says, "If it had been me, I'd have dropped the dish!"

Finally, there is *Jacob,* warily pointing out the dangers in what was being proposed, but as the moment of truth draws near, stifling his forebodings and in the end putting on his mother's effrontery with his brother's clothes and entering his father's tent carrying the fateful dish in his hands.

(iv)

Dramatic irony takes place when an audience at a play or the readers of a novel know more about what is happening than the actors on the stage or the characters in the book. It is a very effective device for increasing tension, and rarely can it have been put to better use than in this old story. Each time as Isaac airs his suspicions—"how is it that you have found it so quickly?", "the voice is Jacob's voice", "are you really my son Esau?", "come near and kiss me, my son"—we wonder how he can be so gullible. But Jacob carries off the deceit with icy aplomb—note particulary his cunning (and indeed blasphemous) "the Lord *your* God granted me success." Whether because of his senility or because of his impatience to be at the savoury food, Isaac is convinced. He eats it and drinks the wine that accompanied it, and with his nose buried in Esau's garments, pronounces Esau's blessing on Jacob.

So to a son who thought nothing of violating filial duty for his own nefarious ends, or indeed of taking God's name in vain, was a priceless blessing imparted by a father who could not see and who would not hear, but who insisted on putting his trust solely in his palate and his nose and his fingertips.

(v)

The last scene when Esau returns is one of harrowing emotional shock and violence. Aghast at what he had done, the old man trembled uncontrollably, but he could not undo it. We cannot say whether he recognized immediately God's hand in what had happened. Probably not. But he knew that a blessing like this, once uttered on his deathbed and in God's name, could not possibly be revoked. The words were already beginning to act (see commentary on 1:3–5, *And God said*). And Esau knew it too. We can hear his despairing cry resounding like a crack of doom round the tent—and down the centuries! In its anguish it matches anything of Lear's or Othello's, nor indeed would it be irreverent to compare it with Our Lord's cry of dereliction from the Cross. A black chasm opened up in that moment before Esau and he could not help himself falling into it. Plaintively he pled, "Have you not reserved a blessing for me?" But even as he asked, he knew it to be hopeless.

All his aged father could do was to spell out the consequences. When he was gone, Jacob would be chief and Esau and his other brothers would be subject to him. He did intone some words over him, but they were tantamount to a curse, not a blessing. If Esau wished to be free of his brother, he would have to leave the land of promise and never again experience its pleasant sights and sounds. There beyond its borders he might, like Ishmael before him, just possibly carve out some success for himself with the sword.

(vi)

That God could have ordained this way for the benefits of election to be passed on from Isaac's generation to the succeeding one almost nauseates us. The word is hardly too strong. What we are witnessing is if anything worse than what happened after Isaac's own birth. Then a helpless woman and her boy were cast into the desert and a sour vindictive Sarah was allowed to celebrate her triumph. But at least Abraham was—in our estimation—worthy of the divine favour, and Isaac was but a child. Now a rash and boorish but a guileless man is vanquished and the field is left to a trio of rogues whose combined crimes of partiality and chicanery and greed and audacity one could search long for and never find again in a single family.

We are not alone in being appalled. It seems to me that the story-teller must have been too. He shows it not by any direct statements but by emptying his story almost completely of God's presence. None of the characters turns to him for guidance, nor does he communicate once with them, as in chapter 21 he had informed Abraham that Hagar's banishment was his will. Yet every bit as much as there, what was at stake was the future of his special people and the continuance of his promises. We are again face to face with the enigma of divine grace. "Yes, and he shall be blessed" is without doubt the chapter's key phrase. The line of election would move on through Jacob and not through Esau. But this time God delays before admitting it. We are left for the moment in the sole company of those who were the objects of his grace so that we may ponder their unworthiness and be led from that to confess our own. This horrendous story is not inviting us to criticize God but to look in a mirror and see ourselves.

FLIGHT

Genesis 27:41–28:9

41 Now Esau hated Jacob because of the blessing with which his father had blessed him, and Esau said to himself, "The days of mourning for my father are approaching; then I will kill my brother Jacob."
42 But the words of Esau her older son were told to Rebekah; so she sent and called Jacob her younger son, and said to him, "Behold,
43 your brother Esau comforts himself by planning to kill you. Now therefore, my son, obey my voice; arise, flee to Laban my brother in
44 Haran, and stay with him a while, until your brother's fury turns
45 away; until your brother's anger turns away, and he forgets what you have done to him; then I will send, and fetch you from there. Why should I be bereft of you both in one day?"

46 Then Rebekah said to Isaac, "I am weary of my life because of the Hittite women. If Jacob marries one of the Hittite women such as these, one of the women of the land, what good will my life be to
1 me?" Then Isaac called Jacob and blessed him, and charged him,
2 "You shall not marry one of the Canaanite women, Arise, go to Paddan-aram to the house of Bethuel your mother's father; and take as wife from there one of the daughters of Laban your mother's
3 brother. God Almighty bless you and make you fruitful and
4 multiply you, that you may become a company of peoples. May he give the blessing of Abraham to you and to your descendants with you, that you may take possession of the land of your sojournings
5 which God gave to Abraham!" Thus Isaac sent Jacob away; and he went to Paddan-aram to Laban, the son of Bethuel the Aramean, the brother of Rebekah, Jacob's and Esau's mother.
6 Now Esau saw that Isaac had blessed Jacob and sent him away to Paddan-aram to take a wife from there, and that as he blessed him he charged him, "You shall not marry one of the Canaanite women,"
7 and that Jacob had obeyed his father and mother and gone to
8 Paddan-aram. So when Esau saw that the Canaanite women did not
9 please Isaac his father, Esau went to Ishmael and took to wife, besides the wives he had, Mahalath the daughter of Ishmael Abraham's son, the sister of Nebaioth.

His hopes so treacherously dashed, it is not surprising that Esau, the hunter used to killing, should vow to be rid of his brother whenever their father was dead. Jacob had won the prize he wanted, but it was not going to be easy for him to keep it.

(i)

It is in this passage that we take our leave of Rebekah and Isaac.

When Rebekah heard of Esau's intention she advised Jacob to flee to her brother Laban in Paddan-Aram (meaning "field of Aram" and another name for the area around Harran). He was to stay there for a while—or as the AV puts it more literally, for "a few days"—until Esau's anger had burned itself out. She knew her older son to be a man of violent passions who would rail for a short time and then accept the inevitable. In this she was right, as events would prove when Jacob returned to Canaan. She even allowed herself as she thought of him a little tenderness, and said to Jacob, "Why should I be bereft of you both in one day?" If Esau slew Jacob, he would himself be executed under the clan code for the crime of fratricide—and he was her son too! Momentarily the mother in her showed through, but it was only momentarily.

Almost immediately she was at her scheming again. Would Isaac let his new heir depart when he knew that he had not long to live? Would he understand the danger he was in? Cunningly she suggested to him that when he was in Mesopotamia Jacob could find a wife for himself among Laban's daughters and not be like Esau, who had married these troublesome Hittite women. At one stroke she reminded the old man of perhaps the only thing he had disapproved of in Esau and turned his thoughts back to perhaps the only happy hour in his own melancholy life when he had met her in the fields as Abraham's servant returned with her from Harran and had fallen in love with her at first sight. (Did she herself, one wonders, shed a silent tear at the memory she was invoking?) Again she was right in her approach, for with a repeated blessing Isaac allowed Jacob to go.

But in one calculation she was wrong. She did not reckon with her brother Laban, who would with *his* scheming turn her "few days" into twenty long years. She would never see her favourite son again. It is fittingly ironic that the last glimpse this redoubtable and relentless woman had of him should be as he scurried ignominiously from the land he had been promised as an inheritance to escape the vengeance of the brother he had defeated. We do not even have a report of her death and burial.

Human pity demands an epitaph for her. It should say something of the carefree, generous and precocious girl whom Isaac loved as well as of the overpossessive mother who, as soon as Jacob was born, forgot all else for his sake and so filled her own life and the lives of those around her with discord and anguish. Perhaps Dante strikes the right balance in his lines:

Nessun maggior dolore
Che ricordarsi del tempo felice
Nella miseria
("There is no greater sorrow than to recall a time of happiness in misery").

(ii)

We have a report of Isaac's death. But if we doubted before that it is misplaced in chapter 35, this passage should convince us. For, of course, Jacob would not have fled had he thought that Isaac's protection would not soon be withdrawn. Nor would Esau have spoken about the "days of mourning" for his father had he thought that they were not almost at hand. Isaac's own final words to Jacob, too, do not contain any hope (as Rebekah's had done) that he would be there when his son returned.

What these words do suggest, however, is that the old man had now reconciled himself to having Jacob as his heir and accepted it as God's will. There is no recrimination in them but rather a quiet confidence that from this enterprise would emerge a "company of peoples" who would through Jacob inherit the "blessing of Abraham" and take possession of the land that was "given" to him. To the very last he is timid, mentioning only Abraham and not bringing himself into it at all. But it is a beautiful blessing, quite lacking the harsh triumphalist tones of so many of Genesis' blessings, including the one just a day or two since forced from his own lips by Jacob's guile.

It seems that as he died this sensuous, timorous and cowardly man could at last say (and again I quote Dante):

E'n la sua volontade e nostra pace
("In his will is our peace").

(iii)

When Esau saw that Jacob had gone to Paddan-Aram with his father's approval, he took a third wife for himself from the daughters of Ishmael, his uncle. Is it being suggested by this brief notice that he was still insensitive to the spiritual implications of the birthright and blessing he had lost? For was not Ishmael, like himself, outside the fold? Or is it hinting exactly the opposite, namely that he was in his own halting way trying to regain the favour of the father who had rejected him and help heal the rift in the family? For, of course, Ishmael was as much "family." as Laban. Was he, in short, still governed by resentment or was he already, as his mother had said he would, acquiescing in the reversal of his and his brother's positions?

As usual, we are left to make up our minds for ourselves. Most Hebrew audiences would probably assume the first. I am inclined to make the second inference and indeed, in making it, to point out its ironic corollary, which is that perhaps Jacob need not have fled at all.

BETHEL I: JACOB'S BETHEL

Genesis 28:10–22

10, 11 Jacob left Beer-sheba, and went toward Haran. And he came to a certain place, and stayed there that night, because the sun had set. Taking one of the stones of the place, he put it under his head and lay
12 down in that place to sleep. And he dreamed that there was a ladder set up on the earth, and the top of it reached to heaven; and behold,
13 the angels of God were ascending and descending on it! And behold, the Lord stood above it and said, "I am the Lord, the God of Abraham your father and the God of Isaac; the land on which you
14 lie I will give to you and to your descendants; and your descendants shall be like the dust of the earth, and you shall spread abroad to the west and to the east and to the north and to the south; and by you and your descendants shall all the families of the earth bless
15 themselves. Behold, I am with you and will keep you wherever you go, and will bring you back to this land; for I will not leave you until
16 I have done that of which I have spoken to you." Then Jacob awoke from his sleep and said, "Surely the Lord is in this place; and I did
17 not know it." And he was afraid, and said, "How awesome is this place! This is none other than the house of God, and this is the gate of heaven."
18 So Jacob rose early in the morning, and he took the stone which he had put under his head and set it up for a pillar and poured oil on

19 the top of it. He called the name of that place Bethel; but the name of
20 the city was Luz at the first. Then Jacob made a vow, saying, "If God
   will be with me, and will keep me in this way that I go, and will give
21 me bread to eat and clothing to wear, so that I come again to my
22 father's house in peace, then the Lord shall be my God, and this
   stone, which I have set up for a pillar, shall be God's house; and of all
   that thou givest me I will give the tenth to thee."

An important part of the meaning of this famous passage to the
many Hebrew audiences who cherished it down the centuries
was the link it forged between the patriarch Jacob and one of
the great centres of Israel's worship. Bethel is mentioned more
often in the Old Testament than any other city except Jerusalem and Samaria. It was captured by Joshua (Josh. 8), recap-
tured by the Canaanites, then captured again by the tribes
(Judg. 1:22ff.). It was there that the Ark was first housed (Judg.
20:27) before being taken to Shiloh (1 Sam. 3:3; 4:3) and in
David's time to Jerusalem. Later on after the division of the
kingdom on Solomon's death it was the northern kingdom's
principal sanctuary and the rival of Judah's Jerusalem. It was
there that Jeroboam placed one of his two golden calves (1 Kgs.
12:28–29) and there that Amos preached his scathing sermon
about false worship (Amos 4:4) and got into trouble for so
doing (Amos 7:10–13). Archaeology confirms that it existed
before Jacob's time when, according to this passage, it was
called Luz. It is probable, however, that the Canaanites had
also called it Bethel, which is a name meaning originally "house
of El", i.e. of the chief Canaanite deity. But this would not have
been acceptable to the Hebrews, so the tradition grew that it
received its second name (reinterpreted to mean "house of
God", i.e. of Israel's God) as a result of Jacob's experience there
as he fled north from Beersheba.

(i)

We do not now share the ancient Hebrews' consuming interest
in recording (and if necessary inventing) the circumstances
under which places and people got their names. In the context
of Genesis' continuing story we are more likely to remember

that Abraham had been at Bethel too. It was one of the first sites he visited in the Holy Land, and he built an altar at it and called on God's name (12:8). But more significantly it was for Bethel he aimed when after disgracing himself in Egypt he wished to renew his allegiance to God and rediscover the secret of his faith (13:3–4). Can we ascribe a similar motive to an apprehensive and despondent Jacob as he now reached it on his way to Harran? I think not.

Apprehensive he must have been, for he was fleeing from his brother's wrath, he was alone, and he did not know whether or not Esau was pursuing him. Despondent he must also have been, for he could not be sure that he would ever enter upon the inheritance he had so underhandedly gained for himself. But I can detect nothing in his demeanour to suggest that he had a bad conscience or desired to mend his ways. Nor when he speaks to him in a vision does God use words that immediately turn our thoughts in that direction.

(ii)

Perhaps it was the craggy shapes of the hills around Bethel as they loomed before him in the hazy twilight that were reproduced in his dream. They would have been unlike anything he had known in the rolling pastures around his home in Beersheba, and could easily have been transmuted by his disturbed imagination into the form of a giant staircase for superhuman beings to clamber over. But more likely it was the *ziggurats* of Mesopotamia that informed his vision, those many tiered towers of Babylonian religion with ramps connecting each tier which were intended by their builders to be just such a ladder as he saw joining earth and heaven, a route by which their gods could descend to them to help them and receive their worship (see further the commentary on 11:1–9 in Volume 1). For not only the name Bethel but the name Babylon, properly *Bab-ilani* meaning "gate of the gods", seem to be reflected in the words which Jacob spoke when he awoke: "This is none other than the *house of God* (Hebrew *Beth-el*) and this is the *gate* of heaven". He had not yet been to Mesopotamia to see the renowned *ziggurats* for himself, but his ancestors had come from there. He must often have heard of them as a boy listening to the tales of his clan. What more natural than that as he himself was going to Mesopotamia, these old tales should have come flooding back into his mind?

But to return to God's address. It repeats the traditional promises given to both Abraham and Isaac. The land on which he lay sleeping would belong to him and his descendants. His descendants would be like the dust for number. Through him and them a blessing would come to all the families of the earth. God then says that though he was leaving the land, he would bring him back to it. He would be with him constantly and would not forsake him until all he had foretold for him was accomplished. Where in all this is there even a vestige of rebuke for sins committed? On the contrary, God appears set on bolstering up Jacob's flagging ego, on confirming to him an inheritance that he thought was slipping from his grasp, and on assuring him of his divine aid in the gaining of it.

(iii)

Jacob was deeply moved by this experience. Of that there can be no doubt. This was the first time God had spoken to him directly and not by proxy in his father's voice, and he was filled with awe. This was something new for him. Only once previously in the epic had he as much as taken God's name on his lips, and that was when he pretended to Isaac that he was Esau back so quickly from the chase "because the Lord *your* God granted me success" (27:20). No prayer to "*my* God" had ever been heard from him. But now God was his God. But no! Rather God would be his God if he carried out his promise and accompanied him on his journey, seeing to his needs, and brought him back safely to this place. Are we hearing aright? I'm afraid we are. Jacob had met God for the first time personally and it had shaken him to the core, but being Jacob he was unable to prevent himself striking a bargain with him, saying in effect that he would only keep his side of it if God first kept his.

The scene at Bethel is a much loved scene, but it has too often been viewed through pious spectacles. It is not a conversion scene, nor is it a confessional scene. It is a scene where God's partisan grace is forwarded. Jacob was his chosen one and must be strengthened for what lay ahead.

At the end of the story Jacob was able to lift up the stone he had used for a pillow and place it on its end as a memorial pillar. If it was the same kind of stone as has been found frequently at excavations of Canaanite holy places it was probably around seven feet high. A considerable feat for one who we have been led to think was physically puny beside his fearsome brother Esau! But now indeed Jacob felt himself to be seven feet tall. The odds were stacked against him and Rebekah was no longer with him. But he had found in the shape of the God of his fathers another "Lady Macbeth" to nerve his arm and fortify his will until final victory was his. This is what in the context of his life so far we must conclude that Bethel meant for Jacob.

BETHEL II: OUR BETHEL

Genesis 28:10-22 *(cont'd)*

As I have suggested, too many interpreters have tended to find in this beautifully worded but in fact very disturbing passage a parable of the sinner confronted by God, hearing his words of forgiveness and having his eyes opened to see what he had been missing, coming to his senses and undertaking with God's help to live a more worthy life in the future. I have tried to show that we misread it if we attempt to explain Jacob's attitude that way. What message then does it have for us?

(i)

Let me begin by quoting as an example of both how to go about it and how not to the second of the Scottish Paraphrases, which is based on the final three verses of the passage:

O God of Bethel! by whose hand
   Thy people still are fed;
Who through this weary pilgrimage
   Hast all our fathers led;

Our vows, our prayers, we now present
   Before thy throne of grace:
God of our fathers! be the God
   Of their succeeding race.

Through each perplexing path of life
   Our wandering footsteps guide;
Give us each day our daily bread,
   And raiment fit provide.

O spread thy covering wings around,
   Till all our wanderings cease,
And at our Father's loved abode
   Our souls arrive in peace.

Such blessings from thy gracious hand
   Our humble prayers implore;
And thou shalt be our chosen God,
   And portion evermore.

I love this great hymn as dearly as any other Scotsman, and if I were an exile from my native land, I would love it even more To the extent that it awakens in us thoughts of home and particularly thoughts of our ancestral faith, it is true to the original. Nor does it extend the original's scope too imaginatively by turning Jacob's exile from his "father's house" into a type or allegory of all men's exile from their "Father's loved abode" in heaven.

But notice how it makes a prayer out of what is essentially a bargain. Whereas Jacob on entering the unknown demands God's aid as a proof that he was on his side, it has us humbly

supplicating his guidance in our bewilderment and his suste-
nance in our need. Implicit in it is a confession of our unworthiness and our inability to reach our goal without his hand in
ours. Jacob's marvellous dream brought him to his knees, but it
was in awe, not repentance, and he was almost immediately on
his feet again trying to bend God's will to his own. His
experience of God increased rather than diminished his self-
sufficiency. These insistent notes of arrogance and of haggling
with God have been excised from the paraphrase, which
marries awe with humility in a manner which the original does
not.

(ii)

Perhaps what strikes us most forcibly about Jacob in his early
life is his quite amazing resilience. A little push from his mother
was in the last chapter all he needed to perpetrate his deceit on a
dying Isaac and gain the blessing. A vision of God on his side is
all he here needs to banish his apprehensions and set out on the
long journey to retain it. It is an account of a man finding God
and hearing his comforting words and basing his life in a real
sense on them, but being too confident by half about it. That
could hardly have been the response God wanted. Not that God
thought for one moment of withdrawing his support because of
it. His grace had chosen this man, and it was not conditional.
But how he must have wished for a kindlier and less selfish and
less bumptious servant!

Seen in this light, the story of Bethel becomes not, as it has so
often been taken to be, a parable of the convicted sinner
discovering the error of his ways, but of the "justified sinner"
too sure that he is "saved". Its message for us therefore is one of
warning rather than of assurance.

Jacob's stance throughout it, indeed, seems to me to smack
just a little too much of another famous Scottish poem for the
comfort of any of us. I am thinking of Burns' cruelly funny
"Holy Willie's Prayer". I quote three of its most sarcastic verses
to underline my point:

O Thou, wha in the heavens dost dwell,
Wha, as it pleases best thysel',
Sends ane to heaven, and ten to hell,
    A' for thy glory,
And no' for any gude or ill
    They've done afore thee!

L---, bless thy chosen in this place,
For here thou hast a chosen race:
But G-- confound their stubborn face,
    And blast their name,
Wha bring thy elders to disgrace
    An' public shame!

But L---, remember me and mine
Wi' mercies temp'ral and divine,
That I for gear and grace may shine,
    Excell'd by nane,
An' a' the glory shall be thine,
    Amen, Amen!

(iii)

But there is a deeper lesson still in the story, and it is a more positive one. It is the lesson suggested by Our Lord himself at his meeting with Nathanael recorded in John 1:43–51. Nathanael was the man who said, "Can anything good come out of Nazareth?" But when he saw Jesus face to face, he had to confess, "Rabbi, you are the Son of God! You are the King of Israel!" As a result of this confession, Jesus said to him, "Truly, truly, I say to you, you will see heaven opened, and the angels of God ascending and descending upon the Son of man." The words are too near those of our passage to have been used by chance. Jesus announces to Nathanael, whom in contrast to wily Jacob he called "an Israelite indeed, in whom is no guile", that he himself is the ladder set up between heaven and earth which Jacob saw.

This is of course well beyond what Jacob himself could have envisaged, but the Christian imagination is able to see the line that extends from Bethel to Nazareth. Jacob thought that he had the ladder as his own private route of access to God. The Jews of Jesus' day, named Israel after him, were tempted to think the same. Over against them both Jesus makes his astonishing claim to Nathanael to be the only real channel of hope and blessing between God and mankind. And there is just a hint in the way that he makes it that the guileless rather than the cunning are the more likely to be given a vision of him in his glory.

EXILE

Genesis 29:1–31:55

The long story of Jacob's sojourn in Paddan-Aram should be read at a sitting if one wishes to savour its folksy atmosphere. It has the usual ethnic overlay, especially in the accounts of the birth of Jacob's children in the middle and of the covenant between him and the "Aramean" Laban at the end. But on the whole it is lightly told, and evinces a wry and sometimes earthy humour which must have made it a firm favourite at many a Hebrew gathering. The opening scenes seem to me to be the crispest, but the story, even though it gets wordier towards the end, never loses its charm. And, as we shall find, it does not lack bite either.

Jacob's arrival at Harran (29:1–14)

1 Then Jacob went on his journey, and came to the land of the people
2 of the east. As he looked, he saw a well in the field, and lo, three flocks of sheep lying beside it; for out of that well the flocks were
3 watered. The stone on the well's mouth was large, and when all the flocks were gathered there, the shepherds would roll the stone from the mouth of the well, and water the sheep, and put the stone back in its place upon the mouth of the well.
4 Jacob said to them, "My brothers, where do you come from?"
5 They said, "We are from Haran." He said to them, "Do you know
6 Laban the son of Nahor?" They said, "We know him." He said to them, "Is it well with him?" They said, "It is well; and see, Rachel his

7 daughter is coming with the sheep!" He said, "Behold, it is still high
day, it is not time for the animals to be gathered together; water the
8 sheep, and go, pasture them." But they said, "We cannot until all the
flocks are gathered together, and the stone is rolled from the mouth
of the well; then we water the sheep."

9   While he was still speaking with them, Rachel came with her
10 father's sheep; for she kept them. Now when Jacob saw Rachel the
daughter of Laban his mother's brother, and the sheep of Laban his
mother's brother, Jacob went up and rolled the stone from the well's
11 mouth, and watered the flock of Laban his mother's brother. Then
12 Jacob kissed Rachel, and wept aloud. And Jacob told Rachel that
he was her father's kinsman, and that he was Rebekah's son; and she
ran and told her father.

13   When Laban heard the tidings of Jacob his sister's son, he ran to
meet him, and embraced him and kissed him, and brought him to his
14 house. Jacob told Laban all these things, and Laban said to him,
"Surely you are my bone and my flesh!" And he stayed with him a
month.

Jacob's marriages to Laban's daughters (29:15–30)

15 Then Laban said to Jacob, "Because you are my kinsman, should
you therefore serve me for nothing? Tell me, what shall your wages
16 be?" Now Laban had two daughters; the name of the older was
17 Leah, and the name of the younger was Rachel. Leah's eyes were
18 weak, but Rachel was beautiful and lovely. Jacob loved Rachel; and
he said, "I will serve you seven years for your younger daughter
19 Rachel." Laban said, "It is better that I give her to you than that I
20 should give her to any other man; stay with me." So Jacob served
seven years for Rachel, and they seemed to him but a few days
because of the love he had for her.

21   Then Jacob said to Laban, "Give me my wife that I may go in to
22 her, for my time is completed." So Laban gathered together all the
23 men of the place, and made a feast. But in the evening he took his
daughter Leah and brought her to Jacob; and he went in to her.
24 (Laban gave his maid Zilpah to his daughter Leah to be her maid.)
25 And in the morning, behold, it was Leah; and Jacob said to Laban,
"What is this you have done to me? Did I not serve with you for
26 Rachel? Why then have you deceived me?" Laban said, "It is not so
done in our country, to give the younger before the first-born.
27 Complete the week of this one, and we will give you the other also in

28 return for serving me another seven years." Jacob did so, and
completed her week; then Laban gave him his daughter Rachel to
29 wife. (Laban gave his maid Bilhah to his daughter Rachel to be her
30 maid.) So Jacob went in to Rachel also, and he loved Rachel more
than Leah, and served Laban for another seven years.

The birth and naming of Jacob's children (29:31–30:24)

31 When the Lord saw that Leah was hated, he opened her womb; but
32 Rachel was barren. And Leah conceived and bore a son, and she
called his name Reuben; for she said, "Because the Lord has looked
33 upon my affliction; surely now my husband will love me." She
conceived again and bore a son, and said, "Because the Lord has
heard that I am hated, he has given me this son also"; and she called
34 his name Simeon. Again she conceived and bore a son, and said,
"Now this time my husband will be joined to me, because I have
35 borne him three sons"; therefore his name was called Levi. And she
conceived again and bore a son, and said, "This time I will praise the
Lord"; therefore she called his name Judah; then she ceased bearing.
1   When Rachel saw that she bore Jacob no children, she envied her
sister; and she said to Jacob, "Give me children, or I shall die!"
2 Jacob's anger was kindled against Rachel, and he said, "Am I in the
place of God, who has withheld from you the fruit of the womb?"
3 Then she said, "Here is my maid Bilhah; go in to her, that she may
4 bear upon my knees, and even I may have children through her." So
she gave him her maid Bilhah as a wife; and Jacob went in to her.
5, 6 And Bilhah conceived and bore Jacob a son. Then Rachel said,
"God has judged me, and has also heard my voice and given me a
7 son"; therefore she called his name Dan. Rachel's maid Bilhah
8 conceived again and bore Jacob a second son. Then Rachel said,
"With mighty wrestlings I have wrestled with my sister, and have
prevailed"; so she called his name Naphtali.
9   When Leah saw that she had ceased bearing children, she took her
10 maid Zilpah and gave her to Jacob as a wife. Then Leah's maid
11 Zilpah bore Jacob a son. And Leah said, "Good fortune!" so she
12 called his name Gad. Leah's maid Zilpah bore Jacob a second son.
13 And Leah said, "Happy am I! For the women will call me happy"; so
she called his name Asher.
14   In the days of wheat harvest Reuben went and found mandrakes
in the field, and brought them to his mother Leah. Then Rachel said
15 to Leah, "Give me, I pray, some of your son's mandrakes." But she

said to her, "Is it a small matter that you have taken away my
husband? Would you take away my son's mandrakes also?" Rachel
said, "Then he may lie with you tonight for your son's mandrakes."
16 When Jacob came from the field in the evening, Leah went out to
meet him, and said, "You must come in to me; for I have hired you
17 with my son's mandrakes." So he lay with her that night. And God
hearkened to Leah, and she conceived and bore Jacob a fifth son.
18 Leah said, "God has given me my hire because I gave my maid to my
19 husband"; so she called his name Issachar. And Leah conceived
20 again, and she bore Jacob a sixth son. Then Leah said, "God has
endowed me with a good dowry; now my husband will honour me,
because I have borne him six sons"; so she called his name Zebulun.
21, 22 Afterwards she bore a daughter, and called her name Dinah. Then
God remembered Rachel, and God hearkened to her and opened her
23 womb. She conceived and bore a son, and said, "God has taken
24 away my reproach"; and she called his name Joseph, saying, "May
the Lord add to me another son!"

Jacob becomes rich (30:25–43)

25 When Rachel had borne Joseph, Jacob said to Laban, "Send me
26 away, that I may go to my own home and country. Give me my wives
and my children for whom I have served you, and let me go; for you
27 know the service which I have given you." But Laban said to him, "If
you will allow me to say so, I have learned by divination that the
28 Lord has blessed me because of you; name your wages, and I will
29 give it." Jacob said to him, "You yourself know how I have served
30 you, and how your cattle have fared with me. For you had little
before I came, and it has increased abundantly; and the Lord has
blessed you wherever I turned. But now when shall I provide for my
31 own household also?" He said, "What shall I give you?" Jacob said,
"You shall not give me anything; if you will do this for me, I will
32 again feed your flock and keep it: let me pass through all your flock
today, removing from it every speckled and spotted sheep and every
black lamb, and the spotted and speckled among the goats; and such
33 shall be my wages. So my honesty will answer for me later, when you
come to look into my wages with you. Every one that is not speckled
and spotted among the goats and black among the lambs, if found
34 with me, shall be counted stolen." Laban said, "Good! Let it be as
35 you have said." But that day Laban removed the he-goats that were
striped and spotted, and all the she-goats that were speckled and

spotted, every one that had white on it, and every lamb that was
36 black, and put them in charge of his sons; and he set a distance of
three days' journey between himself and Jacob; and Jacob fed the
rest of Laban's flock.
37 Then Jacob took fresh rods of poplar and almond and plane, and
38 peeled white streaks in them, exposing the white of the rods. He set
the rods which he had peeled in front of the flocks in the runnels,
that is, the watering troughs, where the flocks came to drink. And
39 since they bred when they came to drink, the flocks bred in front of
the rods and so the flocks brought forth striped, speckled, and
40 spotted. And Jacob separated the lambs, and set the faces of the
flocks toward the striped and all the black in the flock of Laban; and
he put his own droves apart, and did not put them with Laban's
41 flock. Whenever the stronger of the flock were breeding Jacob laid
the rods in the runnels before the eyes of the flock, that they might
42 breed among the rods, but for the feebler of the flock he did not lay
them there; so the feebler were Laban's, and the stronger Jacob's.
43 Thus the man grew exceedingly rich, and had large flocks, maidservants and menservants, and camels and asses.

Jacob's flight (31:1–21)

1 Now Jacob heard that the sons of Laban were saying, "Jacob has
taken all that was our father's; and from what was our father's he has
2 gained all this wealth." And Jacob saw that Laban did not regard
3 him with favour as before. Then the Lord said to Jacob, "Return to
the land of your fathers and to your kindred, and I will be with you."
4 So Jacob sent and called Rachel and Leah into the field where his
5 flock was, and said to them, "I see that your father does not regard
me with favour as he did before. But the God of my father has been
6 with me. You know that I have served your father with all my
7 strength; yet your father has cheated me and changed my wages ten
8 times, but God did not permit him to harm me. If he said, 'The
spotted shall be your wages,' then all the flock bore spotted; and if he
said, 'The striped shall be your wages,' then all the flock bore striped.
9 Thus God has taken away the cattle of your father, and given them
10 to me. In the mating season of the flock I lifted up my eyes, and saw
in a dream that the he-goats which leaped upon the flock were
11 striped, spotted, and mottled. Then the angel of God said to me in
12 the dream, 'Jacob,' and I said, 'Here I am!' And he said, 'Lift up your
eyes and see, all the goats that leap upon the flock are striped,

13 spotted, and mottled; for I have seen all that Laban is doing to you. I
   am the God of Bethel, where you anointed a pillar and made a vow
   to me. Now arise, go forth from this land, and return to the land of
14 your birth.' " Then Rachel and Leah answered him, "Is there any
15 portion or inheritance left to us in our father's house? Are we not
   regarded by him as foreigners? For he has sold us, and he has been
16 using up the money given for us. All the property which God has
   taken away from our father belongs to us and to our children; now
   then, whatever God has said to you, do."

17, 18 So Jacob arose, and set his sons and his wives on camels; and he
   drove away all his cattle, all his livestock which he had gained, the
   cattle in his possession which he had acquired in Paddan-aram, to
19 go to the land of Canaan to his father Isaac. Laban had gone to shear
20 his sheep, and Rachel stole her father's household gods. And Jacob
   outwitted Laban the Aramean, in that he did not tell him that he
21 intended to flee. He fled with all that he had, and arose and crossed
   the Euphrates, and set his face toward the hill country of Gilead.

Laban's pursuit (31:22–35)

22, 23 When it was told Laban on the third day that Jacob had fled, he took
   his kinsmen with him and pursued him for seven days and followed
24 close after him into the hill country of Gilead. But God came to
   Laban the Aramean in a dream by night, and said to him, "Take
   heed that you say not a word to Jacob, either good or bad."
25 And Laban overtook Jacob. Now Jacob had pitched his tent in
   the hill country, and Laban with his kinsmen encamped in the hill
26 country of Gilead. And Laban said to Jacob, "What have you done,
   that you have cheated me, and carried away my daughters like
27 captives of the sword? Why did you flee secretly, and cheat me, and
   did not tell me, so that I might have sent you away with mirth and
28 songs, with tambourine and lyre? And why did you not permit me to
   kiss my sons and my daughters farewell? Now you have done
29 foolishly. It is in my power to do you harm; but the God of your
   father spoke to me last night, saying, 'Take heed that you speak to
30 Jacob neither good nor bad.' And now you have gone away because
   you longed greatly for your father's house, but why did you steal my
31 gods?" Jacob answered Laban, "Because I was afraid, for I thought
32 that you would take your daughters from me by force. Any one with
   whom you find your gods shall not live. In the presence of our

kinsmen point out what I have that is yours, and take it." Now Jacob did not know that Rachel had stolen them.

33 So Laban went into Jacob's tent, and into Leah's tent, and into the tent of the two maidservants, but he did not find them. And he 34 went out of Leah's tent, and entered Rachel's. Now Rachel had taken the household gods and put them in the camel's saddle, and sat 35 upon them. Laban felt all about the tent, but did not find them. And she said to her father, "Let not my lord be angry that I cannot rise before you, for the way of women is upon me." So he searched, but did not find the household gods.

Jacob and Laban make peace (31:36–55)

36 Then Jacob became angry, and upbraided Laban; Jacob said to Laban, "What is my offence? What is my sin, that you have hotly 37 pursued me? Although you have felt through all my goods, what have you found of all your household goods? Set it here before my kinsmen and your kinsmen, that they may decide between us two. 38 These twenty years I have been with you; your ewes and your she-goats have not miscarried, and I have not eaten the rams of your 39 flocks. That which was torn by wild beasts I did not bring to you; I bore the loss of it myself; of my hand you required it, whether stolen 40 by day or stolen by night. Thus I was; by day the heat consumed me, 41 and the cold by night, and my sleep fled from my eyes. These twenty years I have been in your house; I served you fourteen years for your two daughters, and six years for your flock, and you have 42 changed my wages ten times. If the God of my father, the God of Abraham and the Fear of Isaac, had not been on my side, surely now you would have sent me away empty-handed. God saw my affliction and the labour of my hands, and rebuked you last night."

43 Then Laban answered and said to Jacob, "The daughters are my daughters, the children are my children, the flocks are my flocks, and all that you see is mine. But what can I do this day to these my 44 daughters, or to their children whom they have borne? Come now, let us make a covenant, you and I; and let it be a witness between you 45, 46 and me." So Jacob took a stone, and set it up as a pillar. And Jacob said to his kinsmen, "Gather stones," and they took stones, and 47 made a heap; and they ate there by the heap. Laban called it Jegar-48 sahadutha: but Jacob called it Galeed. Laban said, "This heap is a witness between you and me today." Therefore he named it Galeed, 49 and the pillar Mizpah, for he said, "The Lord watch between you

50 and me, when we are absent one from the other. If you ill-treat my
daughters, or if you take wives besides my daughters, although no
man is with us, remember, God is witness between you and me."
51 Then Laban said to Jacob, "See this heap and the pillar, which I
52 have set between you and me. This heap is a witness, and the pillar is
a witness, that I will not pass over this heap to you, and you will not
53 pass over this heap and this pillar to me, for harm. The God of
Abraham and the God of Nahor, the God of their father, judge
54 between us." So Jacob swore by the Fear of his father Isaac, and
Jacob offered a sacrifice on the mountain and called his kinsmen to
eat bread; and they ate bread and tarried all night on the mountain.
55 Early in the morning Laban arose, and kissed his grandchildren
and his daughters and blessed them; then he departed and returned
home.

NEMESIS

Genesis 29:1–30 (cont'd)

The plot of the story centres around Laban's deception of Jacob
and how he in turn is deceived by him. Hebrew audiences,
thinking of the large Aramean populations to their north,
would have enjoyed the idea of one of "them" having once been
outsmarted by one of "us". If it had been a play on the stage,
you could imagine them booing when Laban had his initial
success and cheering when in the end Jacob had his. But the
more perceptive among them would remember how Jacob had
come to be in Mesopotamia in the first place and, though they
may not much have liked it, would have sensed the strong
atmosphere of poetic justice which pervades the opening
scenes. That Jacob eventually turns the tables on Laban does
not cancel out the feeling that in these scenes he is getting what
he deserves.

(i)

As the story begins, the shepherds' indolence as they waited
until there were enough of them to move the huge stone laid
over the well's mouth is neatly contrasted with Jacob's strength
in shifting it by himself. We remember how he had placed the
stone at Bethel upright. There is a contrast too between the

shepherds' gruff and barely civil answers to his questions and his own forwardness and effusiveness when Rachel approaches. In his delight he kisses her before he had even told her who he was. This was the girl for him!

It is a picture of a confident Jacob, fresh from his experience at Bethel and sure of himself again. He is welcomed by an equally effusive Laban, and everything seems set fair for a happy outcome to his enterprise.

(ii)

The audience could have told him otherwise. Laban's welcome was no doubt genuine enough, but it cannot have taken him long to guess from the attention he was paying to Rachel what Jacob's real purpose was. He would recall how all these years before Abraham's servant had brought expensive presents and paid a handsome bride-price for his sister Rebekah to marry Isaac. But this visitor from Canaan had come alone, and there was no sign of rings or jewelry or silver or fine garments. There was something fishy here. He was not going to part with his daughter to this conceited young man for nothing, even though he was Rebekah's son. Jacob would have to pay for by his labour what he could not pay for in money or kind.

Presumably Jacob had not taken any money or gifts with him when he fled because that would have needed a small caravan and would have made it easier for Esau to pursue him. This ought to have made him wary when after a month or so his uncle offered him work and all but asked him to name his own wages. He should have seen what he was at and entered into the spirit of a good oriental bargaining session. Instead he responded immediately, and rashly said he would work for seven years for Rachel. This was a ridiculously high price which reflected his love for the girl rather than her realistic worth in the marriage stakes of the time. Jacob had in effect fallen into the same kind of trap he had laid for his brother Esau when he was after his birthright. He had let it be known that he would pay any price to gain the girl he loved. Laban's reply is suitably generous, "It is better that I give her to you than to any other man", but it is sly as well. It is not quite the definite promise Jacob must have taken it to be.

The seven years' wait, we are informed, seemed to Jacob but "a few days" because of the love he had for Rachel. This is a phrase calculated for once to make us warm to the hero of our epic (though it is not without its irony when we remember that Rebekah had used the same phrase in 27:44). But more importantly for the story's outcome Jacob's devotion would not have been lost on Laban, and he formed his plan to squeeze yet more out of this too willing worker. When the period was up, he assembled his clan and arranged the marriage feast, but in the dark of night he conducted not Rachel but Leah, her older sister, to the nuptial tent. Probably the two sisters were much alike though, as we have just been told, Leah had "weak" eyes, meaning that they lacked the black sparkle which oriental men prize in women. Nevertheless, it is hardly believable that Jacob could have been so easily deceived. We can only put it down to the blind gullibility of a man head over heels in love.

It is impossible not to recall blind old Isaac being gulled in his tent by this same Jacob into mistaking one son for another. Jacob's anger in the morning was as useless as Esau's had been then. Laban answers, "It is not so done in our country, to give the younger before the first-born". It is an evasion, and everybody knows it. This man, we feel, would have sold Rachel to a passing stranger had the price been right. But wait! Had not Jacob himself done just what Laban had said was not done and as the younger taken the place of the first-born? Unwittingly Laban's throw-away remark is the voice of nemesis. The deceiver has himself been deceived, and for once in the Bible an older child has been preferred over a younger.

(iii)

At this point Laban relents a little and lets Jacob have Rachel too after a second series of marriage celebrations. It is these that the word "week" refers to, and presumably Leah's ceremonies had lasted the same time; see Judg. 14:17. He did not insist that Jacob serve another seven years first, but he extracted from him a promise to stay on in the encampment for that period. The first movement of the long story thus ends with the laconic statements that Jacob "loved Rachel more than Leah" and that he "served Laban for another seven years".

How should we take these statements? Should we read them positively as further evidence of Jacob's devotion to Rachel or as evidence that he was learning from his experience and now saw and accepted the ironic justice of what had happened to him? In the context of the rest of the story I do not think so. I believe rather that they reveal a man who (in the phrase applied to Napoleon on his return from Elba) has forgotten nothing and learned nothing. They show us one who had been both the recipient and the victim of partiality, himself openly practising favouritism and not seeing anything wrong in it. They also hint ominously at the long years he has during which to plan carefully how to get back at the wily old uncle who had bested him. Revenge not acquiescence is in the air as we are back with Rebekah's son of old patiently waiting his chance, just as she had so often counselled him to do.

I would justify this interpretation by drawing attention to the remarkable fact that God's name has not yet appeared in the story. It is a silence that is even more eloquent than God's silence in the stolen blessing scene. For Bethel has intervened. He who had promised at Bethel to be with Jacob had nothing to say, but let all this happen to him. And just as remarkable is the fact that he who had received that promise did not at any time think of turning to him who had given it. That silence also speaks volumes.

The voice of nemesis had spoken but, as far as Jacob himself was concerned, I am afraid it went unheeded.

SONS

Genesis 29:31–30:24 *(cont'd)*

(iv)

In the commentary on the genealogies of Abraham and Ketu-

rah and of Ishmael in chapter 25 I made a distinction between
the kind of traditions these genealogies represent and the kind
preserved in the stories of Genesis. The one kind are really
speaking about tribal and ethnic groups under the guise of
individuals. The other kind go back to cherished memories of
the Hebrews about great figures in their past. In the middle part
of the story of Jacob and Laban which tells of the birth of eleven
of Jacob's twelve sons and of his only daughter we have a
mixture of the two kinds. There is genuine reminiscence, but
there is also a genealogy involved, that of Israel itself, and
honesty compels us to regard it as just as artificial an intrusion
into the story as the lists in chapter 25.

It is not that Jacob had sons that we find difficult to swallow
but that he had precisely twelve sons, and that each of them
fathered a family which eventually settled in a specific area of
Palestine and became one of the twelve constituent tribes of the
nation of Israel. This is not the way that nations come into
being. Historically speaking, we have no reason to suppose that
Israel's beginnings were any less complicated than the beginnings of other nation states of ancient or indeed of modern
times. In so far as the latter part of Genesis suggests otherwise,
it must be indulging in oversimplification. It has in effect taken
the name Israel and the names of her twelve tribes, linked them
together in a spurious genealogy as if they had been individuals,
and then found a place for them in the old stories by the neat
fiction that the patriarch Jacob had twelve sons and consquent-
ly received the name Israel as a second name at Peniel (32:28).
The trouble with this particular false genealogy is that it is the
Hebrews' own and has not surprisingly, therefore, invaded the
stories more thoroughly than the genealogies they constructed
for their neighbours. But it is still up to us to detach it from the
stories as far as we can.

There is one clue which may help us here. Although Jacob is
credited with twelve sons, only a few—Joseph pre-eminently
and Reuben, Simeon, Levi, Judah and Benjamin—actually
emerge with any clarity as individuals in the stories to follow in
Genesis. We should concentrate on the activities of this smaller

group if we wish to find the most reliable traces of the family history of the man Jacob.

(v)

Not only is the section 29:30ff. based on a putative genealogy but it positively wallows in another fictional game which the Hebrews loved to play, that of intentionally twisting the meanings of names. From the examples of naming ceremonies which we have looked at previously it should by this time be clear that they had their tongues pretty firmly in their cheeks as they played it. This is so here too, as the following table shows, in which the correct meanings of the names of Jacob's sons—or rather Israel's tribes—are set alongside the ones given in the text. Some of the correct meanings are now beyond recovery, but the Hebrews would have known them. But the relevant fact is that only in a single instance (Simeon) is there much connection between the two sides of the table.

Reuben	"behold a son!" *(re-u ben)*	"he [God] has looked upon my affliction" *(ra-a be-onyi)*
Simeon	"he [God] has heard" *(shim'on)* (longer form)	"he [God] has heard" *(shama')* (normal form)
Levi	uncertain *(lewi)*	"[my husband] shall be joined [to me]" *(yillaweh)*
Judah	uncertain *(yehudah)*	"I will praise [the Lord]" *(odeh)*
Dan	"he [God] has given [favourable] judgment" *(dan)*	"he [God] has judged [me]" *(dan)*
Naphtali	uncertain *(naphtali)*	"I have wrestled" *(niphtalti)*
Gad	title of Canaanite origin, perhaps of the god of "luck" *(gad)*	"good fortune" *(gad)*
Asher	divine name of Canaanite origin *(asher)*	"in my happiness" *(be-oshri)*

Issachar	uncertain *(yissakhar)*	"[God has given me] my hire" *(sikhri)*
Zebulun	"the prince" (divine title) *(zebulun)*	"[my husband] will honour me" *(yizbeleni)*
Joseph	"he [God] adds [blessing]" *(yoseph)*	"may he [God] add [another son]" *(yoseph)*

(vi)

What then in this section tells us of the real feelings and character of the participants? Not, I think, the pious words put in Jacob's mouth in 30:2 as he addresses a barren Rachel, "Am I in the place of God, who has withheld from you the fruit of the womb?" Such sentiments just do not fit with what we have learned so far of him. On the other hand, the way the section dwells on the bitter rivalry between the two sisters does ring true, particularly in the little episode involving the mandrakes found by Leah's son. This fruit was thought by the ancients to possess fertilizing properties. The incident seems to be only loosely connected with the etymology of Issachar's name which follows it, and it may well be a genuine tradition of Jacob's family. It certainly highlights most effectively the one wife's desperate longing for a son and the other's equally desperate desire to win the favour of a husband who, though she had already given him children, did not want to sleep with her.

In its own way the obvious preference of God for the ill-used Leah also strikes an authentic note. His first recorded action since Jacob's arrival in Mesopotamia (well over seven years now) is to open her womb. By his connivance the disdained older sister has several children before Rachel gives birth to Joseph. There is an implied rebuke in this to Jacob—if he was minded to hear it—for his blatant favouring of Rachel. But there is more to it still. It perturbed us greatly that in the previous stories in Genesis God's choice seemed to rest on younger sons who were already the apple of their mothers' eye and to by-pass their elder brothers whom these same mothers had no time for. It didn't sound right that he and these scheming and vindictive women should agree. But here God favours the wife whom Jacob "hated" and keeps the one whom he "loved" waiting. And the favoured one is an elder sister! Moreover, all the sons born to Jacob are included in the chosen line, even those of the handmaids Zilpah and Bilhah, and this time round no one is excluded. This too was God's grace. It is to our way of thinking a more pleasing example of it.

SUCCESS

Genesis 30:25–43 *(cont'd)*

(vii)

We may regard the account of the births of Jacob's sons and his one daughter as an interlude between the first movement of the story and the second, which begins at 30:25 with Jacob's request to Laban to be allowed to return to Canaan now that his double turn of service had been completed.

It has always been something of a mystery why Laban did not let Jacob go and even more of a mystery why Jacob acquiesced so meekly in his decision. The terms of the contract, as far as we have been told them, had been met and Jacob was not, as we have come to know him, a man who would easily have surrendered what he was entitled to, particularly when by Laban's underhand dealing he had been forced to work fourteen years for two wives instead of seven years for one.

The texts discovered at Nuzi throw light on this problem as they did on the legal position behind Abraham's agreement with his slave Eliezer in chapter 15. One of these texts combines within the same legal deed a promise by a father to marry his daughter to a young man if the young man undertook to look after him in his old age, and a promise that the young man would be his heir if he, the father, died without having further issue. If, however, subsequent to the agreement he should have a son, his daughter's husband would have to divide the inheritance with him.

It seems reasonable to assume that the contract entered into by Jacob was of this kind. It would explain why Jacob could not simply get up and go. It would also explain the interest taken later in Jacob by Laban's sons, who are not mentioned until towards the end of this chapter. They must have been born to him after his agreement with Jacob had been sealed.

(viii)

When Jacob made his request to Laban, therefore, he was really asking for the contract to be terminated, and he was, it seems, not unprepared for his request to be turned down. For, as the final paragraphs of chapter 30 make clear, he had a plan ready which must have taken him a long time to put together. Just as he had done so many years before, he made an offer to Laban that he knew his uncle could not resist. But this time it was no love-sick youth willing to go to any lengths to win the girl he had set his heart on who made the offer, but the cunning Jacob of old only pretending to be simple.

He was in command from the start. Laban opened the bargaining by asking Jacob once again to name his wages. And cleverly he gave the credit to Jacob's God, admitting that he had benefited greatly from Jacob's hard work. He realized that he must now let his son-in-law have some independence and be able to earn something that he could call his own, but he was confident that he would not have to part with too much. Jacob in reply undertook to tend his uncle's flocks as before, asking only to be allowed to form his own little flock of sheep and goats on the side. "Fair enough", Laban might have said as he prepared to haggle over the number. Imagine his surprise, then, when Jacob said he would be content with only the mottled sheep and goats from his uncle's flocks and any lamb that was born black. In any normal flock such animals would comprise only a minute proportion of the whole. It was Laban's defences that were down this time. In his amazement he forgot his bargaining instincts and agreed right away. We can almost hear the contempt in his voice as he said, "Good! Let it be as you have said." So contemptuous indeed was he of this "sucker" of a son-in-law that he removed the mottled animals and black lambs from his present flocks. Jacob would only get those that came along in the future.

But Jacob was ready even for this ploy. The audience by now would be smiling broadly. The crooked Laban was about to get his come-uppance. And when they heard how he got it, there would be many audible titters and not a few loud guffaws.

The account as we have it is a little confused, but the two main methods of breeding used by Jacob are clear enough. One was based on the widespread ancient belief that experiences or visions undergone or seen by mothers in pregnancy—human as well as animal—could decisively affect their unborn offspring. To us à load of superstition, but in a superstitious age it was not the method that had the listeners splitting their sides, but the hilarious and rather crude scenes at Jacob's watering troughs that the story conjured up before them. But Jacob did not rely solely on the magical influence of the peeled rods on the females in heat. He backed it up by a more down-to-earth breeding method, seeing to it that the rods were only put in place when the stronger males were at water. The more sceptical in the audience would nod in approval: "A canny lad was our Jacob!"

(ix)

The second movement of the story finishes with the simple statement that as a result of this peculiar but apparently very effective husbandry Jacob "grew exceedingly rich". We are left to savour Jacob's success. No morals are yet drawn, and we have to go on to the first few verses of the third movement in chapter 31 before we are confronted with the sour faces of his victims and have the means to make judgments.

HYPOCRISY

Genesis 31:1–16 *(cont'd)*

(x)

The complaints of Laban's sons are mentioned first, probably because they saw long before their smug and complacent father was himself willing to admit it that he had been hoist with his own petard. How angry they must have been with him, and how they must have hated the simpleton turned shyster who was spiriting away their inheritance before their very eyes! And what about Laban when he finally tumbled to what was happening? The story-teller's masterly understatement says it all: "And Jacob saw that Laban did not regard him with favour as before."

But more importantly what about God? How did he regard his chosen servant's conduct?

(xi)

I hesitate to introduce too censorious a note into what is essentially a piece of Hebrew burlesque. But there is evidence in the way the author phrases his story at this point that, though he may have had his audiences falling about in the aisles, he was himself not at all sure that God was amused.

Firstly, as he had done before, he keeps God's name all but absent from the whole account of Jacob's success. It is mentioned once by Laban (30:27) and once by Jacob himself (30:30), but in both cases it is with reference to Jacob's past service. Is the story-teller hinting that though Laban got what he deserved, God did not like the vengeful and crafty way Jacob went about it? I have the feeling he is because, *secondly,* when he reports God's command to Jacob to return home, he does it most laconically: "Return to the land of your fathers and to your kindred, and I will be with you." There is no repetition here of past fulsome promises. There is no word of censure for Laban and his sons nor of compassion for a Jacob in danger from their wrath. Nor is there the slightest suggestion that at last this man, having been tested in the fires of hard experience, had become a vessel fit for God to use. There is simply God's blunt recognition that he had to be got away from where he was.

Thirdly, there is the way the story-teller paints the scene where Jacob persuades his wives to escape with him. In vivid contrast to the previous episode God's name is all the time on Jacob's lips, but what a mockery of piety his speech to them is! He exaggerates Laban's cheating ways ("ten times") and excuses his own, adding in the first case the comment "but God did not permit him to harm me" and in the second "Thus God has taken away the cattle of your father, and given them to me." He tells them about Bethel and claims to have had a visitation from an angel who had renewed God's promise to be with him, "for I have seen all that Laban is doing to you." What about what he was doing to Laban? How obnoxiously hypocritical and self-righteous can one get?

(xii)

And the self-righteousness is carried forward into Rachel and Leah's reply. They rally immediately to their husband's side and roundly curse their father for his miserliness and greed. It was apparently the done thing in their time for a good father not to spend the "bride-price" paid to him for a daughter but to hold it in trust to be passed on to her when he died. But Laban had used up their "inheritance". He had in effect "sold" them for a profit. Their husband had given him fourteen years' service but all this had achieved was to make him richer. If in more recent years Jacob had won some of this wealth back by his deceit, he had only taken what was rightfully theirs. There is some justice in these accusations, but there is also an unpleasing self-interest. It was loyal of them to support their husband, but did they need to sound, as the story-teller has them doing, so unctuously devout about it? "All the property which God has taken away from our father belongs to us and to our children: now then, whatever God has said to you, do."

There are a lot of pious words around as for a second time Jacob prepares to flee for his life, but we ought not to be misled by them. They come at the end of two decades of duplicity and suspicion and hatred, during which God has for the most part been ignored and has himself remained loudly silent.

VINDICATION

Genesis 31:17–55 *(cont'd)*

(xiii)

The rest of the story is rather long-winded, though the sequence of events is straightforward enough. Jacob and his family flee across the Euphrates, Rachel having stolen her father's household gods. These were little pagan idols which he set up in his tent. We are not told why she took them. Perhaps it was out of spite, but it could have been as a kind of insurance policy should her husband's God fail them (see 35:4). Anyway, the caravan reaches Gilead beyond the Jordan, where a pursuing Laban catches up with them in seven days. But he is immediately warned by God in a dream not to say anything, either good or bad, to Jacob, an idiomatic phrase apparently meaning in this context not to do anything to hinder him. It certainly doesn't stop Laban talking! For when he meets his son-in-law he launches into a lengthy speech upbraiding Jacob for cheating him by running off with his daughters. However, remembering God's warning (he calls him "the God of your father") he promises to do Jacob no harm if only he will return to him his household gods. But Jacob knows nothing of what Rachel has done and protests loudly, inviting Laban to conduct his own search if he does not believe him.

The next scene is pure farce as Laban rummages through the encampment, rushing from tent to tent turning everything upside down, but finding nothing, while an ice-cool Rachel, who had put the idols in her saddle-bag, sits on the saddle and apologizes to her father that she cannot rise up to greet him, "for the way of women is upon me."

Laban's failure to find his idols gives Jacob his cue and he castigates his father-in-law for falsely accusing him, then himself launches into a lengthy speech in which he recounts his twenty years of toil on Laban's behalf, which had gone utterly unappreciated and which but for the intervention of the God of his father—whom interestingly he calls the "fear" of Isaac—would have gone unrewarded as well. This rebuke is accepted by Laban, though not with very good grace, and still protesting, he proposes that the two of them make a treaty or covenant. There is a description of the ceremony, which involves setting up a pillar and a heap of stones, the naming of the place—its location is not certainly known—in Aramaic and Hebrew (both names mean "a heap of witnesses"), a promise by Jacob not to ill-treat Laban's daughters, promises by them both to observe the place where they were as a boundary between their two territories, oaths by "the God of Abraham" and "the God of Nahor" (apparently thought of as the same), and the offering of a sacrifice. Then Laban blesses his daughters and departs for Mesopotamia.

(xiv)

One problem at least in this long narrative can be disposed of with relative ease. Laban could not possibly have reached Gilead in seven days. There must, therefore, be a confusion at the end of the story between a private pact entered into by Jacob and Laban at a place considerably nearer Harran, and a boundary treaty drawn up in Gilead by groups of Hebrews and Arameans at a much later date when in fact the two peoples were present in the area in sufficient numbers to be fighting over territory. Either the two traditions got united carelessly or the second was intentionally read back into the Patriarchal period to give it more weight in Israelite eyes. It is not too difficult to disentangle them. The agreement about Laban's daughters applies obviously to the first, that about not passing "over this heap" equally obviously to the second.

(xv)

But that problem having been cleared away, there remain quite a few others. They mainly concern how we are meant to react to the motives of the characters.

On a surface reading, it looks very much as though Jacob

comes out of this final confrontation with Laban blameless. It was rather vindictive of Rachel to steal her father's household gods, but after all they were pagan idols, and there is irony as well as humour in Laban's frantic search for them. His gods could not be found, whereas Israel's God found him and saw to it that he did no hurt to Jacob. Note also how it is emphasized that Jacob had no knowledge of Rachel's misdemeanour. Jacob was, it seems, fully justified in being angry and, though he may have laid it on a bit thick when retailing his hard years of service ("by day the heat consumed me, and the cold by night"), he was also undoubtedly right in his snide assessment that if he had been able, Laban would have sent him away empty-handed.

I am not sure, however, that I agree entirely with this interpretation. The chief impression I get is the same as I got in the previous scene where Jacob inveigled his wives onto his side. It is of Jacob's insincerity and hypocrisy. He never consulted the "God of my father" when cooking up his scheme to defraud his uncle, yet throughout this episode he could hardly utter a sentence without bringing him in. Forgotten when he was intent on increasing his flocks by chicanery, God was only invoked by him and given the credit for his success when he had to defend his actions to others. Not that we need feel sorry for Laban. He comes over as equally insincere and hypocritical. But is there in the end anything to choose between them? Which statement is the more objectionable, Laban's "all that you see is mine—but what can I do?" or Jacob's "God saw my affliction and the labour of my hands"—and made me rich?

Certainly God does intervene on Jacob's side. Throughout the epic there is never any doubt about that. But it is not a pretty sight as Jacob, once again victorious, returns with his ill-gotten gains to the land which this same God had promised to give to him and his descendants. Surely God's grace has more to it than that? For that reason we can be grateful that the story-teller has made room in his story for the message that God's grace and God's approval are not necessarily the same. It is a message that we would all do well to heed most earnestly as far as our own lives are concerned.

FOREBODING I

Genesis 32:1–21

1, 2 Jacob went on his way and the angels of God met him; and when Jacob saw them he said, "This is God's army!" So he called the name of that place Mahanaim.

3   And Jacob sent messengers before him to Esau his brother in the
4 land of Seir, the country of Edom, instructing them, "Thus you shall say to my lord Esau: Thus says your servant Jacob, 'I have
5 sojourned with Laban, and stayed until now; and I have oxen, asses, flocks, menservants, and maidservants; and I have sent to tell my lord, in order that I may find favour in your sight.' "
6   And the messengers returned to Jacob, saying, "We came to your brother Esau, and he is coming to meet you, and four hundred men
7 with him." Then Jacob was greatly afraid and distressed; and he divided the people that were with him, and the flocks and herds and
8 camels, into two companies, thinking, "If Esau comes to the one company and destroys it, then the company which is left will escape."
9   And Jacob said, "O God of my father Abraham and God of my father Isaac, O Lord who didst say to me, 'Return to your country
10 and to your kindred, and I will do you good,' I am not worthy of the least of all the steadfast love and all the faithfulness which thou hast shown to thy servant, for with only my staff I crossed this Jordan;
11 and now I have become two companies. Deliver me, I pray thee, from the hand of my brother, from the hand of Esau, for I fear him,
12 lest he come and slay us all, the mothers with the children. But thou didst say, 'I will do you good, and make your descendants as the sand of the sea, which cannot be numbered for multitude.' "
13   So he lodged there that night, and took from what he had with
14 him a present for his brother Esau, two hundred she-goats and
15 twenty he-goats, two hundred ewes and twenty rams, thirty milch camels and their colts, forty cows and ten bulls, twenty she-asses and
16 ten he-asses. These he delivered into the hand of his servants, every drove by itself, and said to his servants, "Pass on before me, and put
17 a space between drove and drove." He instructed the foremost,

"When Esau my brother meets you, and asks you, 'To whom do you belong? Where are you going? And whose are these before you?'
18 then you shall say, 'They belong to your servant Jacob; they are a
19 present sent to my lord Esau; and moreover he is behind us.' " He likewise instructed the second and the third and all who followed the droves, "You shall say the same thing to Esau when you meet him,
20 and you shall say, 'Moreover your servant Jacob is behind us.' " For he thought, "I may appease him with the present that goes before me, and afterwards I shall see his face; perhaps he will accept me."
21 So the present passed on before him; and he himself lodged that night in the camp.

As he returns to Canaan after his twenty years in exile Jacob is not exactly brimful of confidence, even though he had come out best in his tussles with Laban and was now rich and surrounded with a numerous family. In fact, the nearer he gets to home the more he is the victim of foreboding as he realizes that he will soon have to meet the brother he had cheated all those years before. And strangely his foreboding persists in spite of an appearance of God to him at a place called Mahanaim.

(i)

According to the story Mahanaim was given its name by Jacob after this appearance, but as we think back on how often in Genesis the Patriarchs are falsely credited with the naming of places, we may be wiser to assume that it was the name that gave rise to the vision. Mahanaim was situated just east of the Jordan and north of its tributary the Jabbok on the caravan route eastwards from the plain of Succoth which is called in Judg. 8:11 the "way of them that dwelt in tents" (AV; see Map 3). The name probably meant originally "the two camps" or "double encampment", the form being what Semitic grammarians call a "dual".

The word, however, does not only mean "camp", but denotes the body of people who habitually live in a camp, that is, either a "company" of nomads or travellers or an "army" of soldiers. Clearly Jacob, as he approached it, took it in this second sense. He formed a picture in his mind's eye of the angelic "company" or "army" of the "Lord of hosts", which he could scarcely avoid contrasting with his own small "company". As a result he was moved to—but what exactly was he moved to?

(ii)

The story-teller does not say, but it is natural for us to turn for guidance to other places in Scripture where similar visionary experiences are related: to Josh. 5:14, for instance, where Joshua was met outside Jericho by a "man" with a drawn sword in his hand who described himself as the "commander of the army of the Lord"; or to 2 Kgs. 6:17 where Elisha, as the king of Syria sent a great force of horses and chariots to capture him, prayed to God to open his fearful servant's eyes and, we are told, "the Lord opened the eyes of the young man, and he saw; and behold, the mountain was full of horses and chariots of fire round about Elisha"; or, perhaps most apposite of all, to chapter 28 and Jacob's own earlier dream at Bethel of the angels of God ascending and descending on the ladder set between heaven and earth.

There is also the impressive testimony of a man like General Gordon of Khartoum. His noble last letter from that desolate place, written just before his betrayal and death, ends with words drawn from our passage: "The angels of God are with me—Mahanaim".

Surely with the good general to guide us and the evidence, too, of these other Scriptural encounters, we must conclude that Jacob's vision was a fortifying one, encouraging him, as danger loomed ahead, to lay hold on the unseen resources available to those who had God on their side, and pointing him away from the "little army" he had with him to the "great army" above and around and beyond him, ready to close in to his defence? That had certainly been the message of Bethel's angels to him as he had fled from the land that had been promised to him and his. What more fitting than that God should now as he returned to it, again in peril, draw near to him and assure him of similar heavenly aid in the confrontation that lay before him?

FOREBODING II

Genesis 32:1–21 *(cont'd)*

(iii)

I cannot agree with this interpretation. It is a tempting one, but
it is over-hasty.

After Bethel Jacob had felt strengthened and invigorated,
and he had arrived at Harran cock-sure and full of confidence.
But after Mahanaim he was, as the rest of this chapter underlines in no uncertain terms, in abject terror, thinking only of
how he could appease an Esau who, he was convinced, must
still be seeking his life. He was even more convinced of this
when the messengers he sent to inform Esau of his arrival—note
how he calls him "my lord" and himself "your servant"—came
back with the news that his brother was already on his way to
meet him and was accompanied by no less than four hundred
men.

In his anxiety Jacob adopted two rather desperate expe-
dients. The first was to arrange that those with him should be
divided into two "companies" on the offchance that should
Esau capture one he would be content and let the other escape.
Is it ironic that the Hebrew word is the same as that which
appears in the place-name Mahanaim and as had been used by
Jacob in his cry at his vision? If it is, it is a pity that the RSV with
"army" in verse 2 and "companies" in verse 7 obscures so
significant a link; the NEB has the same word—"company",
"companies"—in both contexts. The second expedient was to
send on ahead a series of droves of goats, sheep and cattle, each
in the charge of different servants, each of whom was to
announce in turn to Esau as he reached him—again being
careful to address him in Jacob's name as "my lord"—that the
drove was a present to him from Jacob and that Jacob himself
was following behind. By this "softening-up" process, as it
were, he hoped to placate his brother's wrath and win himself
acceptance.

(iv)

Trust Jacob to have had plans even for such an emergency! But it is not his cunning that should strike us this time, but the fact that he thought such extreme measures necessary. So sure was he that Esau meant him harm that he was willing to forego as much of the wealth and property he had brought with him from Mesopotamia as was needed to effect a reconciliation. These are not the actions of a man secure in the faith that he had heaven on his side. On the contrary, they reveal to us a man plagued by doubt and apprehension. His gloom has *not* been lifted as it was at Bethel. For the first time in his life Jacob is deeply uncertain of his own ability to carry an enterprise through to a successful conclusion. He cannot on this occasion so easily bring himself to take God's help for granted.

The little prayer he makes in the middle of his frantic preparations shows this. There is no hint in it of any bargaining with God as in his prayer at Bethel, nor of any of the arrogance and self-justification that had characterized his speeches to Rachel and Leah and to Laban in the previous chapter. Rather—and at long last!—Jacob confesses his unworthiness—he did not deserve "the least of all the steadfast love and all the faithfulness" that God had shown to him since he had left Canaan. with only his staff for company. And he pleads earnestly for God's protection lest his brother "slay us all, the mothers with the children" and bring to naught the promises God had made to him. In the event it was an unnecessary prayer, but it is a touching and—for once—an obviously sincere prayer.

(v)

What then did his experience at Mahanaim mean for Jacob, if it issued not in confidence and comfort but in fear and an acknowledgment of sin?

As I see it, it can only have been understood by him as a warning, as a reminder that the land to which he was now returning was God's special domain and that it was—we could say like Eden (see 3:24)—watched over and guarded by his angels. The vision brought it painfully home to him that such a land was no place for the likes of him, arrogant, scheming, patiently vindictive and, particularly, too confident by half that he had God in his pocket. Mahanaim, in short, had on him the effect which Bethel ought to have had, but didn't. Confronted with God's majesty and power, his response this time was a genuine one, of repentance as well as of awe.

Or to be more truthful, it was genuine as far as it went. We should not, in our gratitude at finding for once a positive lesson in this most disturbing portion of Genesis, exaggerate the vision's effect on Jacob. It led him to pray to God for help with a sincerity and humility he had never previously aspired to, but it did not prevent him, being Jacob, from taking out some insurance on his own behalf with his far-fetched schemes to curry favour with Esau. Nevertheless, it did mark—and not before time—the beginning of a new awareness of God's nature and purposes. And it must have prepared him in some measure for the even more dramatic encounter with God which he was shortly to undergo at Peniel.

PENIEL I: JACOB'S PENIEL

Genesis 32:22–32

22 The same night he arose and took his two wives, his two maids, and
23 his eleven children, and crossed the ford of the Jabbok. He took them and sent them across the stream, and likewise everything that
24 he had. And Jacob was left alone; and a man wrestled with him until
25 the breaking of the day. When the man saw that he did not prevail against Jacob, he touched the hollow of his thigh; and Jacob's thigh
26 was put out of joint as he wrestled with him. Then he said, "Let me go, for the day is breaking." But Jacob said, "I will not let you go,
27 unless you bless me." And he said to him, "What is your name?" And
28 he said, "Jacob." Then he said, "Your name shall no more be called Jacob, but Israel, for you have striven with God and with men, and
29 have prevailed." Then Jacob asked him, "Tell me, I pray, your name." But he said, "Why is it that you ask my name?" And there he
30 blessed him. So Jacob called the name of the place Peniel, saying,

31 "For I have seen God face to face, and yet my life is preserved." The
sun rose upon him as he passed Penuel, limping because of his
32 thigh. Therefore to this day the Israelites do not eat the sinew of the
hip which is upon the hollow of the thigh, because he touched the
hollow of Jacob's thigh on the sinew of the hip.

After despatching his embassy to Esau, Jacob was still deeply
troubled and that very night, without waiting for daylight, he
decided to move his family across a nearby ford of the Jabbok
to a place on the other side. It was as he was crossing over last
and alone that he had his weird and awesome struggle with an
adversary whom at first he thought was human but later
realized was God.

(i)

The story is an intensely dramatic and stirring one, but there are
not a few problems about it which we must deal with before we
can attempt to interpret it.

Firstly, there is the place-name itself. The passage tells us that
it was in commemoration of his encounter that Jacob named
the place Peniel or Penuel, meaning "face of God" (the latter is a
more archaic form). But in fact Peniel like Mahanaim was
probably an older Canaanite name, meaning in pre-Hebrew
times "face of El" (the chief Canaanite god) and referring to
some particularly prominent or fertile piece of ground in the
vicinity on which a settlement had been built. It would be then
the already existing name of the place that suggested to Jacob
the words he used to describe his experience—"I have seen God
face to face, and yet my life is preserved"—rather than these
words that gave him the idea for naming it.

Secondly, the passage adds the information at the end that as
a result of the injury to Jacob's hip ("the hollow of the thigh")
which he received in the struggle, the Israelites "to this day" do
not eat the sinew (probably the sciatic muscle) in this part of the
body. This too is a very dubious statement. We have no
evidence from elsewhere in the Old Testament of such a taboo,
but if it in fact existed, it is much more likely that it derived from
ancient superstitions attaching to an area of the human body

near the sexual organs than from a single accident to a remote ancestor. The tracing of it back to Jacob's injury is probably therefore an afterthought of tradition and not relevant to the story's original meaning.

The same must be true, *thirdly*, of what is at first sight an even more important element in the story, if not its climax. I refer, of course, to the renaming of Jacob as Israel. As we have already seen (in the commentary on the section in chapters 29 and 30 dealing with the birth of Jacob's sons), the name Israel was a racial title which had nothing at first to do with the Patriarch Jacob, but was only later brought into connection with him. Moreover, it means properly "God [El] strives [sc. on behalf of his people]" and not, as it has been made to mean in this passage "he [Jacob] strives [sc. with God]" or (AV, rather inaccurately) "as a prince he has power [with God]". We ought therefore—however regretfully—to leave out this part of the story, if it is what actually happened at the Jabbok that we wish to recover.

(ii)

What then are we left with? I believe the following. As in the dark of night Jacob is crossing the ford after having seen his family and his animals safely over, he is confronted by a "man" who is obviously intent on preventing him from passing. The two fall to wrestling (the Hebrew verb is *ye-abeq*, a rare word clearly chosen because of its assonance with Jabbok—properly *yabboq*—and indeed with Jacob's own name—properly *ya-'qob*), and they fight on till dawn, but with neither gaining the mastery. Just at that point the adversary puts Jacob's hip out of joint. But by then Jacob has guessed his true identity, for when his opponent asks to be released (perhaps because, since it was getting light, Jacob would be able to see him), Jacob says, "I will not let you go, unless you bless me." His adversary blesses him, and Jacob releases him. When later he finds out the name of the area, he is aglow to think he had seen God face to face and survived to tell the tale. But he has not himself escaped unscathed and, as the sun rises over Peniel, he limps slowly away from the battle.

This basic story is so realistically and indeed (from a theological point of view) so crudely told that it must surely go back to Jacob's own description of the event. No later Hebrew story-teller would have dared to have God not only appearing in human form and fighting with a mere man—even a Jacob—but being defeated by him! This goes well beyond the manner in which God's appearance to Abraham as one of three "men" at Mamre was related in chapter 18, and that, as we noted at the time, was strong enough meat for a Hebrew audience to take. Bethel and Mahanaim with their angels seen in dream or vision, yes; God's showing himself, as to Moses, in the midst of a burning bush (Exod. 3), yes, that too; an angel appearing in the guise of a man to Joshua outside the walls of Jericho (Josh. 5:14), yes, even that. But not this—"unless", we can almost hear the audience saying, "we have it in the patriarch's own words".

(iii)

But that the story goes back to Jacob himself is, of course, no reason for us today to accept it as literally true. I doubt whether even the Hebrews went as far as that. What we can undoubtedly say, however, is that Jacob underwent that night at the Jabbok river an experience so unique, an encounter with the divine so profound and real to him, that he could only describe it in physical terms as though he had been wrestling with God as with another man. How can we restate it in terms that make sense to us? We can only try as best we can.

Jacob's fears and forebodings, so graphically drawn in the early part of the chapter, had so overwhelmed him that as he crossed the ford, he felt that God must have rejected him. In a flash it came to him that God, not Esau, was his principal antagonist, and here was he standing in his way, refusing to let him enter the land he had so often promised to his fathers and more than once to Jacob himself. His first thought was to collapse, prostrate and shattered, to the ground. Had he not just a few hours since been brought to confess his unworthiness, to see himself at last in his true colours, and to hate himself for it? This, then, was his punishment being pronounced. But no!

He was not going to let God get away with it. So desperately and long and hard—Gerhard von Rad speaks of his "suicidal courage"—he fought him for his blessing, for a renewal of that blessing which his father had once spoken in God's name and which he himself—how he regretted it now!—had so disgracefully won, and which too all these years in Mesopotamia he had so disdainfully taken for granted. And miraculously God gave in! The blessing was given, the prize which he could now see was the only thing that mattered in his life was his again. Limping, battered and bruised by the struggle, but nevertheless triumphant, a new Jacob was in that moment born.

Again, however, let us beware lest we miss the real point of it. It was not a *good* Jacob that was born. The prophet Hosea, in the use he makes of this incident (12:2-6), was well aware of this. And as we ourselves shall soon see, not even after this scarifying experience do we have a Jacob whom we can genuinely like. The epic of Jacob is not an account of a bad man becoming good. It is on an altogether deeper level than that. But at least we now know what, when the cards were down, this man put first. It was God, and having got hold of him, he was not going to let him go. Therein, in spite of all the sinister traits in his character, traits which sadly persist for many more years to come, lay his greatness. It was perhaps the only mark of real heroism about him, but because of it God could not do other than bless him.

PENIEL II: OUR PENIEL

Genesis 32:22-32 *(cont'd)*

We ought to be extremely chary about applying so unique an experience as Jacob's at Peniel to our own little lives. It is not at all difficult to see in ourselves Jacob's hypocrisies and ingratitude, but have we a right to challenge God as he did? It is not our usual demeanour in God's presence, where more often than not we behave like Uriah Heeps, luxuriating in our humility. Are there times when perhaps we should try to emulate his daring?

(i)

Sir George Adam Smith thought there were when in his great work *The Historical Geography of the Holy Land* he made the following short but spendid comment. He has been describing the fertility of the Jabbok valley and going over the region's place in Israel's history, and he concludes:

> Yet the highest fame of Jabbok will ever be its earliest, and not all the sunshine, ripening harvests along its live length, can be so bright as that first gleaming and splashing of its waters at midnight, or the grey dawn breaking on the crippled patriarch. The history of Gilead is a history of wars and struggle, civilisation enduring only by perpetual strife. But upon the Jabbok its first hero was taught how man has to reckon in life with God also, and that his noblest struggles are in the darkness, with the Unseen.

(ii)

So did A. B. Davidson, another giant among Scottish exegetes, in this rather fuller exposition, also beautifully expressed:

> I daresay we have, all of us, hours like this which Jacob had; times when, after being agitated by some dangerous crisis in our business or relationships, we feel ourselves passing into a personal agitation, engaged in a struggle with a power which we but vaguely see, and at first can hardly name; when we yearn we know not what for, and are sorrowful, though having no outward cause of sorrow; when we are disturbed more deeply than external troubles can account for; when we find ourselves writhing in the darkness, and feel touched to the quick by a hand unknown; when we become aware of something in ourselves greater that we had thought, and unsatisfied; something more mysterious in life, something wider and of greater meaning in the world than the narrow routine in which we had been running. If we could but know it is the Angel of the Covenant that is wrestling with us! He provokes the struggle, that He may conquer us by being overcome. And the weapons of victory in our hands are tears and supplications; and the moment must be seized, or the victory will escape us—"I will not let Thee go, except Thou bless me". The day must not be permitted to dawn upon the conflict. "Let me go", said the angel, "for the day breaketh". And he said, "I will not let Thee

go, except Thou bless me". The moment must be seized, the victory must be won in solitude—the man and we alone, hand to hand, with no onlookers. The first streaks of the world's sun, the first faint sounds of the returning life and thoughts of the world, will rob us of the blessing; and the disappointed Combatant will steal away, and leave us empty, and the strife in vain

from *The Called of God* (Edinburgh, 1902)

(iii)

There is only one comment I would like to add to these two superb interpretations. It is implied in both of them, but perhaps it needs to be emphasized a little more strongly.

It is that the kind of blessing Jacob craved comes not to the well-meaning, but to the desperate, not to man in the ascendant, but to man at the end of his tether. He has to have tried all other routes to happiness and achievement, and to be still in misery and turmoil. He has to have at last recognized that only God can satisfy him, and to be reaching out to him as a drowning man clutches at a straw. He has to admit that God ought not to accept him, and yet refuse to take "No" for an answer, even from him. He has like the importunate widow in Our Lord's parable (Luke 18:1–8) to be ready to hammer at heaven's door and to keep on hammering until it is opened. Only a man in such a case can presume to struggle with God as Jacob struggled at Peniel, for only to a man in such a case will God be willing to surrender the palm of victory. He will know he has been in a battle and will carry God's wounds with him from the field, but only a man in such a case can look upon God and live.

PENIEL III: ISRAEL'S PENIEL

Genesis 32:22–32 *(cont'd)*

We have attempted to reconstruct the individual experience of Jacob at Peniel and to apply it, as far as we can, to ourselves as individuals. But in so doing we have had in all honesty to remove from the story what in its present form is its undoubted high point, the changing of Jacob's name to Israel. Obviously we cannot leave it at that. The renaming may not tell us anything about what happened that fateful night at the Jabbok, but it does tell us, when we think of it, a great deal about Israel's awareness of herself as a people. There must be lessons in this for the Church which claims to be God's people today.

(i)

The Hebrews must have chosen Jacob as their chief ancestor because they felt a close affinity to him. I don't think we are being unkind either to him or to them when we say that they made a good choice. We have found in Genesis quite a few examples of additions to the text where they read back their own selfishnesses and prejudices and hatreds into Patriarchal times and which show them in a distinctly unpleasant light. But this addition is of a quite different kind.

There is a recognition that Jacob's triumphalism is mirrored in their own—"you have striven with God *and with men*, and have prevailed". As Jacob routed all who stood in his way—his father, his uncle, his brother—so Israel saw the mighty Pharaoh off the scene, so she routed the Canaanites and took their land for her own, and so under David and Solomon she carved out for herself a great empire. And yet, as the verses about her name when taken in context make abundantly clear, Israel knew in her heart of hearts that she had nothing in herself to be proud of, sensed even that she was at her best when prostrate and defeated, suffering in slavery in Egypt or in exile in Babylon. It is a remarkable self-appraisal. When we Christians are tempted to criticize the Old Testament for the exclusivist and uncaring parts in it, we should remember to Israel's credit that she placed the first revelation of her own name within a story in which her ancestor has his pride finally brought low and first confesses his desperate need of God.

And we should at the same time try to match Israel's true humility in the Church. It too is a pathetically fallible institution, far too apt to look for success as its divine prerogative, and far too proud for its own health and effectiveness. Are we able to get our priorities right as in her best moments Israel was?

(ii)

But infinitely more remarkable than Israel's seeing herself in microcosm in Jacob the "striver with men"—if you like, Jacob the sinner—is the interpretation she has given her own name as a result of its being linked in tradition with Jacob the "striver with God". That it is linguistically a false interpretation is neither here nor there. What is important is that it means that she had in effect accepted that a large part of her destiny was to fight with him who chose her as his own.

This is an insight of the greatest profundity. There are many, many more triumphalist passages in the Old Testament than there ought to be. There are also many, many passages of touching humility and expectation in God's presence, passsages breathing simple trust and alive with comfort and hope. These are probably our favourites. But perhaps the most glorious passages of all are those in which Hebrew story-teller and prophet and psalmist and wise man go on the offensive against God, protest loudly about his cruelty, and accuse him of ignoring the suffering of his people and indeed of misruling the world.

Abraham shows something of this spirit of protest when he intercedes for Sodom and Gomorrah, and says:

Shall not the Judge of all the earth do right?

(Gen. 18:25)

So does Jeremiah when he says:

Is there no balm in Gilead?
  Is there no physician there?
Why then has the health of the daughter of my people
  not been restored?

(Jer. 8:22)

or:

> O thou hope of Israel,
>> its saviour in time of trouble,
> why shouldst thou be like a stranger in the land,
>> like a wayfarer who turns aside to tarry for a night?
>> (Jer. 14:8)

So does the psalmist as he cries:

> My God, my God, why hast thou forsaken me?
>> Why art thou so far from helping me,
>> from the words of my groaning?
> O my God, I cry by day, but thou dost not answer;
>> and by night, but find no rest.
>> (Ps. 22:1–2)

or:

> O God, why dost thou cast us off for ever?
>> Why does thy anger smoke against the sheep of thy pasture?
> Remember thy congregation, which thou hast gotten of old,
>> which thou hast redeemed to be the tribe of thy heritage!
> How long, O God, is the foe to scoff?
>> Is the enemy to revile thy name for ever?
>> (Ps. 74:1–2, 10)

And so pre-eminently does the book of Job as, for example, when its hero complains:

> Why is light given to a man whose way is hid,
>> whom God has hedged in?
>> (Job 3:23)

or:

> It is all one; therefore I say,
>> he destroys both the blameless and the wicked.
> When disaster brings sudden death,
>> he mocks at the calamity of the innocent.
> The earth is given into the hand of the wicked;
>> he covers the faces of its judges—
>> if it is not he, who then is it?
>> (Job 9:22–24)

It will be recalled that at the end of that book (42:7ff.) it is Job with his sometimes almost blasphemous complainings who is commended by God, not the friends with their splendidly worded defence of orthodox piety. There is more than a suggestion here—as there is in our passage in Genesis—that God welcomes people who argue with him, for it shows that they care. Beside the agony of Job, the sentiments of his friends, however proper, sound cold and bare.

(iii)

In a study appearing in 1946, that is, before the establishment of the modern state of Israel, Margarete Susman, German-Jewish essayist and poet, interpreted Job—she could almost have chosen Jacob—as a prototype of the Jewish people and saw them as carrying on his quarrel with God on behalf of mankind. The kind of things she says in her book do not get much of a hearing among Jews today, when the present Israel seems intent only on "striving with men"—and is doing it very well! They ought to. For Jews today as they strive with men and prevail are in grave danger of forgetting their true destiny, which is to strive with God.

So ought they to get a hearing among us Christians who, perhaps because we believe so passionately that God entered this world in human form in Jesus Christ, have become too familiar with him, and do not nearly often enough reckon with his absence and inaccessibility. There is a "frowning providence" which we ought to be questioning far more often than we do. God wants us to care with an Old Testament fervour and to fight with him not only for our own salvation but for the salvation of the world. For he fears that, unless we do, he may have to withhold his blessing from a world undone.

But let us leave the last word to Margarete Susman:

Job, who in his suffering was delivered by God to his tempter, prefigures in his fate the sorrowful fate of the Jewish people in exile. Like Job the Jews accepted their suffering as something decreed by God. But they do not simply accept it, they want to understand.

They want to understand God for whose sake they suffer. Like Job they demand that God whose bidding and law they have accepted be absolutely just. Here is the reason why life for the Jews in their exile is one long litigation, an incessant quarrel with God.

That she herself sees no end in sight to this quarrel in her own day, but if anything a louder silence from God's side and a bitterer pain for her people in their wrestling with him, may for our purposes be just as well. It should banish from our minds the thought that God's blessing is there for the taking, and concentrate our attention where it ought to be concentrated, on the bruising battle for our own souls and the souls of all men which we in the Church ought to be engaged in, that battle with God which alone can bring his Church "power with God" (AV) and draw from him his blessing for all the families of the earth.

RECONCILIATION

Genesis 33:1–17

1 And Jacob lifted up his eyes and looked, and behold, Esau was coming, and four hundred men with him. So he divided the children
2 among Leah and Rachel and the two maids. And he put the maids with their children in front, then Leah with her children, and Rachel
3 and Joseph last of all. He himself went on before them, bowing himself to the ground seven times, until he came near to his brother.
4 But Esau ran to meet him, and embraced him, and fell on his neck
5 and kissed him, and they wept. And when Esau raised his eyes and saw the women and children, he said, "Who are these with you?" Jacob said, "The children whom God has graciously given your
6 servant." Then the maids drew near, they and their children, and
7 bowed down; Leah likewise and her children drew near and bowed down; and last Joseph and Rachel drew near, and they bowed down.
8 Esau said, "What do you mean by all this company which I met?"
9 Jacob answered, "To find favour in the sight of my lord." But Esau said, "I have enough, my brother; keep what you have for yourself."
10 Jacob said, "No, I pray you, if I have found favour in your sight, then accept my present from my hand; for truly to see your face is like seeing the face of God, with such favour have you received me.

11 Accept, I pray you, my gift that is brought to you, because God has dealt graciously with me, and because I have enough." Thus he urged him, and he took it.

12   Then Esau said, "Let us journey on our way, and I will go before
13 you." But Jacob said to him, "My lord knows that the children are frail, and that the flocks and herds giving suck are a care to me; and
14 if they are overdriven for one day, all the flocks will die. Let my lord pass on before his servant, and I will lead on slowly, according to the pace of the cattle which are before me and according to the pace of the children, until I come to my lord in Seir."

15   So Esau said, "Let me leave with you some of the men who are with me." But he said, "What need is there? Let me find favour in the
16, 17 sight of my lord." So Esau returned that day on his way to Seir. But Jacob journeyed to Succoth, and built himself a house, and made booths for his cattle; therefore the name of the place is called Succoth.

Rarely in Genesis does the story-teller's honesty shine through so disconcertingly as in the chapter which follows Jacob's greatest triumph at Peniel. It cannot have been at all liked by its Hebrew audiences. It tells of the resolution of the conflict between Jacob and Esau with which the epic had begun, and it records (as it must) Jacob's victory, in the sense that Esau returned to Seir and abandoned the land of promise to him. The one whom God "loved" was about to enter upon his inheritance, while the one whom he "hated" (see Mal. 1:2–3; Rom. 9:13) was left outside in the cold. But though in the purpose of God Jacob had to win, the real victor in human terms was undoubtedly Esau.

(i)

The first thing Jacob did as he saw his brother approaching was to put his plan for dividing up his family into operation (see 32:7–8). Only he made three companies instead of two, placing the maids Zilpah and Bilhah with their children in front, then Leah with hers, and at the back Rachel with Joseph. If trouble was coming, it would come to Rachel last. What a time to be showing favouritism!

Then with a deference that in the annals of the time is only recorded of suppliants in the presence of Egypt's Pharaoh, he himself moved slowly forward, prostrating himself seven times as he got nearer to his brother. This was not the elder serving the younger of Rebekah's private oracle (25:23), nor was it his mother's sons bowing down to Jacob as forecast in the blessing he had stolen (27:29). Rather, it was as if Rebekah had been hopelessly deluded and as if Isaac had pronounced the blessing on Esau as he had meant to.

But Jacob had reckoned without a changed Esau. He had expected the worst from his brother and had been for days petrified by fears which were now to prove groundless. The man who, as Jacob was fleeing from Canaan, had sworn to kill him (27:41) and who is called in the New Testament (Heb. 12:16) "immoral and irreligious" for selling his birthright had, it appears, long since renounced his hatred and come to terms with his exclusion. He had already settled in Seir and was prospering there. He had not come for revenge or to fight with his brother over land or inheritance, but to welcome him home. As Jacob stumbled pathetically forward, he ran to meet him and to hug and kiss him. He showed genuine pleasure at Jacob's success and greeted his wives and children with obvious sincerity. He at first declined the droves of animals ("all this company which I met") with which Jacob had hoped to curry his favour—and only accepted them when Jacob pressed them urgently upon him. And to seal the reconciliation, he offered to accompany Jacob on the rest of his journey.

Jacob's relief knew no bounds and, rather extravagantly, he compared the meeting to another meeting with God—"for truly to see your face is like seeing the face of God". But even through his tears of joy, he could not bring himself to accept Esau's offer of company and protection. His excuses sound touching ("the children are frail, and the flocks and herds giving suck are a care to me"), but are they genuine? Probably not; for he promises to follow Esau to Seir, and yet the story ends: "So Esau returned that day on his way to Seir. But Jacob journeyed to Succoth".

(ii)

That laconic and poignant sentence says it all. Embarrassingly almost, the story-teller adds a note that Jacob built a house at Succoth and some "booths" (Hebrew *sukkoth*) to shelter his cattle, from which—if his audience wanted to believe it—the place got its name. But in its context the note rather underlines the fact that Jacob had no intention of having anything to do with his brother again, if he could help it. He was glad to have been reconciled with him, glad too that both of them were prospering and that there would be no unseemly quarrels over property, but glad above all simply that Esau was out of his way. The author's discomfiture is acute, for he knows that all of this was God's will.

We know it was God's will too, but we would be very foolish to try to explain or justify it. We could argue that Jacob sensed that a renewed friendship with his brother would be precariously based and would be bound to lead to fresh disaster, whereas Esau was too blind to see this, that Jacob's clear-headedness was a necessary foil to Esau's impractical and impulsive generosity. But who is going to be convinced? We only need to read the next chapter with its terrible tale of rape and vengeance to see what a nonsense an argument like this is. Esau's presence with him could not possibly have led to more trouble and sorrow than was coming his way in any case.

It would be infinitely more truthful of us to admit that in our human judgment God made the wrong choice or, to put it more circumspectly, that he did not make the choice we would have made. In human terms Esau *does* emerge at the end of their life-long conflict as a better and nicer man than Jacob.

(iii)

I wonder if Jesus had Esau in mind when he told the parable of the Prodigal Son. Lay verse 4 of this chapter

But Esau ran to meet him, and embraced him, and fell on his neck and kissed him, and they wept alongside verse 20 of Luke chapter 15

> And he arose and came to his father. But while he was yet at a distance, his father saw him and had compassion, and ran and embraced him and kissed him

and it looks very much as though he did.

If Our Lord could appreciate the irony of this meeting of Jacob and Esau, if behoves us to recognize it too. It is, of course, the irony of grace, the grace that in this epic story chose the younger and rejected the elder son, that chose the cunning man and rejected the guileless, that chose the suave and rejected the boorish, that chose the vindictive and rejected the forgiving; the grace that in Old Testament times chose Israel and rejected the Edomites, the Moabites, the Canaanites and all the other peoples round about; and the grace that in our day has chosen us and has by-passed so many other men and women better by far than we are.

A final paralysing thought! In the last chapter we were told to fight God's "frowning providence". Here we are being told to acknowledge his "grace". How are we possibly to distinguish between the two? And yet we must!

RAPE AND REVENGE

Genesis 33:18–34:31

18 And Jacob came safely to the city of Shechem, which is in the land of Canaan, on his way from Paddan-aram; and he camped before the
19 city. And from the sons of Hamor, Shechem's father, he bought for a hundred pieces of money the piece of land on which he had pitched
20 his tent. There he erected an altar and called it El-Elohe-Israel.
1 Now Dinah the daughter of Leah, whom she had borne to Jacob,
2 went out to visit the women of the land; and when Shechem the son of Hamor the Hivite, the prince of the land, saw her, he seized her
3 and lay with her and humbled her. And his soul was drawn to Dinah the daughter of Jacob; he loved the maiden and spoke tenderly to
4 her. So Shechem spoke to his father Hamor, saying, "Get me this

5 maiden for my wife." Now Jacob heard that he had defiled his
daughter Dinah; but his sons were with his cattle in the field, so
6 Jacob held his peace until they came. And Hamor the father of
7 Shechem went out to Jacob to speak with him. The sons of Jacob
came in from the field when they heard of it; and the men were
indignant and very angry, because he had wrought folly in Israel by
lying with Jacob's daughter, for such a thing ought not to be done.
8 But Hamor spoke with them, saying, "The soul of my son
Shechem longs for your daughter; I pray you, give her to him in
9 marriage. Make marriages with us; give your daughters to us, and
10 take our daughters for yourselves. You shall dwell with us; and the
land shall be open to you; dwell and trade in it, and get property in
11 it." Shechem also said to her father and to her brothers, "Let me find
12 favour in your eyes, and whatever you say to me I will give. Ask of
me ever so much as marriage present and gift, and I will give
according as you say to me; only give me the maiden to be my wife."
13 The sons of Jacob answered Shechem and his father Hamor
14 deceitfully, because he had defiled their sister Dinah. They said to
them, "We cannot do this thing, to give our sister to one who is
15 uncircumcised, for that would be a disgrace to us. Only on this
condition will we consent to you: that you will become as we are and
16 every male of you be circumcised. Then we will give our daughters to
you, and we will take your daughters to ourselves, and we will dwell
17 with you and become one people. But if you will not listen to us and
be circumcised, then we will take our daughter, and we will be gone."
18, 19 Their words pleased Hamor and Hamor's son Shechem. And the
young man did not delay to do the thing, because he had delight in
Jacob's daughter. Now he was the most honoured of all his family.
20 So Hamor and his son Shechem came to the gate of their city and
21 spoke to the men of their city, saying, "These men are friendly with
us; let them dwell in the land and trade in it, for behold, the land is
large enough for them; let us take their daughters in marriage, and
22 let us give them our daughters. Only on this condition will the men
agree to dwell with us, to become one people: that every male among
23 us be circumcised as they are circumcised. Will not their cattle, their
property and all their beasts be ours? Only let us agree with them,
24 and they will dwell with us." And all who went out of the gate of his
city hearkened to Hamor and his son Shechem; and every male was
circumcised, all who went out of the gate of his city.
25 On the third day, when they were sore, two of the sons of Jacob,
Simeon and Levi, Dinah's brothers, took their swords and came

26 upon the city unawares, and killed all the males. They slew Hamor
   and his son Shechem with the sword, and took Dinah out of
27 Shechem's house, and went away. And the sons of Jacob came upon
   the slain, and plundered the city, because their sister had been
28 defiled; they took their flocks and their herds, their asses, and
29 whatever was in the city and in the field; all their wealth, all their
   little ones and their wives, all that was in the houses, they captured
30 and made their prey. Then Jacob said to Simeon and Levi, "You
   have brought trouble on me by making me odious to the inhabitants
   of the land, the Canaanites and the Perizzites; my numbers are few,
   and if they gather themselves against me and attack me, I shall be
31 destroyed, both I and my household." But they said, "Should he
   treat our sister as a harlot?"

Jacob's stay at Succoth must have lasted a few years, for when
he moved on to Shechem most of his family were grown up. The
first verse of our passage tells us that he arrived there "safely".
There is more than a touch of irony in this adjective, for he
certainly did not leave it in that state. However, he bought a
piece of land there, as if meaning to settle down.

(i)

Shechem was at the time ruled by a family of Hivites or,
according to the Greek translation, Horites. If the Septuagint is
correct, the family was related to the Hurrian people of
northern Mesopotamia and Syria who left us the Nuzi texts,
which we have several times referred to to explain some of the
legal and social customs of the Genesis stories. At any rate,
Hivite or Horite, the family was non-Semitic. It had adopted
some Semitic names, their chief being called Hamor, which
means an "ass" or "donkey"; but, as we find out later, it did not
practise circumcision. Hamor's son seems to have been named
Shechem after the city, but this may be a kind of shorthand like
the English "Norfolk" or "Essex" for the dukes or earls of these
counties.

(ii)

It was Dinah's ill fate to attract this young man's attention, and
like the squire's son in many a modern novel he had his pleasure

of her. But then he fell in love with her, and decided that he must do the right thing. He asked his father to arrange a marriage and to offer an inflated bride-price, in the hope that this would assuage the injured feelings of her family. His father, however, extended this into a general invitation to intermarriage, proposing in effect that Jacob and his clan be absorbed into the indigenous community. Jacob was already a small landowner, and perhaps Hamor thought that this was what he wanted.

At this point the sons of Jacob took over the lead in the negotiations. They appeared to go along with Hamor's proposal, asking only that the men of the city first be circumcised. But it was a subterfuge, for when the male population were still "sore" from the operation, two of them—Simeon and Levi—raided the city, slew all the men, took the women and children captive, carried away as much booty as they could, and rescued Dinah, who had apparently (as part of the arrangement?) gone to live in Shechem's house. Jacob was appalled at this act of treachery, but his sons answered him sharply, "Should he treat our sister as a harlot?"

Some scholars think that mixed up with this story is a record of an alliance between Israelites and Shechemites at a much later period after Joshua's invasion, which went disastrously wrong and led to a local war which the Israelites won. They may well be right, for as we have the account it does seem too large-scale for what must originally have been a private feud between two families. How could two men have wreaked such havoc, and what, for instance, did they do with all the women and children whom they captured? But we need not be too concerned about the minute analysis of the chapter. Whatever additions may have been made to it, any original story must at least have begun with Dinah's rape and resulted in a terrible vengeance being taken by two of her brothers on Hamor and his son and their immediate relatives. How are we meant to react to that?

A Hebrew audience would have been pleased that Jacob and his sons resisted the temptation to intermarry with the people of the land, and they would have approved of his sons rushing to the defence of their sister's besmirched honour. But even they must have been shocked—as Jacob himself was shocked—at their treachery and the savagery of their revenge. To us, who have no national axes to grind, the story is rather another instance of humanity's general barbarity, and alas! it is a barbarity to which God's people contributed just as much as the other side. With its unvarnished picture of raw passion and perfidy, it is one of the darkest tales in the Bible.

Nor can we absolve Jacob himself of guilt, though he protested strongly at what his sons did. He "held his peace" until they arrived on the scene; and his repudiation of their vicious conduct is laced with a cowardly concern for its effect on himself—"you have brought trouble on me by making me odious to [AV, to make me to stink among] the inhabitants of the land . . . I shall be destroyed, both I and my household."

There is a lot of righteous indignation in this chapter, but little if any of the milk of human kindness. Its only gentle moment is when the young man, whose lust sparked off the whole sorry episode, finds himself warming to the girl he had wronged. "He loved the maiden and spoke tenderly to her." Did she, one wonders, seeing his remorse, warm to him in return? Certainly, it never seems to have crossed the minds of her outraged brothers to ask her what she thought.

TRIUMPH TO TRAGEDY

Genesis 35:1–22

1 God said to Jacob, "Arise, go up to Bethel, and dwell there; and make there an altar to the God who appeared to you when you fled
2 from your brother Esau." So Jacob said to his household and to all who were with him, "Put away the foreign gods that are among you,
3 and purify yourselves, and change your garments; then let us arise and go up to Bethel, that I may make there an altar to the God who answered me in the day of my distress and has been with me
4 wherever I have gone." So they gave to Jacob all the foreign gods that they had, and the rings that were in their ears; and Jacob hid them under the oak which was near Shechem.

5 And as they journeyed, a terror from God fell upon the cities that
   were round about them, so that they did not pursue the sons of
6 Jacob. And Jacob came to Luz (that is, Bethel), which is in the land
7 of Canaan, he and all the people who were with him, and there he
   built an altar, and called the place El-bethel, because there God had
8 revealed himself to him when he fled from his brother. And
   Deborah, Rebekah's nurse, died, and she was buried under an oak
   below Bethel; so the name of it was called Allon-bacuth.

9 God appeared to Jacob again, when he came from Paddan-aram,
10 and blessed him. And God said to him, "Your name is Jacob; no
   longer shall your name be called Jacob, but Israel shall be your
11 name." So his name was called Israel. And God said to him, "I am
   God Almighty: be fruitful and multiply; a nation and a company of
12 nations shall come from you, and kings shall spring from you. The
   land which I gave to Abraham and Isaac I will give to you, and I will
13 give the land to your descendants after you." Then God went up
14 from him in the place where he had spoken with him. And Jacob set
   up a pillar in the place where he had spoken with him, a pillar of
   stone; and he poured out a drink offering on it, and poured oil on it.
15 So Jacob called the name of the place where God had spoken with
   him, Bethel.

16 Then they journed from Bethel; and when they were still some
   distance from Ephrath, Rachel travailed, and she had hard labour.
17 And when she was in her hard labour, the midwife said to her, "Fear
18 not; for now you will have another son." And as her soul was
   departing (for she died), she called his name Ben-oni; but his father
19 called his name Benjamin. So Rachel died, and she was buried on
20 the way to Ephrath (that is, Bethlehem), and Jacob set up a pillar
   upon her grave; it is the pillar of Rachel's tomb, which is there to this
21 day. Israel journeyed on, and pitched his tent beyond the tower of
   Eder.
22 While Israel dwelt in that land Reuben went and lay with Bilhah
   his father's concubine; and Israel heard of it.

The first half of this chapter was probably intended to be the
climax of the whole epic, as it describes how Jacob's caravan
moved majestically on to Bethel and the people of Canaan,
frightened, drew aside to let it pass. Here was Israel in foretaste
possessing the promised land! The story-teller does what he can
with it, but he is unable to enlist our enthusiasm. Too sour a

taste remains in our mouths from what had just happened at Shechem. Moreover, there are two further tragedies to befall Jacob before in the third of Genesis' Patriarchal cycles he is replaced in the central role by his son Joseph. These tragedies are mentioned only briefly and tersely, but they rather than the trumped-up triumph of its opening verses set the chapter's atmosphere—and thus the atmosphere of the epic's close.

(i)

Jacob's progress from Shechem to Bethel is presented almost as a pilgrimage. He is instructed by God to "go up" there (compare Ps. 122; 4, "Jerusalem . . . to which the tribes go up") and he calls on those with him to "purify themselves" by getting rid of any remnants of pagan influence among them. This is a remarkable admission—we wonder if Rachel was still holding on to her father's "household gods" (see 31:19, 34)—but not so much is made of it as we might expect. For as the company proceeds, a "terror" from God falls upon the Canaanite cities, so that they do not (as Jacob had been afraid that they would) attack him or hinder his advance. We recall the Lord "discomfiting" the Egyptian hosts at the Red Sea (Exod. 14:24) or, as the trumpets blew, "setting every man's sword against his fellow" in the mighty army that opposed Gideon's hundred (Judg. 7:22). This is God fighting for his own with no questions asked. Finally Jacob arrives at Bethel, builds an altar there, is given a second vision to match the one he had received all those years before and a renewal of the promises ("kings shall spring from you"), and erects a pillar and pours out a drink offering on it.

It is a most impressive scene, especially the picture of God's "terror" guaranteeing his people safe passage through a hostile territory. But is the writer not allowing his Hebrew pride to outrun his judgment more than a little?

(ii)

There is some evidence that he was aware that he had been exaggerating. For right in the middle of his triumphant account he inserts a little note about the death at Bethel of Rebekah's nurse Deborah, who has only been mentioned once before (24:59). Had this old, old woman, who had perhaps dandled him on her knee as a baby, come north to Jacob from Hebron when he had returned to Canaan to tell him of Rebekah's own earlier death, the mother who, it will be remembered, had expected him back from Mesopotamia in a "few days" (27:44, AV), but had not lived to see it? If so, the note prepares us for a quick descent from triumph to pathos; for hardly has Jacob left Bethel than his beloved Rachel dies giving birth to Benjamin.

Genesis' women—Sarah, Hagar, Rebekah, Leah, Rachel, Dinah, Tamar (chapter 38)—are almost without exception tragic figures. Whether themselves the perpetrators of trouble or simply its victims, none of them has a very happy life. Rachel was in many ways the most fortunate of them all. She envied Leah's fruitfulness and had to wait long years for her own child. She was cruel to her father when she stole his idols and crueller still when she let him search for them in vain. She may even have had half a belief in them herself. But she won early the love of Jacob and retained it through thick and thin, and here at last some success was coming his way, and she was expecting another baby. How unutterably sad—how ironic too—that she should die just at that moment! It is not surprising that Rachel came to represent for future generations of Hebrews the embodiment of suffering motherhood, the *mater dolorosa* grieving over her family's tragedies. "Rachel weeping for her children" became a proverb in Israel. It is quoted by the prophet Jeremiah (31:15), and in the New Testament by Matthew (2:18) to express the horror felt at the massacre of the innocents by Herod.

We are not told that Jacob wept for her, as Abraham had wept for Sarah (23:2). Maybe his grief was too deep for tears. He must have been sorely tempted to let the name the dying woman gave her new-born son stand—*Ben-oni,* meaning "son of my sorrow". But he changed the name to Benjamin (Hebrew *ben-yamin),* meaning "son of the south" (the quarter of greatest sunshine) or "son of the right hand" (the side of honour—see

Ps. 110:1—and of good fortune). What was he thinking of? Some commentators suggest he may merely have been resisting the bad omens that Rachel's name could have drawn in its trail. For once I cannot agree. We often have cause to suspect Jacob's motives, but this time, I feel, we see him, though heartbroken, glimpsing some sunshine through the darkness that was at that moment enveloping him. We see him this time, though generally scheming on his own behalf, genuinely putting his trust for the future in God.

I think we can say that in the instant of Rachel's death the hollow mockery of his "triumph" was brought shatteringly home to Jacob. Because of it his life after this could not but be shot through with an infinite sorrow (see 48:7). Yet he was able to hope that this child, born as his mother died, would see the blossoming of the blessing of which he now knew he himself, for all his trying, possessed only the green bud.

(iii)

What a dramatic ending to the epic that magnificent act of faith would have made! But there is one sentence to come, and what it tells of must have made the naming of his last-born son "son of good fortune" seem to Jacob but the wildest flight of fancy. For Reuben—his first-born son—is found in incest with Bilhah, his concubine and the maid of Rachel! How much more could this doughty fighter be expected to take? What price now the promises and blessing he had struggled so long and so hard to win for himself and pass on to his sons?

We must also ask whether Jacob in any way blamed himself as he surveyed the disintegration of his family and the wreckage of his hopes. Perhaps he did, perhaps he didn't. All the writer of the chapter says is "and Israel [Jacob] heard of it." It is yet another of these oh! so laconic statements in which Genesis abounds, which so frustratingly transfer the burden of interpretation onto the reader's shoulders and leave him all but helpless in the face of the divine will. We know that the story of God's people did not end at this point. We cannot help wondering why it didn't.

THE PARTING OF THE WAYS

Genesis 35:23–36:43

23 Now the sons of Jacob were twelve. The sons of Leah: Reuben (Jacob's first-born), Simeon, Levi, Judah, Issachar, and Zebulun.
24, 25 The sons of Rachel: Joseph and Benjamin. The sons of Bilhah,
26 Rachel's maid: Dan and Naphtali. The sons of Zilpah, Leah's maid: Gad and Asher. These were the sons of Jacob who were born to him in Paddan-aram.
27 And Jacob came to his father Isaac at Mamre, or Kiriath-arba
28 (that is, Hebron), where Abraham and Isaac had sojourned. Now
29 the days of Isaac were a hundred and eighty years. And Isaac breathed his last; and he died and was gathered to his people, old and full of days; and his sons Esau and Jacob buried him.
1, 2 These are the descendants of Esau (that is, Edom). Esau took his wives from the Canaanites: Adah the daughter of Elon the Hittite, Oholibamah the daughter of Anah the son of Zibeon the Hivite, and
3, 4 Basemath, Ishmael's daughter, the sister of Nebaioth. And Adah
5 bore to Esau, Eliphaz; Basemath bore Reuel; and Oholibamah bore Jeush, Jalam, and Korah. These are the sons of Esau who were born to him in the land of Canaan.
6 Then Esau took his wives, his sons, his daughters, and all the members of his household, his cattle, all his beasts, and all his property which he had acquired in the land of Canaan; and he went
7 into a land away from his brother Jacob. For their possessions were too great for them to dwell together; the land of their sojournings
8 could not support them because of their cattle. So Esau dwelt in the hill country of Seir; Esau is Edom.
9 These are the descendants of Esau the father of the Edomites in
10 the hill country of Seir. These are the names of Esau's sons: Eliphaz the son of Adah the wife of Esau, Reuel the son of Basemath the
11 wife of Esau. The sons of Eliphaz were Teman, Omar, Zepho,
12 Gatam, and Kenaz. (Timna was a concubine of Eliphaz, Esau's son; she bore Amalek to Eliphaz.) These are the sons of Adah, Esau's
13 wife. These are the sons of Reuel: Nahath, Zerah, Shammah, and
14 Mizzah. These are the sons of Basemath, Esau's wife. These are the

sons of Oholibamah the daughter of Anah the son of Zibeon, Esau's wife: she bore to Esau Jeush, Jalam, and Korah.

15 These are the chiefs of the sons of Esau. The sons of Eliphaz the 16 first-born of Esau: the chiefs Teman, Omar, Zepho, Kenaz, Korah, Gatam, and Amalek; these are the chiefs of Eliphaz in the land of 17 Edom; they are the sons of Adah. These are the sons of Reuel, Esau's son: the chiefs Nahath, Zerah, Shammah, and Mizzah; these are the chiefs of Reuel in the land of Edom; they are the sons of Basemath, 18 Esau's wife. These are the sons of Oholibamah, Esau's wife: the chiefs Jeush, Jalam, and Korah; these are the chiefs born of 19 Oholibamah the daughter of Anah, Esau's wife. These are the sons of Esau (that is, Edom), and these are their chiefs.

20 These are the sons of Seir the Horite, the inhabitants of the land: 21 Lotan, Shobal, Zibeon, Anah, Dishon, Ezer, and Dishan; these are 22 the chiefs of the Horites, the sons of Seir in the land of Edom. The sons of Lotan were Hori and Heman; and Lotan's sister was Timna. 23 These are the sons of Shobal: Alvan, Manahath, Ebal, Shepho, and 24 Onam. These are the sons of Zibeon: Aiah and Anah; he is the Anah who found the hot springs in the wilderness, as he pastured the asses 25 of Zibeon his father. These are the children of Anah: Dishon and 26 Oholibamah the daughter of Anah. These are the sons of Dishon: 27 Hemdan, Eshban, Ithran, and Cheran. These are the sons of Ezer: 28 Bilhan, Zaavan, and Akan. These are the sons of Dishan: Uz and 29 Aran. These are the chiefs of the Horites: the chiefs Lotan, Shobal, 30 Zibeon, Anah, Dishon, Ezer, and Dishan; these are the chiefs of the Horites, according to their clans in the land of Seir.

31 These are the kings who reigned in the land of Edom, before any 32 king reigned over the Israelites. Bela the son of Beor reigned in 33 Edom, the name of his city being Dinhabah. Bela died, and Jobab 34 the son of Zerah of Bozrah reigned in his stead. Jobab died, and 35 Husham of the land of the Temanites reigned in his stead. Husham died, and Hadad the son of Bedad, who defeated Midian in the country of Moab, reigned in his stead, the name of his city being 36 Avith. Hadad died, and Samlah of Masrekah reigned in his stead. 37 Samlah died, and Shaul of Rehoboth on the Euphrates reigned in 38 his stead. Shaul died, and Baal-hanan the son of Achbor reigned in 39 his stead. Baal-hanan the son of Achbor died, and Hadar reigned in his stead, the name of his city being Pau; his wife's name was Mehetabel, the daughter of Matred, daughter of Mezahab.

40 These are the names of the chiefs of Esau, according to their

families and their dwelling places, by their names: the chiefs Timna,
41, 42 Alvah, Jetheth, Oholibamah, Elah, Pinon, Kenaz, Teman, Mibzar,
43 Magdiel, and Iram; these are the chiefs of Edom (that is, Esau, the
father of Edom), according to their dwelling places in the land of
their possession.

The epic of Jacob draws to its distressing close with the short
notice of Reuben's incest. What follows is mainly genealogies,
chroniclers' work tying up loose ends before the epic of Joseph
begins.

(i)

There is a brief genealogy of Jacob himself—more exactly a list
of the twelve tribes—in which Benjamin's birth is carelessly
mentioned as having taken place in Paddan-Aram along with
the rest and Dinah's is not mentioned at all, and then, taking up
most of chapter 36, a genealogy of prominent Edomites, many
of whom are supposed to have descended from Esau. In this too
there are some careless mistakes; for instance, the daughter of
Ishmael whom he married is called Basemath, whereas in 28:9
she was called Mahalath. For a detailed treatment of the
chapter and its problems interested readers are referred to one
of the larger Commentaries. Here it is enough to note that the
lists in the first half of the chapter are of the same kind as the
genealogies in chapter 25, supplying us, that is, with information about tribes and places in or near Edom (e.g. Teman,
Amalek) rather than historical relatives of Esau. See also Map
2. Those in the second half may well contain the names of actual
kings and chiefs of the region at a much later date. The only real
connection of Esau, son of Jacob, with Edom and Seir is that it
was in that area that he settled when he left Canaan.

(ii)

Along with the genealogies we have, however, a report of two
events which as they are placed here may seem to have occurred
after Rachel's death and Reuben's incest, but which from the
content of previous stories we must suspect had occurred long
before. The first of these is the death of Isaac, the second the

aforementioned departure of Esau. We argued in the commentary on chapter 27 that Isaac must have died not long after Jacob left for Mesopotamia; and we saw that on his return to Canaan, Esau came to meet him from Seir (32:3), so he must already have made his home there. The chroniclers responsible for the genealogies probably moved Isaac's death to this point because they wanted to fit in a tradition available to them that Isaac lived a hundred and eighty years; and having had Esau present at the funeral, they naturally had to have him depart once more for Seir. It is much more satisfactory and more in line with the force of the story in chapter 33 to suppose that the two brothers never met again after their reconciliation.

(iii)

It is nevertheless very appropriate that we should be reminded in chapter 36 of the parting of the ways between Jacob and Esau. For it is this parting which poses in its acutest form the basic dilemma of the whole epic.

The dilemma is not that of deciding whether Jacob deserved his success and Esau his failure. We can, if we wish, try to draw up the balance sheets. Jacob was most of the time uncaring of others, vindictive, selfish, plotting, partial—yet he loved Rachel with an undying love and was ready to suffer anything to win her. Most of the time he never gave a thought for God—and yet when at Peniel the crunch came, he put God first and showed it by being ready to fight God himself for his blessing. Esau sold his birthright for a single meal—yet his cry of despair when he found Isaac had blessed Jacob instead of him proved that he was not careless of his heritage. He vowed to kill Jacob—and yet with the passing of the years he came to accept his exclusion from the blessing as God's will, and he made amends nobly for the sins of his youth by forgiving the brother whom he had wronged far less than he was wronged by him.

If we judge the epic by such human standards, we may well conclude that Jacob was a greater man than Esau, and Esau a nicer man than Jacob. And as we look at the outcome of their conflict we may well conclude that each got the prize he merited. Jacob got the chieftainship of the clan and a free entry into the land of Canaan but, as we have just seen, it was a victory that turned very quickly to ashes in his hands. Esau, on the other hand, was obviously at their parting a man at peace with himself. He had been forced from the land of his birth, but he was happy in Seir and prospering. It seems a just distribution of the spoils, and we are content enough.

It is only when we lift the reckoning onto a higher level that we begin to lose our bearings. For Genesis does not allow us to rest in our human judgment, but presses insistently upon us the judgment of God. The grace of God bestrides the epic like a colossus, and it is centred on Jacob and makes no room for Esau. It was through Jacob and the people he fathered that God intended one day to save the world, but he had no special task for Esau to perform. To put it at its crudest (with Mal. 1:2–3 and Paul in Rom. 9:13), he "loved" Jacob and "hated" Esau.

If at this level of reckoning we cry "unfair", we only reveal the terrifying gap that separates our human judgment from God's. Therein lies the real dilemma of the chapters we have been studying. As men we cannot help crying "unfair"; as believers we know we ought to trust and accept God's grace. We cannot therefore go from this turbulent tale uplifted and heartened and satisfied. It flings our human balance sheets contemptuously back in our faces. But there is perhaps in our bewilderment and perplexity, our resentment even, one glorious prospect which it holds out before us. This has to do with that picture of a desperate sinner at Peniel clawing his way to blessing. It belongs to God's peculiar grace not only to lay us in the dust but to challenge us to stand on our feet like men and dare him to save us. Have we got what it takes to do that?

JOSEPH : AN EPIC OF DESTINY

DISCORD

Genesis 37:1-4

1 Jacob dwelt in the land of his father's sojournings, in the land of
2 Canaan. This is the history of the family of Jacob.
    Joseph, being seventeen years old, was shepherding the flock with
his brothers; he was a lad with the sons of Bilhah and Zilpah, his
father's wives; and Joseph brought an ill report of them to their
3 father. Now Israel loved Joseph more than any other of his children,
because he was the son of his old age; and he made him a long robe
4 with sleeves. But when his brothers saw that their father loved him
more than all his brothers, they hated him, and could not speak
peaceably to him.

The third of Genesis' Patriarchal epics is introduced as the
history of Jacob's family. We usually call it the story of Joseph
after its chief character, or the story of Joseph and his brethren, but in many ways the Biblical title is a more accurate one. It
keeps in our minds the old chief of the clan, who contributes a
full share to its troubled opening and who, though not so
prominent later, is always there in the background. Moreover,
the epic does not reach its climax until not only Joseph and his
brothers but their aged father and all their dependents are
reunited on Egyptian soil.

(i)

As the epic begins everything appears quiet and peaceful.
Jacob's older sons have been joined by their younger brother
Joseph, now seventeen, as they tend their flocks. But under-
neath the surface three of the nastiest of human passions are
festering, ready with deadly effect to break out at the first
opportunity. These are tale-bearing, favouritism, and envy.

The tale-bearing is Joseph's, the favouritism Jacob's, and the envy the brothers'.

(ii)

No one likes a gossip, even if his tales be true, and the Hebrews were no exception. The book of Proverbs is full of warnings against intemperate and slanderous speech and constantly counsels the wise man to keep his silence; and in quite a few verses it has tale-bearing obviously in mind, as in:

> The words of a whisperer are like delicious morsels;
>> they go down into the inner parts of the body.
>
> (Prov. 18:8)

In view of this so deep-seated Hebrew aversion to the mischievous use of words, it is very unlikely that any of this story's original audiences could have been tempted to justify Joseph's conduct as stemming from a respect for truth, or filial loyalty, or some other admirable sentiment. Nor should we. The storyteller in the Joseph epic is on the whole very kind to his hero and often, indeed, he comes near to idealizing him (something rare in the Bible). But here at the beginning there is little doubt that he is presenting him as a rather naive and unfeeling young man, who still has a lot to learn. The fact that he doesn't bother to inform us what (if any) evil the brothers had been doing is a sure indication of this. Joseph is not yet the man of praiseworthy sagacity and tact he later becomes, but a foolish youth who carries tales back to his father and causes much distress thereby.

(iii)

Jacob's partiality we are acquainted with from of old. He "loved" Rachel and "hated" Leah, and now, it seems, he could not prevent himself from showing favouritism to Rachel's son. He had learned nothing from his own experience as a child, when he had been his mother's favourite and Esau his father's, and what tragedy had followed then! That catastrophe ensues this time too can come as no surprise to us. It comes about after he gives a specially valuable garment to Joseph as a gift. The reader will notice with some regret that the AV's coat "of many colours" has become in the RSV a robe that was "long" and "had sleeves". This removes a magical phrase from Scripture, but unfortunately accuracy demands it. The point seems to be that the robe was not a suitable dress for a working man, but one more appropriate to the leisured classes. The Hebrew word only occurs once elsewhere, in 2 Sam. 13:18, significantly of the garb of a princess.

It should be noted also that the phrase "son of his old age", applied to Joseph, is a rather careless exaggeration, probably introduced for dramatic effect. The story-teller must have been well aware that Joseph had been born in Paddan-Aram when Jacob was in his prime. At this time he was probably about sixty. If anyone should have been called a "son of his old age", it was the recently born Benjamin. See 44:20.

(iv)

Envy is a more destructive passion than either gossiping or partiality, and so in this story it turns out. Nevertheless, it is difficult not to feel some sympathy for the brothers. Charles Dickens catches beautifully the anguish of a family where favouritism is practised when he writes:

> In the little world in which children live there is nothing so finely perceived and so finely felt as an injustice. It may be only small injustice that the child is exposed to; but the child is small and its world is small.

For years the brothers had had to put up with a father who made no pretence that he liked one of them more than the others. And here he was compounding his unfairness by treating Joseph as a pampered prince, at the very time, too, that he was approaching manhood and should have been taking an increasing share of the work of the clan. And the pampered prince, when he did deign to go out to the pastures with them, was spying on them and whispering who knows what scurrilous things about them into an already biased ear when he got home.

It is little wonder that they "could not speak peaceably to him" or, as NEB has it, "could not say a kind word to him". It was harsh of them, but if their encampment was a bitter and unhappy place, it was—at least thus far—less their fault than that of a foolishly fond Jacob and a foolishly ingenuous Joseph.

DREAMS

Genesis 37:5–11

5 Now Joseph had a dream, and when he told it to his brothers they
6 only hated him the more. He said to them, "Hear this dream which I
7 have dreamed: behold, we were binding sheaves in the field, and lo, my sheaf arose and stood upright; and behold, your sheaves
8 gathered round it, and bowed down to my sheaf." His brothers said to him, "Are you indeed to reign over us? Or are you indeed to have dominion over us?" So they hated him yet more for his dreams and
9 for his words. Then he dreamed another dream, and told it to his brothers, and said, "Behold, I have dreamed another dream; and behold, the sun, the moon, and eleven stars were bowing down to
10 me." But when he told it to his father and to his brothers, his father rebuked him, and said to him, "What is this dream that you have dreamed? Shall I and your mother and your brothers indeed come to
11 bow ourselves to the ground before you?" And his brothers were jealous of him, but his father kept the saying in mind.

There is another bout of seeming innocence on Joseph's part to come before his brothers are spurred beyond envy to action against him. Joseph has two dreams and he cannot resist retailing them eagerly to his brothers, or indeed to his father.

(i)

To understand the brothers' reaction we have to realize that people in ancient times were much more affected by dreams than we are in this scientific age. It is almost impossible nowadays, when everybody knows at least a little about psychology and the subconscious, to take seriously the idea that dreams are a message from God and a portent of the future. If anything, we think of them as telling us more about our past. People in the age of the Bible, however, were never able to be sure that their dreams were not communications from the unseen world, insights into the future fraught with danger or hope that were almost bound to come true.

When Joseph blurted out the content of his two dreams, therefore, both his father and his brothers would have regarded them with genuine trepidation. This was especially the case when they were so transparent in meaning. No professional interpreter was needed to explain them, and there was no scope for introducing uncertainties and ambiguities. Plainly and crudely they spoke of a time when Joseph would be wearing a real prince's apparel and all of them would have to do obeisance before him.

It was this fear and anxiety as much as jealousy and envy that made the brothers seize the opportunity when it presented itself of getting rid of Joseph. It seems to us a terribly violent response to a young man's fancies, but to them it was the only certain way of preventing what were tantamount to prophecies from coming to pass. Jacob's response is also instructive. He was naturally annoyed, but he no more than the brothers was inclined to disregard the dreams. He had enough evidence from his own earlier life of God's peculiar behaviour to be other than circumspect as well as irritated. Can you imagine a modern father, even a doting one, countenancing such boasting from a son?

(ii)

The mention in the first dream of men who were shepherds harvesting sheaves of corn may strike us at first as odd, but not when we think about it a little. Like the reference to Isaac sowing seed at Gerar in 26:12, it is a reminder to us that the Patriarchs were semi-nomads rather than full Bedouin. Their main activity was the constant search for pasture for their flocks, which sometimes took them long distances. Thus in the next episode Joseph was sent by Jacob from Hebron to

Shechem far to the north to see how his brothers were getting on, and when he arrived there had to go on some miles further to Dothan to find them. But even that story tells us that the clan encampment was for the time being fixed at Hebron. It seems that the clansmen took the chance whenever they stayed in a place long enough to plant and harvest some grain crops, which were of course required for bread and for animal fodder in the winter. At other times they would obtain grain by barter from the settled farming population.

There is a surface problem in the second dream, too, in that it seems to presuppose that Rachel was still alive at the time. But this is not the only possible sense. Probably the "moon" of the dream was Leah, now without question Jacob's chief wife, and called "your mother" by him in his complaint to Joseph because that was the only convenient designation when he was referring to him along with all his brothers. There is a similar "shorthand" in verse 35 of the chapter, where "daughters" must mean Dinah along with the wives of Jacob's older sons. It would be making a mountain out of a molehill to argue from such a simple remark that sisters must have been born for Dinah after Jacob's return from Mesopotamia. See also Ruth 1:11-13.

(iii)

We all know that the dream of the brothers bowing down to Joseph is fulfilled later in the epic. Not once but four times they prostrate themselves before him, without recognizing him in 42:6, 43:26, and 44:14 during their two visits to Egypt, and fully conscious of who he was in 50:18 after their father's death. These are high points in the drama. They forcibly turn our thoughts back to the dream of the sheaves. No one could possibly miss their import.

It is not so commonly pointed out, however, that the second dream is *not* fulfilled in the epic. How could it be when the later stories picture Joseph as the ideal son? It would be turning upside down the appropriate relationships within the family. So on his arrival in Egypt, far from his father having to bow before him, Joseph goes out to meet him in his chariot, gets down and "presents himself" to him, falls on his neck, and weeps "a good while" (46:29).

But the sting in the tail of that touching scene is that Joseph's dream of the sun and moon and stars must have been a false one, suggested by his own arrogance and ambition and not at all by God's prompting. It is another subtle indication that there was a pride in the young Joseph that needed to be humbled.

REVENGE

Genesis 37:12–36

12 Now his brothers went to pasture their father's flock near Shechem.
13 And Israel said to Joseph, "Are not your brothers pasturing the flock at Shechem? Come, I will send you to them." And he said to
14 him, "Here I am." So he said to him, "Go now, see if it is well with your brothers, and with the flock; and bring me word again." So he
15 sent him from the valley of Hebron, and he came to Shechem. And a man found him wandering in the fields; and the man asked him,
16 "What are you seeking?" "I am seeking my brothers," he said, "tell
17 me, I pray you, where they are pasturing the flock." And the man said, "They have gone away, for I heard them say, 'Let us go to Dothan.'" So Joseph went after his brothers, and found them at
18 Dothan. They saw him afar off, and before he came near to them
19 they conspired against him to kill him. They said to one another,
20 "Here comes this dreamer. Come now, let us kill him and throw him into one of the pits; then we shall say that a wild beast has devoured
21 him, and we shall see what will become of his dreams." But when Reuben heard it, he delivered him out of their hands, saying, "Let us
22 not take his life." And Reuben said to them, "Shed no blood; cast him into this pit here in the wilderness, but lay no hand upon him"— that he might rescue him out of their hand, to restore him to his
23 father. So when Joseph came to his brothers, they stripped him of
24 his robe, the long robe with sleeves that he wore; and they took him and cast him into a pit. The pit was empty, there was no water in it.
25 Then they sat down to eat; and looking up they saw a caravan of Ishmaelites coming from Gilead, with their camels bearing gum,
26 balm, and myrrh, on their way to carry it down to Egypt. Then Judah said to his brothers, "What profit is it if we slay our brother

27 and conceal his blood? Come, let us sell him to the Ishmaelites, and let not our hand be upon him, for he is our brother, our own flesh."

28 And his brothers heeded him. Then Midianite traders passed by; and they drew Joseph up and lifted him out of the pit, and sold him to the Ishmaelites for twenty shekels of silver; and they took Joseph to Egypt.

29 When Reuben returned to the pit and saw that Joseph was not in
30 the pit, he rent his clothes and returned to his brothers and said,
31 "The lad is gone; and I, where shall I go?" Then they took Joseph's
32 robe, and killed a goat, and dipped the robe in the blood; and they sent the long robe with sleeves and brought it to their father, and said, "This we have found; see now whether it is your son's robe or
33 not." And he recognized it, and said, "It is my son's robe; a wild beast has devoured him; Joseph is without doubt torn to pieces."
34 Then Jacob rent his garments, and put sackcloth upon his loins, and
35 mourned for his son many days. All his sons and all his daughters rose up to comfort him; but he refused to be comforted, and said, "No, I shall go down to Sheol to my son, mourning." Thus his father
36 wept for him. Meanwhile the Midianites had sold him in Egypt to Potiphar, an officer of Pharaoh, the captain of the guard.

How ably this story of the brothers' revenge builds up the tension! Will Joseph find his brothers? What will they decide in the end to do with him? How will they explain things to Jacob? But then in the very last verse the writer seems to spoil it all by making what looks like an obvious and glaring blunder. Earlier in the story we had been told that the Midianites who found Joseph in the pit sold him to some Ishmaelites, who then took him with them to Egypt. Yet in this verse it is the Midianites who take him to Egypt and sell him to Potiphar, the captain of Pharaoh's guard.

(i)

Let us assume first that we are in fact dealing here with a careless mistake on the story-teller's part, and see how that affects our reading of the story. We do now and again find such errors in Scripture, which the scribes who copied out the scrolls over the centuries knew perfectly well were errors but refused to correct because by their time what they were copying had

changed from being just traditional literature into "Holy Writ".
In this case the mistake could have arisen from a confusion
between two related nomadic peoples who came from much the
same area; see Judg. 8:24.

As Joseph approached ("this dreamer" his brothers called
him, but the Hebrew is more suggestive, meaning "this master
of dreams"), they decided to kill him and throw his body into a
pit (properly the shaft of a well that had gone dry). Reuben,
however, counselled against this, not wanting to have anything
to do with open fratricide, and suggested instead that they
merely leave him in the pit to die of hunger and exposure. Or so
the other brothers would understand his words, but in fact he
had made up his mind to return later, and rescue him and
"restore him to his father".

These words are probably significant. They put Reuben's
solicitude in devastating perspective. He had no more cause
than the other brothers to feel any affection for Joseph. But as
Jacob's eldest son and therefore the one in charge of the
expedition and, perhaps even more to the point, as the erstwhile
defiler of Bilhah's bed (35:22), he had much more cause than
they to fear his father's wrath if they should return to Hebron
without him.

At this juncture we must suppose that Reuben arranged to be
called away to attend to some emergency in the flocks The
other brothers must also have retired some distance from the pit
to have their meal. As they were eating they caught sight of a
caravan of Ishmaelites wending its way along the trade route
from Gilead to Egypt. This would be a westward continuation
of the "way of the tent dwellers", mentioned earlier in connection with Jacob at Mahanaim, and would join the great
international "way of the sea" nearer the coast (see Maps 1 and
3). The gum and ointments the Ishmaelites carried would be in
great demand in Egypt both for medicinal purposes (see Jer.
8:22) and for use in embalming.

It was then that Judah brought forward his alternative plan.
It was if anything even more repulsive than Reuben's. Instead
of leaving Joseph to die, could they not sell him to these

Ishmaelites? In this way they wouldn't only assuage their consciences—after all "he is our brother, our own flesh"—but would make a profit out of the deal as well! But—a nice irony this—he was forestalled. Some Midianite traders, whom the brothers had not noticed, had come across Joseph and hauled him out of the cistern, and they had already sold him to the Ishmaelites.

Meanwhile Reuben, who had returned after what he thought was a suitable interval, found Joseph gone and collapsed in a paroxysm of grief and self-pity—"and I, where shall I go?" He could only now fall in with the others' scheme. They dipped the long robe, which in their rage they had naturally stripped from Joseph as soon as he had arrived, in a goat's blood and took it back to their father at Mamre, pretending to have found it by the wayside. Jacob immediately assumed that his favourite son had been torn to pieces by a wild beast, gave himself over to uncontrollable mourning in the extravagant Oriental manner, and refused to be comforted. Nothing was left for him but to join his son among the shades in the underworld, and until that day he would not remove his mourner's garb.

(ii)

As so reconstructed, the story is a complicated one but perfectly understandable. However, there is another way of explaining the awkward reference to Midianites in the last sentence. This brings in the so-called "documentary hypothesis" of the scholars. According to them we have in this chapter what is essentially a conflation of two accounts, one deriving from the "E" source and involving Reuben and a caravan of Midianites, the other from the "J" source and involving Judah and a caravan of Ishmaelites. In the one Reuben proposes to leave Joseph in the pit, where he is found by the Midianites and sold by them to Potiphar when they reach Egypt (verse 36). In the other the brothers on Judah's suggestion sell Joseph to the Ishmaelites, and it is they who take him to Egypt (last part of verse 28) and in turn sell him to Potiphar (first verse of chapter 39).

This theory not only removes the mistake in the final verse, but has the merit of simplifying the story line. But it hardly matters whether we decide to live with an error or with a conflation of sources. The end result in either case is the same. The brothers engineer Joseph's disappearance and make out to their old father that he is dead. What should concern us more is the motives and characters of the participants, particularly perhaps Joseph who, it will be noticed, is given nothing at all to do or say throughout the whole of this scene. It is there that the lessons of this frightening story of a family hopelessly at odds with itself are to be found.

SILENCE

Genesis 37:12–36 *(cont'd)*

(iii)

We do not need to say much more about Reuben and Judah and the other brothers. Even to contemplate fratricide was in the society of fierce clan loyalties to which they belonged a heinous crime (see the commentary on the Cain and Abel story in Volume 1, especially pp. 149ff.). But to sell a brother Hebrew into slavery was almost as bad; see Lev. 25:46 and 2 Chr. 28:8–15. When at the same time the audience sees them so selfishly and cravenly concerned to escape the consequences of their actions, it soon abandons any sympathy it may have had for them.

Moreover, there is an unsavoury whiff of Prometheus about the brothers' attitude, which is well exemplified by the agitated manner in which they argued with each other and the cynicism with which, after the deed was done, they deceived their father, even joining the comforters around him. At first tentatively and then brazenly they did what they had to do to prevent the fulfilment of Joseph's dream even though, as we saw earlier, they were aware that they could be tampering with "fate" and opposing the divine will. It was a risk they were prepared to take to rid themselves of a brother they detested.

(iv)

Jacob comes out of the episode a little better than the brothers, but only just. Pathetic is perhaps the best word to describe his behaviour. Was he so blind as not to see the peril he was placing his favourite in by sending him so far away from home to enquire about his brothers? Didn't he guess that they would regard it as another spying mission? Was he not even a little suspicious when they came home with Joseph's robe all bloody but no Joseph? And why such a frenzy of grief, contrasting so sharply with the faith in the future he had been able to hold onto when his beloved Rachel had died? It would be too harsh to say that he had lost his faith, but he had certainly lost his amazing resilience of old. The aged Jacob of the Joseph stories is but a pale reflection of the battler of the earlier stories, who would not even let God say "No!" to him. He touches our hearts, but the grudging respect we had for him is gone.

Dr. Strahan in his book *Hebrew Ideals* offers this penetrating commentary on the sad scene, drawing his example from the infamous "Killing Times" in Scotland:

> Jacob looks too much at the gloomy face of death, too little at the glorious face of God. Men of stronger faith have learned to answer even such questions as, "Is this thy son's coat?" without rending their garments and refusing to be comforted. Richard Cameron's head and hands were carried to the old Covenanter, his father, Allan Cameron. "Do you know them?" asked the cruel men who wished to add grief to the father's sorrow. And he took them on his knee, and bent over them, and kissed them, and said, "I know them! I know them! They are my son's, my dear son's." And then, weeping and yet praising, he went on, "It is the Lord! Good is the will of the Lord, who cannot wrong me and mine, but has made goodness and mercy to follow us all our days."

(v)

And what finally of Joseph? He was certainly foolish to have worn the offending robe on this particular errand. On the other hand, he did what was required of him well, refusing to be put off when he arrived at Shechem to find his brothers had moved on. But why are we given nothing about his behaviour and reactions after he caught up with the brothers and was brought face to face with death? We find out later that Joseph did in fact plead for his life (see 42:21), yet not a word is said about it here.

It seems to me that the author, having none too gently exposed his hero's arrogance and boastfulness earlier in the chapter, is beginning to prepare us for the noble Joseph of the stories that come next, whom he wants to set before us as the suffering servant of God, one who accepts injustice and imprisonment uncomplainingly in the sure faith that he has divine aid on his side. He is not yet quite ready to praise him, but he wants us to believe that he acted with considerable dignity. At the same time, he makes none of the asides with which he so liberally peppers the story of Joseph's stay in Potiphar's house, informing us that God was with him, guiding him and protecting him (see 39:2, 5, 21, 23). He is in short inviting us to witness the beginning of a change in Joseph, but he allows the atmosphere of disapproval to linger over him just a little longer before his heroism becomes unmistakably apparent. It is a delicate portrayal of a man learning the lessons of life.

INTERLUDE

Genesis 38:1–30

1 It happened at that time that Judah went down from his brothers,
2 and turned in to a certain Adullamite, whose name was Hirah. There Judah saw the daughter of a certain Canaanite whose name was
3 Shua; he married her and went in to her, and she conceived and bore
4 a son, and he called his name Er. Again she conceived and bore a
5 son, and she called his name Onan. Yet again she bore a son, and she
6 called his name Shelah. She was in Chezib when she bore him. And Judah took a wife for Er his first-born, and her name was Tamar.
7 But Er, Judah's first-born, was wicked in the sight of the Lord; and
8 the Lord slew him. Then Judah said to Onan, "Go in to your brother's wife, and perform the duty of a brother-in-law to her, and
9 raise up offspring for your brother." But Onan knew that the offspring would not be his; so when he went in to his brother's wife

he spilled the semen on the ground, lest he should give offspring to
10 his brother. And what he did was displeasing in the sight of the Lord,
11 and he slew him also. Then Judah said to Tamar his daughter-in-law, "Remain a widow in your father's house, till Shelah my son grows up"—for he feared that he would die, like his brothers. So Tamar went and dwelt in her father's house.

12 In course of time the wife of Judah, Shua's daughter, died; and when Judah was comforted, he went up to Timnah to his sheep-
13 shearers, he and his friend Hirah the Adullamite. And when Tamar was told, "Your father-in-law is going up to Timnah to shear his
14 sheep," she put off her widow's garments, and put on a veil, wrapping herself up, and sat at the entrance to Enaim, which is on the road to Timnah; for she saw that Shelah was grown up, and she
15 had not been given to him in marriage. When Judah saw her, he
16 thought her to be a harlot, for she had covered her face. He went over to her at the road side, and said, "Come, let me come in to you," for he did not know that she was his daughter-in-law. She said,
17 "What will you give me, that you may come in to me?" He answered, "I will send you a kid from the flock." And she said, "Will you give
18 me a pledge, till you send it?" He said, "What pledge shall I give you?" She replied, "Your signet and your cord, and your staff that is in your hand." So he gave them to her, and went in to her, and she
19 conceived by him. Then she arose and went away, and taking off her veil she put on the garments of her widowhood.

20 When Judah sent the kid by his friend the Adullamite, to receive
21 the pledge from the woman's hand, he could not find her. And he asked the men of the place, "Where is the harlot who was at Enaim
22 by the wayside?" And they said, "No harlot has been here." So he returned to Judah, and said, "I have not found her; and also the men
23 of the place said, 'No harlot has been here.'" And Judah replied, "Let her keep the things as her own, lest we be laughed at; you see, I sent this kid, and you could not find her."

24 About three months later Judah was told, "Tamar your daughter-in-law has played the harlot; and moreover she is with child by harlotry." And Judah said, "Bring her out, and let her be burned."
25 As she was being brought out, she sent word to her father-in-law, "By the man to whom these belong, I am with child." And she said, "Mark, I pray you, whose these are, the signet and the cord and the
26 staff." Then Judah acknowledged them and said, "She is more righteous than I, inasmuch as I did not give her to my son Shelah." And he did not lie with her again.

27 When the time of her delivery came, there were twins in her
28 womb. And when she was in labour, one put out a hand; and the
    midwife took and bound on his hand a scarlet thread, saying "This
29 came out first." But as he drew back his hand, behold, his brother
    came out; and she said, "What a breach you have made for
30 yourself!" Therefore his name was called Perez. Afterward his
    brother came out with the scarlet thread upon his hand; and his
    name was called Zerah.

Chapter 38 is usually regarded by modern scholarship as an
independent tradition which originally had nothing to do with
the epic of Joseph. According to some indeed it belongs
properly with the genealogies of Genesis rather than with the
Patriarchal stories, giving us hidden information about the
early history of the tribe of Judah but not telling us anything
about a real son of Jacob.

(i)

There is good cause for this opinion. For one thing, it is not easy
to find room for the events it relates within the time-scale
supplied for Joseph's life.

According to that time-scale Jacob's sons (including Judah)
went to Egypt to buy grain some twenty years after Joseph's
disappearance (see 41:46 and add seven years for the years of
plenty). Since the first sentence of this chapter suggests that
Judah married his Canaanite wife just after Joseph's departure,
this leaves only a couple of decades or so for her to bear three
sons, for Er the oldest to grow up and marry Tamar and then
die (according to the text because of some unspecified wickedness "in the sight of the Lord"), for Onan the second oldest to
fail in his duty as next-of-kin and be struck down for it, for
Tamar to return to her father's house and wait until Shelah, the
third son, was old enough to take her to wife, for Judah's own
wife to die ("in course of time", the story says), for Tamar to
adopt her desperate expedient of playing the harlot when
Shelah, having reached his maturity, was not given to her, for
Judah himself in search of sexual relief to pick her up by the
wayside and get her with child, for the twins Perez and Zerah to

be born, and for Judah thereafter to rejoin his father's clan at
the latest around the time the famine struck. Of course, we need
not take Joseph's dates as literally exact, but we would have to
stretch them considerably to accommodate all these happenings. Three decades rather than two would seem more appropriate.

This is a not impossible solution, but only if we are willing to
accept its serious corollaries for the Joseph story. In this the
"lad" Benjamin, for example, would then be around thirty
rather than twenty when he met Joseph, and the aged Jacob
with seventeen years still to live (47:28) a nonagenarian rather
than an octogenarian when he went down to Egypt. Is it
sensible in order to fit in this minor story to tamper so
extensively with the internal logic of the major Joseph story?

But more damaging still to efforts to align this story with the
larger story around it is the fact that the names of Judah's sons
and grandsons all appear elsewhere in genealogical lists as the
names of branches or subdivisions of tribes, usually of the tribe
of Judah but on occasion of different, even non-Israelite,
groupings. See for Er 1 Chr. 4:21 (linked with Shelah); for Onan
or Onam Gen. 36:23 (an Edomite clan); for Shelah, Perez and
Zerah Num. 26:20; for Zerah again Gen. 36:13 (an Edomite
clan) and Num. 26:13 (a Simeonite). It does look as if we are
faced in this chapter with an intrusion of tribal categories into
the Patriarchal narratives just as artificial as the passages using
the name Israel for Jacob and specifying the number of his sons
as precisely twelve.

(ii)

In view of these difficulties, it is not surprising that some
scholars argue that what we have in chapter 38 is an invented
story to account, first, for the separation of Judah as an entity
on its own in the south of Canaan over against all the northern
tribes (who retained the title Israel), second, for the surprisingly
close links that existed between Judah and the indigenous
population and, third, for the fluctuating fortunes of Judah's
clans, notably the disappearance early on of the clans of Er and

Onan and the emergence of the clan of Perez (in this tale the pushing twin of Tamar) as the dominant group within the confederation. It may not be without significance for the preservation of this tradition, moreover, that Perez was the branch of Judah to which King David belonged (Ruth 4:18). In other words, developments which could only have taken place on Palestinian soil after the Conquest are being given legitimacy in the form of a tradition about individuals which traces them back to the time of the Patriarchs.

And yet what a powerful tale this is! We have already acknowledged that a twelve tribe scheme has been foisted onto the later stories in Genesis, but have not let that stop us insisting that there is a historical basis to these stories. Why could something similar not have happened here? It is well nigh unthinkable to read this chapter and not believe that behind it lies a story of real family tragedy and intrigue. The observation of detail is so precise, the delineation of character so sharp, the tapestry of human motive and endeavour so richly woven that something within us tells us that the scholars who regard it as a mere fiction are going too far. We may not be able to solve all the problems attached to it, but that is no reason for setting it completely aside.

JUSTICE

Genesis 38:1-30 *(cont'd)*

(iii)

Let us concentrate then on the "human" core of the story, which revolves around the custom of "levirate" marriage. Under this it was the duty of a brother-in-law to marry the widow of a brother who had died childless (*levir* is Latin for "brother-in-law"). The first son of this marriage was regarded as his dead brother's and inherited his property and carried on his name. Such an institution may not have caused insuperable difficulties in a society like the Patriarchal where polygamy was permitted, and the duty was in that ancient period, as in this chapter, obligatory. But in a monogamous society, as later Israel seems on the whole to have been, it cannot have been easy to maintain. This was probably the reason for the law in Deut. 25:5–10 which allowed the brother-in-law to decline the obligation, though only after a public procedure in which the widow was entitled to spit in his face for refusing to honour the name of the dead. The custom was still known in New Testament times, for it figures in one of the controversies between Jesus and the Sadducees (Matt. 22:24–26), but we have no means of telling how far it was practised.

Be that as it may, Onan the brother of Er had no choice in the matter, and when he refused to consummate his enforced match with Tamar, he was struck down by the Lord for his sin. The term "onanism" has passed into our language as a euphemism for masturbation, but it is in the context much more likely that the means used by Onan to evade his responsibilities was what is now known as *coitus interruptus* or withdrawal before completion of the sexual act. That those in previous generations who coined the English term did not realize this is a revealing commentary both on their ignorance of sexual matters and their view of sexual deviations. It does not call for much effort to imagine the fears aroused in the minds of adolescent boys who were referred to this chapter of Genesis by over-zealous parents or teachers.

(iv)

The judgments which should primarily interest us, however, are not those passed quickly on Er and Onan, but those passed at length in the story on Judah and Tamar.

Judah emerges as an appalling hypocrite, but he has the grace in the end to acknowledge it. As head of the family he sees to it that Onan marries Tamar but, though after Onan's death he lets her think that she would be given to Shelah, he does not in the event give her to him. We are not told his reason, but presumably he had come to the conclusion that Tamar herself had something to do with his two sons' early deaths and did not want his third son exposed to the same risk. But then his own wife died, and after the mourning rites were completed, he paid a visit to his flock and while there accosted a woman by the wayside who he thought was a prostitute but was in fact his daughter-in-law disguised. He promised to give her a kid in return for her services and agreed to leave with her a pledge till it was sent. The pledge consisted of his private seal and the cord by which he carried it round his neck, and his staff. Probably the staff was inscribed or decorated in some distinctive way. Certainly these were items that would instantly have identified him, and not unnaturally he wanted them back. But when he sent the kid and the harlot could not be found, he preferred to lose them rather than make a fuss in public, hoping that the woman would not reappear.

Three months later he heard that Tamar was with child by an unknown man. Without thinking he assumed she had been playing the harlot, and peremptorily he pronounced sentence of death on her. But Tamar at that point sent him the insignia she had as a pledge, and he was forced publicly to confess the wrong he had done her. Whether in other circumstances such a man would have been so contrite we may take leave to doubt, but at least, when forced to it, he admitted that he had been guilty of the double standards which men have always down the ages used to distinguish between their own sexual misdemeanours and those of their womenfolk.

Tamar, like Sarah and Rebekah before her, strikes us as a *femme formidable* indeed. As a childless widow she could hardly have been more vulnerable in the society of the time. Only a child, preferably a son, would have given her standing and security. Yet both her brother-in-law and her father-in-law had refused—and in the cruellest possible manner—to give her the minimal rights prescribed for her by clan custom. But Tamar was no Hagar weeping in her solitude. She was not going to rot in widow's weeds for the rest of her life if she could help it. The stratagem she adopted was certainly a desperate one. It was also a perceptive one, in that she guessed correctly what Judah would do, both when he met her by the way and when later he was confronted with the truth. The taking of so incriminating a pledge in particular was a masterstroke.

This woman did wrong, but I detect in the story none of that vindictiveness that had so characterized Sarah and Rebekah's actions. They were successful women intent on hanging on to their success at all costs. Tamar was a defenceless widow fighting for common justice in a situation where even such rights as she possessed were being denied her. We may have to condemn her for what she did, but our condemnation is swallowed up in sympathy and admiration.

(v)

The issue of the incestuous union between Judah and Tamar was the twins Perez and Zerah. There is the same kind of play on Perez's name as we have frequently seen associated with birth stories in Genesis and which have long ceased to impress us. But there is one further feature of this compelling and elemental story which is worth remarking upon. It shows none of that hatred of foreigners which so mars not a few of Genesis' stories. Unlike Isaac and Jacob, both of whom had to find wives among relatives in Mesopotamia, Judah marries a hated Canaanite and the heroine of the story is herself a Canaanite woman. We are reminded of the Moabitess Ruth who, as a young widow in not dissimilar circumstances to Tamar, also contrived to shame God's people by her single-mindedness and quiet loyalty. It is a fitting irony that both these women should figure in the chosen line that led to King David.

A final comment. This chapter may have been placed in its present position after the epic of Joseph was complete. It has nevertheless been placed there with considerable dramatic sense. It creates suspense for the reader at a moment when Joseph's future hangs in the balance. It fills out the character of Judah and prepares us a little for this brother's generous gesture in chapter 43. But chiefly and most effectively it underscores the drastic straits into which Jacob's family has been plunged, rent asunder as it now was by strife and shame. To that extent it does belong under the heading "history of the family of Jacob" which prefaces the epic.

TEMPTATION

Genesis 39:1–23

1 Now Joseph was taken down to Egypt, and Potiphar, an officer of
Pharaoh, the captain of the guard, an Egyptian, bought him from
2 the Ishmaelites who had brought him down there. The Lord was
with Joseph, and he became a successful man; and he was in the
3 house of his master the Egyptian, and his master saw that the Lord
was with him, and that the Lord caused all that he did to prosper in
4 his hands. So Joseph found favour in his sight and attended him,
and he made him overseer of his house and put him in charge of all
5 that he had. From the time that he made him overseer in his house
and over all that he had the Lord blessed the Egyptian's house for
Joseph's sake; the blessing of the Lord was upon all that he had, in
6 house and field. So he left all that he had in Joseph's charge; and
having him he had no concern for anything but the food which he
ate.
7 Now Joseph was handsome and good-looking. And after a time
his master's wife cast her eyes upon Joseph, and said, "Lie with me."
8 But he refused and said to his master's wife, "Lo, having me my
master has no concern about anything in the house, and he has put
9 everything that he has in my hand; he is not greater in this house
than I am; nor has he kept back anything from me except yourself,
because you are his wife; how then can I do this great wickedness
10 and sin against God?" And although she spoke to Joseph day after
11 day, he would not listen to her, to lie with her or to be with her. But
one day, when he went into the house to do his work and none of the
12 men of the house was there in the house, she caught him by his
garment, saying, "Lie with me." But he left his garment in her hand,
13 and fled and got out of the house. And when she saw that he had left
14 his garment in her hand, and had fled out of the house, she called to
the men of her household and said to them, "See, he has brought
among us a Hebrew to insult us; he came in to me to lie with me, and
15 I cried out with a loud voice; and when he heard that I lifted up my
voice and cried, he left his garment with me, and fled and got out of
16 the house." Then she laid up his garment by her until his master
17 came home, and she told him the same story, saying, "The Hebrew
servant, whom you have brought among us, came in to me to insult

18 me; but as soon as I lifted up my voice and cried, he left his garment
with me, and fled out of the house."

19   When his master heard the words which his wife spoke to him,
"This is the way your servant treated me," his anger was kindled.

20 And Joseph's master took him and put him into the prison, the place
where the king's prisoners were confined, and he was there in prison.

21 But the Lord was with Joseph and showed him steadfast love, and

22 gave him favour in the sight of the keeper of the prison. And the
keeper of the prison committed to Joseph's care all the prisoners
who were in the prison; and whatever was done there, he was the

23 doer of it; the keeper of the prison paid no heed to anything that was
in Joseph's care, because the Lord was with him; and whatever he
did, the Lord made it prosper.

We now return to the story of Joseph. Like one much greater
than he (though I do not press the comparison), Joseph has to
face and conquer temptation before he can become a true
servant of God. It is the purpose of this chapter to show him
passing the test with flying colours, and enduring with equa-
nimity the suffering that results. The story is serenely told, but I
do not think it quite comes off. The story-teller idealizes Joseph
too much.

(i)

The theme of a young and industrious slave being promoted to
a position of high trust in his owner's household can be
paralleled throughout history and fiction. So can that of a
bored and frustrated lady of rank trying to seduce a handsome
young servant and crying "Rape!" when her advances are
repulsed.

It seems to me that the second theme is far more colourfully
presented in this story than the first. Joseph rises to eminence
because his master—an Egyptian!—recognizes that the Lord—
to him surely a foreign god—was with him. His house prospers
under Joseph's judicious management, and again we are reminded that the Lord was with him. Indeed, Potiphar was able to
leave everything in Joseph's care and himself only turn up at
meal-time! We get the message, but did the story-teller need to
lay it on quite so thick?

It is in story terms quite a relief when Potiphar's wife comes on the scene. Right away the atmosphere changes. The nymphomaniac's curt command "Lie with me" contrasts nicely with Joseph's rather wordy and moralizing reply. But when eventually she makes a grab for him, he flees, leaving his outer garment in her hand—and this time round there are no sermons! This, we cannot but feel, is more like a real man's reaction. Then comes the screaming and the vitriol. An appeal to the other servants to back up her story is accompanied by a clever hint that as Egyptians they too must have felt resentment at this upstart Hebrew. Note also the none too flattering way she refers to her husband with an unadorned "he". The Genesis story-teller is back at his sparkling best, giving us his own savage instance of the truth of Congreve's adage:

Heav'n has no rage, like love to hatred turn'd,
Nor Hell a fury, like a woman scorn'd.

(ii)

From what we have learned of Potiphar's character—the one who was glad to have Joseph more or less take over the nonmilitary side of his duties and the "he" of his wife's shrill complaint—it comes as no surprise that instead of instantly executing him, he should merely consign him to prison. It is fortunate for Joseph, but there is a nice irony in the thought of Pharaoh's captain of the guard being such a shuffler. (The prison in which Joseph was put was one for which Potiphar seems to have been responsible; it was for political or military offenders—the "king's prisoners" they are called—and was apparently in the same complex of buildings as his own house.) Joseph offers no defence. Presumably his silence in face of calumny and an unmerited punishment was meant to elicit our admiration—and of course it does.

But hardly does he have him in prison than the story-teller becomes pious again. The Lord was with Joseph and showed him steadfast love, and it was not long before the gaoler too had him doing his work for him. And again our hero needed no supervision, for again the Lord was with him and "whatever he did, the Lord made it prosper." With a final sentence like that we almost forget that this man was languishing in prison and that we are supposed to be sympathizing with his courage in adversity.

There is plenty of evidence of the writer's skill and keen eye for character in the middle of this chapter, but in my opinion that skill deserts him at the beginning and end of the story. He is so concerned to get over his lesson of God's providence following Joseph at every step that he turns him into a bit of a plaster-saint. We are not as moved as we ought to be. The flawed hero of chapter 37 has become flawless a little too soon. It is much the same in the next story of Joseph as the interpreter of dreams. We have to wait till in chapter 42 Joseph meets his brothers before the story-teller is sufficiently sure of himself to make his hero appear human and therefore less than perfect again.

A Note on Structure and Style in the Joseph Epic

We have just judged a story to be not as good as we thought it ought to be. Perhaps this is an appropriate moment, then, to look more closely at the way the author tells the Joseph epic as a whole. In earlier parts of Genesis we found that considering matters of style and structure could help us to understand better the story-teller's intentions. I believe this to be true in the case of this part as well.

No more than the stories about Abraham and Jacob are the stories about Joseph history in our sense of the word. There are a number of indications that their Egyptian background is authentic (I shall say something about these later), but by and large they are just as reserved with regard to background information about people, events and places as the stories earlier in Genesis, and just as often the reader is left frustratingly in the dark. Nevertheless, there are some striking and very instructive differences both in plot formation and verbal style between this epic and the two preceding ones.

The Joseph epic is much more carefully constructed. Where in the Abraham and Jacob cycles we had what was in effect a series of single narratives loosely joined together, there is here (if we leave aside chapter 38) a sustained plot in which one episode leads naturally into the other and everything moves purposefully towards a controlled denouement. It is rather like a long-distance race compared with a succession of short sprints.

The style is also more diffuse and leisurely. There are less awkward pauses for genealogical lists and notices about the founding of holy places and the meaning of names, more repetitions, more references or allusions backwards and forwards, more extended conversations in the oriental fashion. But perhaps most noticeable of all, there is a change in the way the deity is portrayed. In the Joseph stories God hardly ever interferes in the action directly, appearing embarrassingly as a man or a little less so as an angel and addressing the Patriarchs face to face. We are never in doubt that he is the controlling influence behind what is happening, but it is the story-teller or one of the characters speaking who tells us this, not God himself. He is no longer, as it were, a member of the cast on stage.

It is at this point that we begin to see the connection between plot and style on the one hand and theme and theology on the other. For the themes of the three epics are also very different, and the different literary treatments in fact reflect these different themes. The first two epics are epics of challenge and crisis, in the Abraham epic the challenge of faith, in the Jacob the crisis of grace. God meets the two heroes personally in the hurly-burly of life, demanding an instant response, interfering outrageously with their human plans and ambitions, constantly confronting them—and through them us— with the ironies and paradoxes of choice and decision. The theme of the Joseph epic, however, is the overriding providence of God in the affairs of men. He disposes things gradually and gently, overruling rather than interfering, working behind the scenes to bring good out of evil.

In story terms the themes of the first two epics—faith and grace— preclude an even pace and a happy ending; the theme of the third— God's providence—demands both. The story of Abraham has to finish with him—and us—uncertain, because faith is not knowledge. The story of Jacob has to conclude with him—and us—bewildered, for God's grace cannot be tied to our understanding. But the story of Joseph can end with him—and us—content and perhaps even a little smug, for it rests on the conviction that all things work together for good to them that love God.

I think we can agree that in each case the style and structure of the

Genesis epics beautifully match their theme. In all three there are superb stories and stories which seem to us less than effective, but each by the way in which it is written gets our imaginations working in the right direction and forcibly turns our thoughts towards the relevant aspect of the divine nature and activity.

INSPIRATION

Genesis 40:1–41:45

At the beginning of this story Joseph is in prison and has reached the nadir of his fortunes. By the end of it he is master of all Egypt, second only to the Pharaoh himself. His elevation is due to his ability to understand and explain dreams, an ability which we are frequently reminded derives not from the wisdom of the mighty land in which he was exiled but from the inspiration of the God of the Hebrews. The story is for the most part well told and the suspense well sustained, but sometimes there is an artificial flavour to it and where there are ironies they are noticeably at the Egyptians' expense, not at Joseph's. Only in the very last paragraph is it possible to detect a veiled criticism of the hero.

The butler's dream (40:1–15)

1 Some time after this, the butler of the king of Egypt and his baker
2 offended their lord the king of Egypt. And Pharaoh was angry with
3 his two officers, the chief butler and the chief baker, and he put them in custody in the house of the captain of the guard, in the prison
4 where Joseph was confined. The captain of the guard charged Joseph with them, and he waited on them; and they continued for
5 some time in custody. And one night they both dreamed—the butler and the baker of the king of Egypt, who were confined in the prison—each his own dream, and each dream with its own meaning.
6 When Joseph came to them in the morning and saw them, they were
7 troubled. So he asked Pharaoh's officers who were with him in custody in his master's house, "Why are your faces downcast
8 today?" They said to him, "We have had dreams, and there is no one to interpret them." And Joseph said to them, "Do not interpretations belong to God? Tell them to me, I pray you."

9   So the chief butler told his dream to Joseph, and said to him, "In
10 my dream there was a vine before me, and on the vine there were
three branches; as soon as it budded, its blossoms shot forth, and the
11 clusters ripened into grapes. Pharaoh's cup was in my hand; and I
took the grapes and pressed them into Pharaoh's cup, and placed the
12 cup in Pharaoh's hand." Then Joseph said to him, "This is its
13 interpretation: the three branches are three days; within three days
Pharaoh will lift up your head and restore you to your office; and
you shall place Pharaoh's cup in his hand as formerly, when you
14 were his butler. But remember me, when it is well with you, and do
me the kindness, I pray you, to make mention of me to Pharaoh, and
15 so get me out of this house. For I was indeed stolen out of the land of
the Hebrews; and here also I have done nothing that they should put
me into the dungeon."

The baker's dream (40:16–19)

16 When the chief baker saw that the interpretation was favourable, he
said to Joseph, "I also had a dream: there were three cake baskets on
17 my head, and in the uppermost basket there were all sorts of baked
food for Pharaoh, but the birds were eating it out of the basket on
18 my head." And Joseph answered, "This is its interpretation: the
19 three baskets are three days; within three days Pharaoh will lift up
your head—from you!—and hang you on a tree; and the birds will
eat the flesh from you."

The dreams come true (40:20–23)

20 On the third day, which was Pharaoh's birthday, he made a feast for
all his servants, and lifted up the head of the chief butler and the
21 head of the chief baker among his servants. He restored the chief
butler to his butlership, and he placed the cup in Pharaoh's hand;
22 but he hanged the chief baker, as Joseph had interpreted to them.
23 Yet the chief butler did not remember Joseph, but forgot him.

The Pharaoh's two dreams (41:1–8)

1 After two whole years, Pharaoh dreamed that he was standing by
2 the Nile, and behold, there came up out of the Nile seven cows sleek
3 and fat, and they fed in the reed grass. And behold, seven other
cows, gaunt and thin, came up out of the Nile after them, and stood
4 by the other cows on the bank of the Nile. And the gaunt and thin

5 cows ate up the seven sleek and fat cows. And Pharaoh awoke. And
  he fell asleep and dreamed a second time; and behold, seven ears of
6 grain, plump and good, were growing on one stalk. And behold,
  after them sprouted seven ears, thin and blighted by the east wind.
7 And the thin ears swallowed up the seven plump and full ears. And
8 Pharaoh awoke, and behold, it was a dream. So in the morning his
  spirit was troubled; and he sent and called for all the magicians of
  Egypt and all its wise men; and Pharaoh told them his dream, but
  there was none who could interpret it to Pharaoh.

The butler remembers Joseph (41:9–13)

9 Then the chief butler said to Pharaoh, "I remember my faults today.
10 When Pharaoh was angry with his servants, and put me and the
11 chief baker in custody in the house of the captain of the guard, we
   dreamed on the same night, he and I, each having a dream with its
12 own meaning. A young Hebrew was there with us, a servant of the
   captain of the guard; and when we told him, he interpreted our
   dreams to us, giving an interpretation to each man according to his
13 dream. And as he interpreted to us, so it came to pass; I was restored
   to my office, and the baker was hanged."

Joseph interprets the Pharaoh's dreams and gives him advice (41:14–36)

14 Then Pharaoh sent and called Joseph, and they brought him hastily
   out of the dungeon; and when he had shaved himself and changed
15 his clothes, he came in before Pharaoh. And Pharaoh said to
   Joseph, "I have had a dream, and there is no one who can interpret
   it; and I have heard it said of you that when you hear a dream you
16 can interpret it." Joseph answered Pharaoh, "It is not in me; God
17 will give Pharaoh a favourable answer." Then Pharaoh said to
   Joseph, "Behold, in my dream I was standing on the banks of the
18 Nile; and seven cows, fat and sleek, came up out of the Nile and fed
19 in the reed grass; and seven other cows came up after them, poor and
   very gaunt and thin, such as I had never seen in all the land of Egypt.
20, 21 And the thin and gaunt cows ate up the first seven fat cows, but when
   they had eaten them no one would have known that they had eaten
22 them, for they were still as gaunt as at the beginning. Then I awoke. I
   also saw in my dream seven ears growing on one stalk, full and good;
23 and seven ears, withered, thin, and blighted by the east wind,

24 sprouted after them, and the thin ears swallowed up the seven good
ears. And I told it to the magicians, but there was no one who could
explain it to me."

25 Then Joseph said to Pharaoh, "The dream of Pharaoh is one; God
26 has revealed to Pharaoh what he is about to do. The seven good
cows are seven years, and the seven good ears are seven years; the
27 dream is one. The seven lean and gaunt cows that came up after
them are seven years, and the seven empty ears blighted by the east
28 wind are also seven years of famine. It is as I told Pharaoh, God has
29 shown to Pharaoh what he is about to do. There will come seven
30 years of great plenty throughout all the land of Egypt, but after them
there will arise seven years of famine, and all the plenty will be
31 forgotten in the land of Egypt; the famine will consume the land, and
the plenty will be unknown in the land by reason of that famine
32 which will follow, for it will be very grievous. And the doubling of
Pharaoh's dream means that the thing is fixed by God, and God will
33 shortly bring it to pass. Now therefore let Pharaoh select a man
34 discreet and wise, and set him over the land of Egypt. Let Pharaoh
proceed to appoint overseers over the land, and take the fifth part of
the produce of the land of Egypt during the seven plenteous years.
35 And let them gather all the food of these good years that are coming,
and lay up grain under the authority of Pharaoh for food in the
36 cities, and let them keep it. That food shall be a reserve for the land
against the seven years of famine which are to befall the land of
Egypt, so that the land may not perish through the famine."

Joseph enters the service of Pharaoh (41:37–45)

37, 38 This proposal seemed good to Pharaoh and to all his servants. And
Pharaoh said to his servants, "Can we find such a man as this, in
39 whom is the Spirit of God?" So Pharaoh said to Joseph, "Since God
has shown you all this, there is none so discreet and wise as you are;
40 you shall be over my house, and all my people shall order themselves
as you command; only as regards the throne will I be greater than
41 you." And Pharaoh said to Joseph, "Behold, I have set you over all
42 the land of Egypt." Then Pharaoh took his signet ring from his hand
and put it on Joseph's hand, and arrayed him in garments of fine
43 linen, and put a gold chain about his neck; and he made him to ride
in his second chariot; and they cried before him, "Bow the knee!"
44 Thus he set him over all the land of Egypt. Moreover Pharaoh said
to Joseph, "I am Pharaoh, and without your consent no man shall

45 lift up hand or foot in all the land of Egypt." And Pharaoh called
Joseph's name Zaphenath-paneah; and he gave him in marriage
Asenath, the daughter of Potiphera priest of On. So Joseph went
out over the land of Egypt.

WISDOM

Genesis 40:1–41:45 *(cont'd)*

(i)

The first step on Joseph's God-guided ascent to eminence was
when at the end of the last story he was entrusted with the
oversight of the other prisoners in the military gaol. When,
however, two of the Pharaoh's highest domestic officers,
themselves probably former slaves, fell foul of their royal
master and were delivered into Potiphar's custody, Joseph was
taken out of the prison to attend them. Apparently they were
not put in the actual prison but detained pending investigation
in some part of Potiphar's house. It was another step upwards
for Joseph, though only a temporary one; for it seems that when
his services were no longer required he was returned to his cell
or, as he calls it, his "dungeon" (see 40:15 and 41:14). The word
is the same as was used to describe the "pit" into which he had
been cast by his brothers and provides a vivid flash-back to the
beginning of the epic.

After a time the chief butler and the chief baker dreamed two
similar dreams in the same night and were perturbed by them.
Joseph, now the sympathetic attendant, asked them why they
were so downcast and they told him it was because they had no-
one to interpret their dreams. This may seem to us a rather lame
complaint, but we have again to remember the fascination of all
antiquity with dreams. If this was true of the Hebrews, how
much more was it true of the Egyptians! We know of the
compilation of Egyptian "dream books", and we will shortly
encounter the magicians and wise men of the Pharaoh's court,
among whose many duties in the area of the occult was clearly
that of giving suitable interpretations of their master's dreams.

What the butler and baker were complaining about, then, was that in their present disgrace they were unable to call upon these experts. It is a nice insight in foretaste into the superstitious dread that in the next scene so patently rules the Pharaoh's household and the paralysis of all its members, including the Pharaoh and his so-called experts, when confronted with phenomena they could not explain. And of course it is against that background that we are to understand Joseph's role as an interpreter. Though he was able easily to explain all the dreams, he was himself no expert—but he had access to One who was! He was like the great prophets of later times, not a trained professional, but a man who stood in the secret counsel of God, to whom all "interpretations" belonged.

(ii)

The main lesson of the story is to be found here. Only those in tune with the mind of God could interpret dreams; for it was he who caused them to be dreamed and he who disposed the future of which they spoke. It is the same lesson as we find in the Book of Daniel. Its hero also rose to a high position in a foreign court. He too endured much unjust suffering for his faith, and he too was a mouthpiece of God, who could with supreme ease explain the dreams of important people.

One of the ironies which the stories of Joseph and Daniel share is the same subtle use of the word *Elohim* or "God". This, we know, is grammatically a plural form (see further the commentary on 1:26–31, *Let us make* . . . , in Volume 1). We are meant then to think of the pagans around the hero—Egyptians here, Babylonians in Daniel's case—understanding it (or to be more exact, its Egyptian or Babylonian equivalent) to refer to "the gods" and agreeing with sentiments like Joseph's. Of course "the gods", who spoke to men through dreams, knew what they were about. But how did that help them? For in dreams "the gods" spoke in riddles.

By *Elohim,* however, Joseph and Daniel meant something very different. They were referring to the one God who had

created and who even now sustained the world and who alone
controlled the destiny of both individuals and nations. And this
God had made his mysteries clear, even the mysteries of
dreams, to his special people—or at any rate to the "wise"
among them. Alongside such direct inspiration what could all
the science of pagan professors achieve?

All this we have to infer from Joseph's simple question in
chapter 40, "Do not interpretations belong to God?", and from
a few similar short statements in chapter 41; see verses 16, 25,
28, 32 and, on the Pharaoh's lips, 38–39. Daniel, in his great
hymn in chapter 2, spells it out more fully:

> Blessed be the name of God for ever and ever,
>   to whom belong wisdom and insight.
> He changes times and seasons;
>   he removes kings and sets up kings;
> he gives wisdom to the wise
>   and knowledge to those who have understanding;
> he reveals deep and mysterious things;
>   he knows what is in the darkness,
>   and the light dwells with him.
> To thee, O God of my fathers,
>   I give thanks and praise,
> for thou hast given me wisdom and strength,
>   and hast now made known to me what we asked of thee.
>
> (verses 20–23)

See also Dan. 2:27–28; 4:34–37.

We today are not likely to take so kindly as the Hebrews did
to all this talk of dreams and mysteries and secrets needing to be
interpreted or revealed. But if we can make allowance for that,
there is much to which we can heartily assent. For take away the
superstition and the message is essentially a simple one, and it is
also a vital one. It is that God and God alone proposes and God
and God alone disposes; yet he does not leave his people
ignorant of his purposes. The "signs of the times" are always
there for the spiritually sensitive to read.

(iii)

Another lesson which comes over at the beginning of the Book of Daniel and in this part of the Joseph epic is that God's people *can* live a life of faith in an alien environment. They can be loyal both to God and to the state of which they are citizens as long as that state respects their religious rights. It is only when such a state arrogates God's role and demands from its citizens a "worship" that is God's alone that his people must call a halt and be prepared, if necessary, to suffer for their faith. That time is not yet for the Hebrews in Egypt, though there are some ominous asides later in the Joseph epic (e.g. 43:32; 46:34) which prepare us for the distant day when (Exod. 1:8) "there arose a new king over Egypt, who did not know Joseph". In Daniel, however, the change comes with startling rapidity and from being tolerated the Jews were subjected to the fiercest persecution.

For the Bible's message to believers in such a dire situation readers may refer to Mr. Ellison's Commentary on Exodus and Dr. Russell's Commentary on Daniel in the present series. For just now we have before us the happier case of a young Hebrew who, without being disloyal to the faith of his fathers, yet achieved worldly success and distinction in a society which had no time for his religion, though it shrewdly recognized that it could provide able and trustworthy administrators.

Jews down the centuries must have drawn immense comfort from the example of Joseph, and many of them have in their various ways emulated his success. So can Christians today who live in most parts of the world. But a second's thought should warn us not to take too much comfort from it. Daniel's experience is probably more apposite. At this very moment many Jews and many Christians are citizens of countries where the thin line separating toleration from persecution has been crossed and where no believer can hope to climb up the social ladder as Joseph did and still remain a believer. And the societies in which we live may soon go the same way. With his proneness to idealize his hero's progress the story-teller in this part of the Joseph epic could be accused of hiding some of life's more unpleasant realities from his audience's eyes. Where in it all is the "pilgrim" emphasis of the Abraham and Jacob stories?

INGRATITUDE

Genesis 40:1–41:45 *(cont'd)*

(iv)

But let us now look at some of the details of the story. Its lessons are, as we have seen, ones that a modern audience can only appreciate with difficulty and not a little revamping. I feel also that as a story it is far from being one of Genesis' best. The story-teller seems strangely reluctant to make the most of his opportunities.

For one thing, the dreams of the butler and baker and of the Pharaoh are not all that complicated. They have the right mixture of reality and fantasy that one expects in dreams. The butler dreams of giving the Pharaoh wine, but the vines he sees blossom and ripen and ferment in an instant. The baker dreams of taking cakes in baskets to his master's table, but he sees birds eating the cakes as he carries the baskets through the palace. Pharaoh dreams of thin cattle and blighted ears of corn, but he sees the thin cattle devouring fat ones and remaining thin and the wasted ears swallowing full ones and remaining wasted. But we cannot help wondering why the two officials should have had so little idea of what their dreams were about that without an interpreter they felt helpless. Nor is it obviously apparent why the magicians and wise men should have been so flummoxed by Pharaoh's dreams that they had not a word to say to him. Because of this Joseph's success in interpreting them is in each case diminished. How much better the author of the Book of Daniel manages the scenes in chapters 2 and 4! Nebuchadnezzar's dreams are very much more complex and grotesque than Pharaoh's. The frantic incapacity of the Babylonian professors thus makes sense and the achievement of Daniel in explaining them comes over with more dramatic punch. Joseph is made to appear too nonchalant.

There is an even more revealing contrast between the end of Daniel's speech in chapter 2 and the end of Joseph's address to the Pharaoh here. Daniel interprets Nebuchadnezzar's dream at length and stops. It is Nebuchadnezzar who, after acknowledging that Daniel's God is truly God of gods and Lord of kings and a revealer of mysteries, decides to honour Daniel and make him ruler over the whole province of Babylon. In Genesis, however, Joseph gives his simple explanation of the dreams and then more or less invites the Pharaoh to promote him. "God has shown to Pharaoh what he is about to do" hardly sounds right on the lips of a man who had just a moment before been brought before him from a prison cell. The story-teller of course wishes to emphasize the Pharaoh's utter feebleness over against the One who in fact controls the future. But he overdoes it, and the scene is thus emptied of realistic impact. The writer of the Book of Daniel makes essentially the same point a lot more effectively.

(v)

Fortunately, however, there are a couple of places where things come to life.

The first is towards the end of the scene with the two officials in custody. There is a clever play on words in Joseph's replies to them. The butler's head will be "lifted up"; that is, the investigation into his misconduct will result in him being declared innocent, he will be able to stand in his master's presence once more and will be given his old job back. Compare 2 Kgs. 25:27 where "graciously freed" is literally "lifted up the head". The baker's head will also be "lifted up"—but from him!; he will be found guilty and decapitated, and his body left hanging for the birds to eat. There is also Joseph's plaintive request to the butler to mention him favourably to Pharaoh after he is restored: "for I was indeed stolen out of the land of the Hebrews; and here also I have done nothing that they should put me into the dungeon". These are moving words—and Joseph is actually asking someone for help! This scene has all the crispness of Hebrew story-telling at its best. Not a word is said of the reactions of the two men to their fate, and at the end of it all we get is a brief statement that the sentences were duly carried out and an even briefer one that the butler forgot his promise to Joseph.

The second place is when in the Pharaoh's court two years later the butler remembered about Joseph. "I remember my faults today" is not a good translation, since it could make us think he was sorry that he had let Joseph down. He is not in the slightest. The "faults" he speaks of are his offences against Pharaoh or, to be more exact, the offences of which he had been unjustly accused, though he is too tactful to say that to his master's face. It is a beautiful example of a twisted diplomat at work. He mentions "faults" which are no faults and without a qualm of conscience "remembers" a man he had cruelly wronged.

These two little scenes ring true, I am sure, because the story-teller himself is caught up in their human appeal. Though in true Hebrew fashion he does not dwell on the emotions of the participants, it is these emotions—of despair and longing on Joseph's part, of relief and then of supercilious forgetfulness on the butler's part, of stark fear on the baker's part—that move him and make him unconsciously sharpen his writing. In the later confrontation between Pharaoh and Joseph he is far too interested in making his theological point about all wisdom deriving from God and consequently the characters become artificial and the writing flat.

Let the reader ask himself honestly what about this long and tedious tale stays clearest in his mind, and I think he will agree with my assessment. It is not the emphasis on dreams nor the formalised proceedings in the Pharaoh's court. It is the cold and thankless ingratitude of a high Egyptian official towards a lowly Hebrew who when he himself was low had been kind to him but for whom when he was on top again he spared not a single thought.

Shakespeare says all that needs to be said about this most typical and most foul of human characteristics in his caustic song from *As You Like It:*

Blow, blow, thou winter wind,
Thou art not so unkind
　As man's ingratitude;
Thy tooth is not so keen
Because thou art not seen,
　Although thy breath be rude.

Freeze, freeze, thou bitter sky,
That dost not bite so nigh
　As benefits forgot;
Though thou the waters warp,
Thy sting is not so sharp
　As friend remember'd not.

(vi)

Finally, Pharaoh does what he is told—what else?—and pro-
motes Joseph as his vizier or prime minister to organize his
domains against the coming famine. Joseph dons the trappings
of his authority and all Egypt "bows the knee" before him as he
goes out over the land. Pharaoh also gives him an Egyptian
name and the daughter of an Egyptian priest in marriage. It is a
magnificent climax. Or is it? I suspect that the story-teller by the
way he piles up the details in this last paragraph may be
beginning obliquely to criticize Joseph again. But more about
that in the next section.

FORGETFULNESS

Genesis 41:46–57

46 Joseph was thirty years old when he entered the service of Pharaoh
　king of Egypt. And Joseph went out from the presence of Pharaoh,
47 and went through all the land of Egypt. During the seven plenteous
48 years the earth brought forth abundantly, and he gathered up all the
　food of the seven years when there was plenty in the land of Egypt,
　and stored up food in the cities; he stored up in every city the food
49 from the fields around it. And Joseph stored up grain in great
　abundance, like the sand of the sea, until he ceased to measure it, for
　it could not be measured.

50 Before the year of famine came, Joseph had two sons, whom Asenath, the daughter of Potiphera priest of On, bore to him.
51 Joseph called the name of the first-born Manasseh, "For," he said, "God has made me forget all my hardship and all my father's house."
52 The name of the second he called Ephraim, "For God has made me fruitful in the land of my affliction."
53 The seven years of plenty that prevailed in the land of Egypt came
54 to an end; and the seven years of famine began to come, as Joseph had said. There was famine in all lands; but in all the land of Egypt
55 there was bread. When all the land of Egypt was famished, the people cried to Pharaoh for bread; and Pharaoh said to all the
56 Egyptians, "Go to Joseph; what he says to you, do." So when the famine had spread over all the land, Joseph opened all the storehouses, and sold to the Egyptians, for the famine was severe in the
57 land of Egypt. Moreover, all the earth came to Egypt to Joseph to buy grain, because the famine was severe over all the earth.

This passage links the two main parts of the Joseph epic, the story of his rise to fame in Egypt and that of his restoration to his family (or rather, as it turns out, theirs to him). It passes quickly over Joseph's arrangements to fill Egypt's granaries with food and the coming of the famine as he had foretold. The story-teller obviously wants to move us on as soon as possible to the encounter between Joseph and his brothers. But he has not lost his dramatic feel. In the middle of his catalogue of events he relates the birth of two sons to Joseph. It seems to be just another piece of information among the rest, but he cunningly contrives to use it to teach his audience a valuable lesson, indeed, to cut his hero down to size. In the view of some of us it is not before time.

(i)

Joseph could hardly have risen higher. In order to do what had to be done, he was installed by Pharaoh in the two chief offices of state, that of director of the palace, who had charge of the Pharaoh's finances, and that of grand vizier or authorized representative of the Pharaoh, who carried his seal and whose commands would thus automatically be obeyed as though they were his own. He wore the great chain of state, rode in one of the Pharaoh's chariots, and was preceded by a guard who called on everyone to "make way" or "bow the knee" (the word seems to be Egyptian, though its precise meaning is uncertain).

Naturally a Hebrew audience would rejoice in so glorious an achievement. At the same time it is hard to believe that they would not feel some tremors of unease. Joseph had been given an Egyptian name and he had married an Egyptian woman. But Egyptian names as much as Hebrew ones were heavily religious in their connotations (Zaphenathpaneah is thought to mean "the god speaks and he lives"). Nor was the woman he married any ordinary Egyptian woman, but the daughter of the high-priest at On (later Heliopolis), the holy city of the mighty sun-god Re (see Map 4). And now, to cap it all, Joseph was being accorded an adulation that was distinctly un-Hebraic. It was almost as if the divine honours that in Egyptian belief belonged to the Pharaoh as a son of the gods were being transferred to him. Was the story-teller not overdoing it? What could he be getting at?

(ii)

We get a strong hint of his purpose in the report of the birth and naming of Joseph's two sons. The name Manasseh means "[God is] the one who makes [us] forget", so for once in Genesis the interpretation of a name is not far removed from the original sense. It is the kind of name that parents who had previously lost a child might have chosen. On the other hand, Ephraim is only connected with the verb "be fruitful" by a couple of consonants in common; its original meaning is unknown. But the important thing is that in explaining the names Joseph gives full credit to his own God for all that had happened. It was the Hebrews' God, not the Pharaoh or the gods of Egypt, for all their prominence in the story, who had brought him to his present success and happiness and caused him to forget all his former life of hardship and affliction.

There was no danger then of Joseph betraying the faith of his fathers. We can almost hear the audience's sigh of relief.

Nevertheless, did he need to sound quite so smug and self-satisfied? Did he need to give the impression of enjoying quite so heartily his first taste of the "fleshpots" of Egypt (see Exod. 16:3)? Why did he appear to relish so much his new-found authority? And why did he have to mention "all my father's house", as if it were solely they and in no way himself who had been responsible for his long years of suffering?

I think that the author intentionally leaves a nasty taste in our mouths at this point. He seems to me to be at last recognizing that the way he has been portraying his hero was making him out too good to be true—the conscientious slave, the irresistibly handsome youth, the silent and uncomplaining victim of calumny, the considerate steward, the nonchalant interpreter of dreams, the easy superior of all Pharaoh's wise men, the instantly efficient prime minister! So he subtly, by the way he describes his triumph, lets it be noticed that Joseph was still more arrogant by half than he ought to have been. His humility before God was not yet a fully genuine humility. In particular he had still to learn that his promotion to affluence was not an end in itself, but only part of a grander design, and that grander design included the family he had forgotten about. Did he not recall the haughty butler who had forgotten him?

(iii)

A perturbing imbalance in the epic has at last been put right. It is not as a paragon of virtue but as an imperfect human being like the rest of us that Joseph enters the epic's second act. In this he will not only be the viceroy of Egypt but a member of a family finding health and wholeness after two decades and more of hatred and discord. The very first sentence of the next story effectively reminds us of this other—and in God's purpose much more important—role of Joseph's by suddenly transporting us from a rich, well-managed and well-fed Egypt to the small land of Canaan where because of the famine people were already dying of hunger. If in his affluence Joseph had forgotten his father's house, God had not forgotten it.

NOT YOU BUT GOD

Genesis 42:1–45:28

The story of the two confrontations between Joseph and his brothers sparkles with subtlety and finesse. Even though it is long, it ought to be read over slowly at a single sitting, so that we catch at least some of the nuances and paradoxes in which it abounds. Much of its attractiveness resides in the clever use which the story-teller makes of the device of dramatic irony. We have already seen in the story of the stolen blessing in chapter 27 how devastating a weapon this device could be in short compass. Here it is employed over no less than four chapters, sometimes with more than a dash of vitriol but on the whole gently and unobtrusively as step by step what the participants know and what we know—and, we could add, what God knows—come together in a denouement that is as moving as it is satisfying. Joseph's words in chapter 45 sum up the story's secret meaning—"not you, but God". What in effect we are privileged to witness through the story-teller's imaginative skill is the providence of God at work in human lives.

The brothers descend to Egypt (42:1–5)

1 When Jacob learned that there was grain in Egypt, he said to his
2 sons, "Why do you look at one another?" And he said, "Behold, I
have heard that there is grain in Egypt; go down and buy grain for us
3 there, that we may live, and not die." So ten of Joseph's brothers
4 went down to buy grain in Egypt. But Jacob did not send Benjamin,
Joseph's brother, with his brothers, for he feared that harm might
5 befall him. Thus the sons of Israel came to buy among the others
who came, for the famine was in the land of Canaan.

Their first meeting with Joseph (42:6–17)

6 Now Joseph was governor over the land; he it was who sold to all the
people of the land. And Joseph's brothers came, and bowed
7 themselves before him with their faces to the ground. Joseph saw his

brothers, and knew them, but he treated them like strangers and spoke roughly to them. "Where do you come from?" he said. They

8 said, "From the land of Canaan, to buy food." Thus Joseph knew his

9 brothers, but they did not know him. And Joseph remembered the dreams which he had dreamed of them; and he said to them, "You

10 are spies, you have come to see the weakness of the land." They said

11 to him, "No, my lord, but to buy food have your servants come. We are all sons of one man, we are honest men, your servants are not

12 spies." He said to them, "No, it is the weakness of the land that you

13 have come to see." And they said, "We, your servants, are twelve brothers, the sons of one man in the land of Canaan; and behold, the

14 youngest is this day with our father, and one is no more." But Joseph

15 said to them, "It is as I said to you, you are spies. By this you shall be tested: by the life of Pharaoh, you shall not go from this place unless

16 your youngest brother comes here. Send one of you, and let him bring your brother, while you remain in prison, that your words may be tested, whether there is truth in you; or else, by the life of

17 Pharaoh, surely you are spies." And he put them all together in prison for three days.

Simeon is left hostage (42:18–25)

18 On the third day Joseph said to them, "Do this and you will live, for I

19 fear God: if you are honest men, let one of your brothers remain confined in your prison, and let the rest go and carry grain for the

20 famine of your households, and bring your youngest brother to me; so your words will be verified, and you shall not die." And they did

21 so. Then they said to one another, "In truth we are guilty concerning our brother, in that we saw the distress of his soul, when he besought us and we would not listen; therefore is this distress come upon us."

22 And Reuben answered them, "Did I not tell you not to sin against the lad? But you would not listen. So now there comes a reckoning

23 for his blood." They did not know that Joseph understood them, for

24 there was an interpreter between them. Then he turned away from them and wept; and he returned to them and spoke to them. And he

25 took Simeon from them and bound him before their eyes. And Joseph gave orders to fill their bags with grain, and to replace every man's money in his sack, and to give them provisions for the journey. This was done for them.

The money discovered (42:26-28)

26, 27 Then they loaded their asses with their grain, and departed. And as one of them opened his sack to give his ass provender at the lodging
28 place, he saw his money in the mouth of his sack; and he said to his brothers, "My money has been put back; here it is in the mouth of my sack!" At this their hearts failed them, and they turned trembling to one another, saying, "What is this that God has done to us?"

Jacob is inconsolable (42:29-38)

29 When they came to Jacob their father in the land of Canaan, they
30 told him all that had befallen them, saying, "The man, the lord of the
31 land, spoke roughly to us, and took us to be spies of the land. But we
32 said to him, 'We are honest men, we are not spies; we are twelve brothers, sons of our father; one is no more, and the youngest is this
33 day with our father in the land of Canaan.' Then the man, the lord of the land, said to us, 'By this I shall know that you are honest men: leave one of your brothers with me, and take grain for the famine of
34 your households, and go your way. Bring your youngest brother to me; then I shall know that you are not spies but honest men, and I will deliver to you your brother, and you shall trade in the land.' "
35 As they emptied their sacks, behold, every man's bundle of money was in his sack; and when they and their father saw their bundles of
36 money, they were dismayed. And Jacob their father said to them, "You have bereaved me of my children: Joseph is no more, and Simeon is no more, and now you would take Benjamin; all this has
37 come upon me." Then Reuben said to his father, "Slay my two sons if I do not bring him back to you; put him in my hands, and I will
38 bring him back to you." But he said, "My son shall not go down with you, for his brother is dead, and he only is left. If harm should befall him on the journey that you are to make, you would bring down my grey hairs with sorrow to Sheol."

Reluctantly the brothers return (43:1-15)

1, 2 Now the famine was severe in the land. And when they had eaten the grain which they had brought from Egypt, their father said to them,
3 "Go again, buy us a little food." But Judah said to him, "The man solemnly warned us, saying, 'You shall not see my face, unless your
4 brother is with you.' If you will send our brother with us, we will go
5 down and buy you food; but if you will not send him, we will not go

down, for the man said to us, 'You shall not see my face, unless your
6 brother is with you.' " Israel said, "Why did you treat me so ill as to
7 tell the man that you had another brother?" They replied, "The man
questioned us carefully about ourselves and our kindred, saying, 'Is
your father still alive? Have you another brother?' What we told him
was in answer to these questions; could we in any way know that he
8 would say, 'Bring your brother down'?" And Judah said to Israel his
father, "Send the lad with me, and we will arise and go, that we may
9 live and not die, both we and you and also our little ones. I will be
surety for him; of my hand you shall require him. If I do not bring
him back to you and set him before you, then let me bear the blame
10 for ever; for if we had not delayed, we would now have returned
twice."
11   Then their father Israel said to them, "If it must be so, then do this:
take some of the choice fruits of the land in your bags, and carry
down to the man a present, a little balm and a little honey, gum,
12 myrrh, pistachio nuts, and almonds. Take double the money with
you; carry back with you the money that was returned in the mouth
13 of your sacks; perhaps it was an oversight. Take also your brother,
14 and arise, go again to the man; may God Almighty grant you mercy
before the man, that he may send back your other brother and
15 Benjamin. If I am bereaved of my children, I am bereaved." So the
men took the present, and they took double the money with them,
and Benjamin; and they arose and went down to Egypt, and stood
before Joseph.

The conversation with Joseph's steward (43:16–25)

16 When Joseph saw Benjamin with them, he said to the steward of his
house, "Bring the men into the house, and slaughter an animal and
17 make ready, for the men are to dine with me at noon." The man did
18 as Joseph bade him, and brought the men to Joseph's house. And
the men were afraid because they were brought to Joseph's house,
and they said, "It is because of the money, which was replaced in our
sacks the first time, that we are brought in, so that he may seek
occasion against us and fall upon us, to make slaves of us and seize
19 our asses." So they went up to the steward of Joseph's house, and
20 spoke with him at the door of the house, and said, "Oh, my lord, we
21 came down the first time to buy food; and when we came to the
lodging place we opened our sacks, and there was every man's
money in the mouth of his sack, our money in full weight; so we have

22 brought it again with us, and we have brought other money down in
our hand to buy food. We do not know who put our money in our
23 sacks." He replied, "Rest assured, do not be afraid; your God and
the God of your father must have put treasure in your sacks for you;
24 I received your money." Then he brought Simeon out to them. And
when the man had brought the men into Joseph's house, and given
them water, and they had washed their feet, and when he had given
25 their asses provender, they made ready the present for Joseph's
coming at noon, for they heard that they should eat bread there.

Joseph's banquet (43:26–34)

26 When Joseph came home, they brought into the house to him the
present which they had with them, and bowed down to him to the
27 ground. And he inquired about their welfare, and said, "Is your
28 father well, the old man of whom you spoke? Is he still alive?" They
said, "Your servant our father is well, he is still alive." And they
29 bowed their heads and made obeisance. And he lifted up his eyes,
and saw his brother Benjamin, his mother's son, and said, "Is this
your youngest brother, of whom you spoke to me? God be gracious
30 to you, my son!" Then Joseph made haste, for his heart yearned for
his brother, and he sought a place to weep. And he entered his
31 chamber and wept there. Then he washed his face and came out; and
32 controlling himself he said, "Let food be served." They served him
by himself, and them by themselves, and the Egyptians who ate with
him by themselves, because the Egyptians might not eat bread with
33 the Hebrews, for that is an abomination to the Egyptians. And they
sat before him, the first-born according to his birthright and the
youngest according to his youth; and the men looked at one another
34 in amazement. Portions were taken to them from Joseph's table, but
Benjamin's portion was five times as much as any of theirs. So they
drank and were merry with him.

The arrest of Benjamin (44:1–13)

1 Then he commanded the steward of his house, "Fill the men's sacks
with food, as much as they can carry, and put each man's money in
2 the mouth of his sack, and put my cup, the silver cup, in the mouth of
the sack of the youngest, with his money for the grain." And he did
3 as Joseph told him. As soon as the morning was light, the men were
4 sent away with their asses. When they had gone but a short distance

from the city, Joseph said to his steward, "Up, follow after the men; and when you overtake them, say to them, 'Why have you returned
5 evil for good? Why have you stolen my silver cup? Is it not from this that my lord drinks, and by this that he divines? You have done wrong in so doing.' "
6, 7 When he overtook them, he spoke to them these words. They said to him, "Why does my lord speak such words as these? Far be it from
8 your servants that they should do such a thing! Behold, the money which we found in the mouth of our sacks, we brought back to you from the land of Canaan; how then should we steal silver or gold
9 from your lord's house? With whomever of your servants it be
10 found, let him die, and we also will be my lord's slaves." He said, "Let it be as you say: he with whom it is found shall be my slave, and
11 the rest of you shall be blameless." Then every man quickly lowered
12 his sack to the ground, and every man opened his sack. And he searched, beginning with the eldest and ending with the youngest;
13 and the cup was found in Benjamin's sack. Then they rent their clothes, and every man loaded his ass, and they returned to the city.

The brothers confess their guilt (44:14–17)

14 When Judah and his brothers came to Joseph's house, he was still
15 there; and they fell before him to the ground. Joseph said to them, "What deed is this that you have done? Do you not know that such a
16 man as I can indeed divine?" And Judah said, "What shall we say to my lord? What shall we speak? Or how can we clear ourselves? God has found out the guilt of your servants; behold, we are my lord's slaves, both we and he also in whose hand the cup has been found."
17 But he said, "Far be it from me that I should do so! Only the man in whose hand the cup was found shall be my slave; but as for you, go up in peace to your father."

Judah's intercession (44:18–34)

18 Then Judah went up to him and said, "O my lord, let your servant, I pray you, speak a word in my lord's ears, and let not your anger burn
19 against your servant; for you are like Pharaoh himself. My lord
20 asked his servants, saying, 'Have you a father or a brother?' And we said to my lord, 'We have a father, an old man, and a young brother, the child of his old age; and his brother is dead, and he alone is left of
21 his mother's children; and his father loves him.' Then you said to

your servants, 'Bring him down to me, that I may set my eyes upon
22 him.' We said to my lord, 'The lad cannot leave his father, for if he
23 should leave his father, his father would die.' Then you said to your
servants, 'Unless your youngest brother comes down with you, you
24 shall see my face no more.' When we went back to your servant my
25 father we told him the words of my lord. And when our father said,
26 'Go again, buy us a little food,' we said, 'We cannot go down. If our
youngest brother goes with us, then we will go down; for we cannot
27 see the man's face unless our youngest brother is with us.' Then your
servant my father said to us, 'You know that my wife bore me two
28 sons; one left me, and I said, Surely he has been torn to pieces; and I
29 have never seen him since. If you take this one also from me, and
harm befalls him, you will bring down my grey hairs in sorrow to
30 Sheol.' Now therefore, when I come to your servant my father, and
the lad is not with us, then, as his life is bound up in the lad's life,
31 when he sees that the lad is not with us, he will die; and your servants
will bring down the grey hairs of your servant our father with sorrow
32 to Sheol. For your servant became surety for the lad to my father,
saying, 'If I do not bring him back to you, then I shall bear the blame
33 in the sight of my father all my life.' Now therefore, let your servant,
I pray you, remain instead of the lad as a slave to my lord; and let the
34 lad go back with his brothers. For how can I go back to my father if
the lad is not with me? I fear to see the evil that would come upon my
father."

Joseph discloses his identity (45:1–3)

1 Then Joseph could not control himself before all those who stood by
him; and he cried, "Make every one go out from me." So no one
stayed with him when Joseph made himself known to his brothers.
2 And he wept aloud, so that the Egyptians heard it, and the house-
3 hold of Pharaoh heard it. And Joseph said to his brothers, "I am
Joseph; is my father still alive?" But his brothers could not answer
him, for they were dismayed at his presence.

He acknowledges the providential purpose of God in all that has happened (45:4–15)

4 So Joseph said to his brothers, "Come near to me, I pray you." And
they came near. And he said, "I am your brother, Joseph, whom you
5 sold into Egypt. And now do not be distressed, or angry with
yourselves, because you sold me here; for God sent me before you to

6 preserve life. For the famine has been in the land these two years;
and there are yet five years in which there will be neither ploughing
7 nor harvest. And God sent me before you to preserve for you a
8 remnant on earth, and to keep alive for you many survivors. So it
was not you who sent me here, but God; and he has made me a father
to Pharaoh, and lord of all his house and ruler over all the land of
9 Egypt. Make haste and go up to my father and say to him, 'Thus says
your son Joseph, God has made me lord of all Egypt; come down to
10 me, do not tarry; you shall dwell in the land of Goshen, and you shall
be near me, you and your children and your children's children, and
11 your flocks, your herds, and all that you have; and there I will
provide for you, for there are yet five years of famine to come; lest
you and your household, and all that you have, come to poverty.'
12 And now your eyes see, and the eyes of my brother Benjamin see,
13 that it is my mouth that speaks to you. You must tell my father of all
my splendour in Egypt, and of all that you have seen. Make haste
14 and bring my father down here." Then he fell upon his brother
15 Benjamin's neck and wept; and Benjamin wept upon his neck. And
he kissed all his brothers and wept upon them; and after that his
brothers talked with him.

The Pharaoh invites Jacob to Egypt (45:16–28)

16 When the report was heard in Pharaoh's house, "Joseph's brothers
17 have come," it pleased Pharaoh and his servants well. And Pharaoh
said to Joseph, "Say to your brothers, 'Do this: load your beasts and
18 go back to the land of Canaan; and take your father and your
households, and come to me, and I will give you the best of the land
19 of Egypt, and you shall eat the fat of the land.' Command them also,
'Do this: take wagons from the land of Egypt for your little ones and
20 for your wives, and bring your father, and come. Give no thought to
your goods, for the best of all the land of Egypt is yours.' "
21   The sons of Israel did so; and Joseph gave them wagons, according to the command of Pharaoh, and gave them provisions for the
22 journey. To each and all of them he gave festal garments, but to
Benjamin he gave three hundred shekels of silver and five festal
23 garments. To his father he sent as follows: ten asses loaded with the
good things of Egypt, and ten she-asses loaded with grain, bread,
24 and provision for his father on the journey. Then he sent his brothers
away, and as they departed, he said to them, "Do not quarrel on the
25 way." So they went up out of Egypt, and came to the land of Canaan

26 to their father Jacob. And they told him, "Joseph is still alive, and he
   is ruler over all the land of Egypt." And his heart fainted, for he did
27 not believe them. But when they told him all the words of Joseph,
   which he had said to them, and when he saw the wagons which
   Joseph had sent to carry him, the spirit of their father Jacob revived;
28 and Israel said, "It is enough; Joseph my son is still alive; I will go
   and see him before I die."

REMORSE

Genesis 42:1–25 *(cont'd)*

(i)

The drama of the opening scenes is sharply etched. There is
Jacob's command to his sons to go down to Egypt to seek grain,
"that we may live and not die". There is his refusal to send
Benjamin. There is the emphasis that the ten and Benjamin are
Joseph's brothers. There is their arrival as "they came to buy
among those that came" (AV). There is the obsequious way they
bow before the governor of the land, "with their faces to the
ground". There is the telling play on words, impossible to catch
in English:

wayyakkirem wayyitnakker alehem
"and he knew them, but he treated them like strangers".

There is Joseph recalling his dreams.

We are left in no doubt that this was a fulfilment, partial
maybe but real, of the dreams in chapter 37. From the brothers'
side it is as yet an unconscious fulfilment, but Joseph is fully
cognisant of its importance.

(ii)

Yet how few of our other questions about Joseph are satisfac-
torily answered! Did he as vizier actually supervise the distribution of supplies in person, or should we infer that he turned up
on this occasion because he heard that a band of Hebrews had
arrived from Canaan? If the latter, did it pass through his mind

that they might be his brothers or was he at first more concerned, at a time when foreigners were pouring into Egypt, to verify that they posed no threat to the state's security? Was he in the habit of detaining such groups while checking their credentials, so that those around could have noticed nothing unusual in him clapping these men in gaol? Or was this a special punishment thought up by him on the spur of the moment to get back at them for what they had done to him so many years ago?

We can only speculate on the answers to these questions. Nevertheless, I think there is enough evidence in what we are given to absolve Joseph of pure vindictiveness in his response. His first ploy may well have had a good element of pique in it. He knew that his brothers were not spies, but in spite of that he treated them as though they were. He put them in prison and proposed to send one of their number back to bring (in the person of Benjamin) a proof of their innocence he did not need. But then he changed his mind and decided to keep only one behind as hostage. And he claimed, "I fear God". Once again in translating *Elohim* we are aware of the differences between English and Hebrew. It was in fact the God of Israel that Joseph meant, but he was speaking in Egyptian and the brothers were hearing him through an interpreter, and they did not yet know who he was. A more colourless translation like NEB's "I am a god-fearing man" would be safer in the context. But however we render the phrase, it has to signal a shift on Joseph's part from a solely emotional to a more coolly considered attitude.

At that point the brothers engaged in a private and heated conversation with no idea that the great official could understand them. They were comparing their predicament, as he must surely have meant them to, with the events of twenty years before. As then they were to go back to Jacob minus one brother! But Joseph did not gloat. Tears came into his eyes and he had to withdraw in order to compose himself. It is impossible to construe this as the reaction of a vengeful man, nor was it all that cool either. In fact it is the story-teller's way of letting the audience know that Joseph was genuinely fond of his brothers and that from now on he was, as the proverb has it, being "cruel to be kind". We find ourselves able to make allowance for any bitter satisfaction he may have drawn from their discomfiture. We are even willing to go along with his next turn of the screw which is, as they leave, to instruct his servants to put their money back into their sacks when they were filled with grain. For we are now convinced that he meant them no permanent harm.

(iii)

What, then, of the brothers? It is much more likely that they were thinking from the start of the events of twenty years past. Would they hear any rumour of Joseph when they were in Egypt? That—and of course their father's refusal to send Benjamin with them—was probably why, when this supercilious Egyptian accused them of spying, they did not only deny it and say they were honest men but told him about Jacob and about Benjamin and about the brother who was "no more". They were not to know that by this reply they would not only intensely annoy Joseph—the last time he had been with them they had been anything but honest!—but would give him a credible excuse to embarrass them where they were most vulnerable. It must have come as a fearful shock to them when the grand official, swearing by the life of Pharaoh, fastened on the mention of a younger brother and demanded that he be brought to him before he would believe them.

But then after three days in prison they were hauled before him once more. This time he talked not of Pharaoh's life but of "the gods" whom he feared. He obviously meant what he said, but surprisingly instead of sending only one back home to fetch Benjamin, he was letting them all go except one. What a merciful release! But almost immediately relief gave way to dread as they realized that if anything this was worse. For it meant that for a second time they would have to return to their old father with a brother missing. It is little wonder that they began to wish they had listened to Joseph's pleas all those years before and that Reuben in particular saw in it a reckoning, long delayed but none the less deserved for that For, needless to say,

Jacob would not let Benjamin return with them and if they did not return themselves to be executed, then certainly whoever was chosen as hostage was doomed. Finally, so as not to let them doubt his seriousness, the Egyptian, having picked out Simeon, the second oldest of them, had him fettered before their very eyes.

For all the poetic justice of it, it seems an almost unbelievable series of disasters to launch on a group of men already worried enough about how they might feed their families—or rather it would have been did not the audience already know that the punishment would never be carried out. It is because we know this that we can at one and the same time sympathize with the brothers and savour their temporary distress. We can even begin to warm to them as haltingly but unmistakably they are moved to ask each other whether they might not themselves be to blame for what had befallen them.

GRIEF

Genesis 42:26–43:15 *(cont'd)*

(iv)

But whether wittingly or not, Joseph, by having the brothers' money covertly returned to their sacks, had overdone things and, by so doing, had lost control of the situation. He had reckoned without the old father back in Canaan who was, as his brothers could have told him, a very different man from the Jacob he had once known.

He must by his plan have intended the brothers to return in a few weeks with Benjamin in an even more chastened frame of mind. But when they discovered the money at one of the camping sites (this rather than AV's "inn" or RSV's "lodging place") where they stopped on their way home, they knew immediately that that was out of the question. There were no thoughts of their own guilt this time, but a complete failure of nerve in the face of "this that God has done to us". And it turned out exactly as they feared. Indeed, they themselves stumblingly made matters worse. In their embarrassment they could not bring themselves to tell the old man about the money as well as about Simeon and Benjamin. Instead they went through a macabre charade of opening their sacks in front of him as though for the first time. Right away Jacob collapsed in convulsions of grief. Not even Reuben's offer to let Jacob slay his own two sons (we have not been told before about these) if he did not bring Benjamin safely back to him could persuade him to entertain the idea.

The money in their sacks was for him the last straw. Could he ever trust this lot again? For all he knew they had even tried to cheat the powerful "lord of the land" they had pictured as so fierce. Two of his sons were dead or as good as dead. The rest of them, guilty or innocent, were thieves in the eyes of the Egyptians. No way could he let Benjamin go now. If anything were to happen to him, his grey hairs would be brought down in sorrow to the grave.

(v)

But in time hunger worked its insidious power over even this wretched octogenarian. For amazingly it was Jacob himself who, when the supplies were used up, suggested that they go back for more, and Judah had to remind him that Benjamin would have to go with them. He made only a half-hearted protest, "Why did you treat me so ill as to tell the man that you had another brother?" But he accepted Judah's guarantee, though it was far less binding than Reuben's had been, for it spoke only of him "bearing the blame for ever". The brothers were to take some choice nuts and honey and ointments as a present (apparently only the cereal crops had failed) and a double sum of money and suggest to the Egyptian that the original money had perhaps found its way into their sacks by "an oversight"!

The parallel with an aged Isaac in the blessing scene in chapter 27 is too close to be ignored. He had suspected that mischief was afoot, yet in the end he gave the blessing to Jacob in order to be at the savoury dish he was carrying. Now Jacob

himself was senile and forgetful, paralysed by grief and apprehension—but he and his clan had to have food. He commended
the enterprise touchingly enough to "God Almighty" (*El
Shaddai;* see at 17:1) and hoped that both Simeon and Benjamin might be restored to him. But then almost in despair he
added, "If I am bereaved of my children, I am bereaved". We
are reminded of Job's great cry of faith, "The Lord gave, and
the Lord has taken away; blessed be the name of the Lord"
(1:21). But Jacob's was a whining rather than a lofty resigna-
tion.

It is hard to be sorry for this lugubrious old man, so intent on
holding on to life while talking so incessantly of death, and
positively wallowing in his misery. But knowing what is to
happen, we can scarcely begrudge even him the few moments of
peace and happiness he is to have before he at last dies. His life
had been all turmoil and struggle. It deserved in God's mercy a
quiet ending.

(vi)

We react much more cordially to the brothers in this scene
Their concern for their aged father seems genuine, in vivid
contrast to their lack of it when reporting to him on that other
occasion in the past. Moreover, it is peculiarly fitting that the
two brothers who had then been most prominent in deciding
Joseph's fate should take the lead on this occasion. Reuben had
been the only one then to feel qualms of conscience and now too
he goes further with his gesture, pledging his own sons against
the return of Jacob's son. Judah then had been despicably
profit-seeking and now too he emphasizes the material—"for if
we had not delayed, we would now have returned twice". His
noblest moment is still to come (see 44:18ff.), but at least he is
now willing to take some responsibility on his shoulders.

It is a distinct pleasure to see two men who had each been
guilty in the past of heinous crimes (in addition to chapter 37,
see for Reuben 35:22, and for Judah 38:15–16) recognizing that
there was more to life than selfish passion. Indeed, from this
point on in the story our hearts are, if we be truthful, more with

the brothers than with Joseph. Men who had once been seething with jealousy and hatred, they were learning life's lessons quicker than he, in his zeal to prevent a premature calamity, was willing to give them credit for. There are still question marks against them. For one, none of them during this long and depressing stay in Canaan seems to have spared much thought for Simeon. The more they delayed, the more he was in mortal danger, if the Egyptian governor was as stern a man as he had made himself out to be. For another it needed the pangs of hunger in their case too to screw up their courage sufficiently to make them go back. But go back to Egypt they did something we cannot imagine the brothers of chapter 37 doing

A Note on "Sources" in Chapters 42 and 43

There are some indications in the section we have been studying of a similar combination of two traditions to that the scholars found in chapter 37. We have two accounts of the sacks being opened, once at a halt the night after the brothers' departure from Egypt and once when they arrived home, and both times we are told that they trembled or were dismayed. There are also two accounts of one of the brothers offering a security against Benjamin's safe return, Reuben immediately after their arrival in Canaan and Judah some time later when a return was mooted. But only in the first of these is Simeon mentioned by the brother, while in the second it looks on the surface as though, when Judah spoke, he was breaking the news about Benjamin to Jacob for the first time.

On these grounds not a few scholars would reconstruct two separate stories, both of which knew about the money in the sacks and about the condition that Benjamin should be taken back to Egypt, but only the first of which knew about Simeon having been kept behind as a hostage. This first story like that with Reuben in it in chapter 37 is assigned by them to the "E" document or source; in it the brothers do not open the sacks till they get home and they return immediately, if reluctantly, with Benjamin to redeem Simeon from gaol. In the second, belonging to "J", the brothers discover the money at the camping site and in their fear they tell their father neither about it nor about Benjamin; only when their grain is finished and Jacob suggests that they go down for more do they, with Judah as their spokesman, confess the truth.

This theory would certainly remove some of the stutters in the story as we now have it, but it would also remove much of its tension and drama which, as we have just seen, resides precisely in the brothers and their father being so mesmerised and confused that they hardly know which way to turn. It has its merits, but I am even less inclined to accept that two traditions have got mixed up in this section than I was in the case of the betrayal story in chapter 37.

THE CALM...

Genesis 43:16–34 *(cont'd)*

(vii)

Swiftly the scene shifts to Joseph's house in Egypt, where the brothers were told to report on their arrival. As they stood in the courtyard, he saw that Benjamin was with them and gave orders to his steward to take the men to the guest room and prepare a banquet. And then he left. As he would have spoken in Egyptian, the brothers did not know what he had said, and naturally they assumed the worst. Had they been too long a time in coming back? But they had brought Benjamin with them and their lives at least were safe—or so they hoped. Then there was their carefully rehearsed but woefully thin-sounding excuse about the purchase money. That it was true was neither here nor there. He would be bound to treat it with contempt and at best turn them into slaves and—a naive touch this!—purloin their donkeys.

So in some trepidation they approached the steward and tried him with their speech. They had no idea who had put the money in their sacks, but they had brought it back with them and a second sum as well to buy more grain. Imagine their delight—though it cannot have been unmixed with a new kind of consternation—when he replied that "your God" must have put a treasure-trove in their sacks, for he had received their payment in full. And then he brought Simeon out to them—they had almost forgotten him!—, invited them to wash and saw to the needs of their animals. They were told they were to dine with the great man at noon and got their presents ready.

When Joseph arrived, they did obeisance, handed over their gifts, and answered his questions—would he never stop asking them?—about their father and about Benjamin. As he looked at close quarters on Benjamin, his only full brother, whom he had last seen as an infant, he again almost broke down before them and had to rush from the room to try to regain control of his emotions. In their surprise at being so kindly received, the brothers may not have noticed this, though it was the second time he had interrupted a conversation between them. After all, a vizier was a busy man.

But how must they have felt during the strange banquet that followed? The vizier ate by himself in splendid isolation. All right, he was grand vizier of Egypt. But the Egyptian guests had a table to themselves, and they had a table to themselves. They were being reminded that they were aliens, belonging to an inferior race and in Egypt on sufferance. But why then had so great a man bothered to dine with them at all? Finally, Benjamin was on his explicit instructions served with helpings five times the size of theirs! The scene ends with the wine flowing and them making merry with him, but it is the previous comment that in its typically laconic Hebrew way speaks loudest: "and the men looked at one another in amazement".

(viii)

It is a most peculiar scene. What was the audience supposed to make of it? At the level of narrative technique it serves, of course, to build up the suspense. We know all through it, though the brothers do not, that the worst is still to come. But I believe that in its simple—one could almost say simplistic —way it makes several other very telling points.

Firstly, it contrasts a magnificent Egypt and a homespun Canaan and this in more than one way. The brothers are shown as crude peasants, indeed as little men thinking little thoughts; for what conceivable importance could their asses have had in Egyptian eyes? Yet was their fear that they would be turned into slaves so naive? The audience's imagination would jump some generations forward to a time when the descendants of these men would in very fact be slaves in Egypt. But at the moment the Egyptians were being kind to them. Or were they? The seating arrangements suggest that it was a surface tolerance only. There was too much disdain mingled with the kindness for them to be completely at ease.

Secondly, it at the same time contrives to suggest that the brothers, rough-hewn and perplexed though they may have been, were still changing for the better. There was nothing that they could do about the special favours accorded to Benjamin. Nevertheless, they accepted them without demur and later, when they found out who the high Egyptian really was, they never as much as hinted that they had noticed them. Yet it had been just such favouring of Joseph by Jacob that had so rankled with them at the beginning and had indeed sparked off the whole traumatic train of events that had led to this hour.

Thirdly, it gets us questioning Joseph's intentions again. He had retreated with moist eyes when he saw Benjamin. But did he nevertheless share some of the Egyptians' contempt for these peasants, though they were his kinsmen? Did he still at heart feel as superior to them as he had at the beginning? Or is there an indication in him eating alone that for all his exalted rank he too, as a Hebrew by birth, was a victim of Egyptian *apartheid*? Did he secretly despise those whom he now led, and they him? Can we detect in him something of the spirit of Moses, another prince of Egypt, who, in the splendid words of the Letter to the Hebrews (11:25, AV), chose "rather to suffer affliction with the people of God, than to enjoy the pleasures of sin for a season; esteeming the reproach of Christ greater riches than the treasures of Egypt"?

I doubt the last very much, but it is impossible to be quite sure, just as Joseph's next action strikes us as enigmatic in the extreme. At first glance the banquet seems to present an auspicious opportunity for him to make himself known to his brothers. They had done, if a little tardily, all that he had asked of them. He and they were suitably softened by wine. He had just wept copious tears on seeing Benjamin. But he does not. Almost wantonly in our view he decides to toy with them yet once more. In this sense the scene emerges in context as I have headed it, a veritable calm before the storm. For in front of the brothers lies another and even more horrendous bout of stark and naked terror. If there is a moment in this long and essentially pleasing and uplifting story when our smiles from offstage threaten to freeze on our faces, it is this. It will be well through chapter 44 before we can bring ourselves to resume them.

... BEFORE THE STORM

Genesis 44:1–17 *(cont'd)*

(ix)

The stratagem which Joseph this time adopts to trap his unwary brothers is not only cunning but diabolical—and I use the word in a literal, not a metaphorical sense. His steward was again to put their money back in their sacks, but in addition he was to place his vizier's silver cup in Benjamin's sack. We begin to catch a glimpse of what was in Joseph's mind. It was not enough that the brothers as a whole should suffer for what they had done to him, or even that they should have had to return without Simeon. After all, he had been one of them on that fateful day so long ago. To make the punishment fit the crime, an unsuspecting and innocent younger son (did he say to himself, "like I was then"?) had to be exposed to direst peril while in their keeping.

The steward must have carried out his instructions later the same night, for it was at dawn the next morning that the brothers set off for home, probably still in a rather befuddled state after the banquet, certainly mightily relieved that a mission so fraught with hazard had been successfully accomplished. But hardly were they out of the city than Joseph ordered the steward to pursue them and accuse them straight out of stealing the cup. Vehemently they protested their innocence and rashly (had the wine affected their memories?) they invited him to search the sacks. If it was found in one of them, the guilty man deserved to die, and the rest of them would be Joseph's slaves.

In their confused indignation they probably did not hear the steward's reply, which mitigated the sentence they had pronounced on themselves. His lord wished only to enslave the guilty brother; the others would be blameless. The search began and inevitably the cup was discovered in Benjamin's sack. In an instant their hangovers vanished. Neither they nor the steward as much as mentioned the purchase money, which lay in full view of them all. It hardly mattered now. Benjamin's fate was sealed, he of all of them, the very one they had almost had to prize out of his old father's protecting arms. And it was they who had condemned him out of their own mouths. They rent their clothes as though he were already dead and, dazed and shattered, made their way with their stern escort back to the city.

(x)

It has to be clearly understood that Joseph's silver cup was no ordinary cup. It was not its value in money that made it so precious to him. It was the cup from which, as we are told, he practised "divination". This was an ancient variant of the game of reading tea-leaves which old ladies sometimes like to play today. But to the Egyptians divination was no harmless pastime. From what we know of the practice, it involved mixing a few drops of oil with the water in the cup or throwing in a small object or two and finding hidden references to the future from the resulting configurations or ripples. Like the interpretation of dreams it was a skilled art, part of the stock-in-trade of the "magicians" who, it will be recalled, were so pointedly lampooned in the earlier scene in the Pharaoh's court (see 41:8, 24). There Joseph, the untrained man of God, had done what they with all their learning were unable to do and by God's direct inspiration had explained the Pharaoh's dreams.

It now transpired that he was taking up another and much more sinister practice of theirs and taking it up on their terms. For there were no other. In later Israel divination was a heathen "abomination" carrying the death penalty; see Lev. 20:6; Deut. 18:9–14. See also Num. 23:23 where with AV (margin) and NEB "against" should be rendered "in". There is no way in which we can shrug off this feature of the story as incidental to it. We could argue that the dangers of the practice may not have been so apparent in Patriarchal times as later, but it can hardly have been commended. It is also possible that as grand vizier Joseph was expected to acquire such skills, and had done so without necessarily himself approving of them. But is anyone going to be convinced by these arguments? The cup plays a crucial role in the narrative and its role cannot be separated from its religious associations. Joseph plainly wanted the brothers to be aware of these associations. He had to that extent intentionally enlisted pagan religion on his side and to that extent he was playing with fire. That is what I meant when I said earlier that Joseph's final scheme had something of the devil in it.

(xi)

In this light the outraged response of the brothers to the steward's accusation takes on a more ominous colouring. It was not simply a semi-drunken stupor that made them bridle so fiercely. As men of their time they too were susceptible to superstition. It was not in their case, as in Joseph's, a matter of indulging in or at any rate making use of the black arts. The cup was a sacred cup to the Egyptians and that in itself was enough to send shivers of terror down their spines. Anyone who stole such a cup was not only committing a crime but a sacrilege.

And when the cup was found in Benjamin's sack, their terror could only have been compounded. They felt themselves caught up in things far beyond their ability to fathom, the helpless victims of a man who, as he himself claimed, could foretell the future. Heathen though he was, his powers were manifestly divine. They could not see how he could be, but God—yes, even their God—must be implicated in this overwhelming catastrophe that had come upon them. How in such a case could they even begin to think of themselves as guiltless? The particular charge against them might be false, but their guilt against heaven was there plain for all to see. Let this Egyptian ally of his, then, finish once and for all his cat-and-mouse game with them! Judah with his agonized cry spoke for them all as, broken and at their wit's end, they positively implored him to put them to death.

At last Joseph had them where he wanted them, confessing their guilt to his face. It was not their guilt of the moment, which was no guilt. It was not even the guilt of their betrayal of himself so many years ago though, if they had thought of it, they would without any question have included it. It was the guilt of their whole lives exposed by his machinations. And here they were crying out in despair to him to sentence them to death as they had once sentenced him! The wheel had come round full circle. He could afford to relax. He repeated the lesser sentence which his steward had pronounced—only Benjamin was to become a slave (as he had once been a slave!)—and paused to see what would happen.

We in the audience also thankfully wait for what we know will be a happy outcome. It cannot come too soon, for in this last scene Joseph has on any reckoning been taking terrible risks with the workings of destiny and coming within a hair-breadth of making a mockery of his vaunted faith in God. He has been tampering with forces too potent and too ambiguous for even a grand vizier and stand-in for the mighty Pharaoh to keep in check and all but putting himself—and his brothers with him—beyond the pale of a good God's protection. At this instant he is in fact in his hubris peering into the depths of Hell. He does not fall in, but it is a close call.

RECONCILIATION

Genesis 44:18–45:28 *(cont'd)*

(xii)

The story's most glorious and delicious irony is at hand. In a speech of simple but dignified eloquence one of the accused

becomes the judge's judge and in effect puts Joseph in the dock.
When Judah rises and rather daringly walks up to Egypt's
governor, Joseph has his brothers like puppets on a string,
twitching defencelessly to his every tug. They will be released
from their agony only when he decides. By the time Judah stops
talking, Joseph has been beautifully put in his place. He and his
brothers both are humbled before God.

In a flash everything appears to him in a new light. The very
act of theirs for which he had been straining so long and latterly
so questionably to discover an appropriate chastisement,
becomes a mercy of God's, a good thing, not a bad. As God's
man he had always tried to give God credit for his successes.
Now he is able to look back beyond these to the pain and
conflict that had preceded them and to see these too as God's
doing. There had all the time been a puppet-master greater by
far than he pulling the strings and he as well as his brothers had
all along been dancing to his tune.

(xiii)

Judah's speech was neither obsequious nor defiant. He accepted that Pharaoh's *alter ego* had spoken both justly and graciously in condemning Benjamin and letting the rest of them
return. But back in Canaan he had solemnly promised their
father to bring Benjamin home unharmed, and he had no
recourse but to try a last gambit on his behalf. He asks that he
instead of Benjamin should bear the punishment of slavery. It is
a noble offer, nobly made, with not a trace of self-regard in it.
At a stroke it cancels out the meanness and shame of what he
had done more than twenty years before (see 37:26-27).

But leading up to this honourable request is a description,
charged with emotion, of an aged father doting on Benjamin
because his older brother was dead, afraid to let him out of his
sight lest harm befall him too; of ten harassed brothers not
knowing what to do as disaster after disaster overtakes them; of
an Egyptian official whose insistent questioning it was that had
set the whole sorry series of events in motion; and again, at the
end, of the old man in Canaan turning his face to the wall and

giving up life's struggle when he finds that Benjamin is not with them. How, he concludes, could I—but he also means how could you—cause him such grief and anguish.

No one could have failed to be pierced to the quick by such a heart-felt plea, accompanied as it was by such a selfless gesture. But the man listening was not no one. He was that son who had died. Jacob was that father, and he had not seen him during that long, long time. The one speaking to him was his brother, and Benjamin and his other brothers were standing suppliant in front of him. Judah was right in his implied rebuke. He had not started out so to humiliate and crush them. He had gone much too far, and they were all better men than he. We are not told in so many words that these were his thoughts. But there can be little doubt that they were, for all of a sudden we find that God, not Joseph, occupies the centre of the stage.

(xiv)

The room was quickly cleared and in a shaking voice he cried, "I am Joseph", and immediately asked, "Is my father still alive?" A stupid question, we think, but Joseph was really castigating himself bitterly; we have to add, "after all I have done to him". Similarly when he told his brothers not to reproach themselves for selling him into slavery, he was almost saying, "I deserved it". There is a profound sense of agitation as well as of inexpressible joy behind his stumbling words, and it is shared by the brothers. So dismayed were they that they could not utter a word.

But as he proceeded, imperceptibly the tension slackened. He could at last understand it all, the partialities, the boasting, the jealousies, the hatred, the excuses, the scheming, the testing, the surprises, the horrors, the fears, the betrayals, the posturings, the glories and the shame—his brothers' and his own. Their whole lives had been nothing other than God's preparation of them for this hour. God's hidden purposes were fast becoming clear to him. He, not they, had sent him to Egypt to preserve for them all a remnant in the earth, and to keep alive for them many survivors. The famine was still raging in Canaan, so they must all come down to Egypt and settle amid its plenty.

The brothers, too, as they listened, felt God's calm spreading over them. For the first time in two bitter years, perhaps in twenty-two, they were at peace. After some kissing and hugging, they could talk freely and naturally with Joseph. When last had they done that?

(xv)

It remains only for Jacob and the rest of the clan to be summoned to Egypt. It is a nice touch that the Pharaoh allies himself with the invitation and lavishly plies the brothers with gifts both for themselves and their father. The story-teller can allow this, since he has revealed who it was that truly disposed human destinies, be it in Egypt or in Canaan or anywhere else in the world. It is another nice touch that a newly composed and practical Joseph should be slightly wary again. He makes a special mention of Benjamin's eyes having seen him so that he could confirm to Jacob what the others said and, as they depart, he calls after them, "Do not quarrel on the way". He suspects that Jacob will need some convincing: and so he does. But when he sees the special waggon sent to transport him, his spirits revive. An intolerable burden of gloom, much of it of his own making, is in that moment lifted from the old misanthrope's shoulders. Soon he will see his beloved Joseph again, and then he can die content. The audience earnestly echoes his "It is enough!" It sets a fitting seal on one of the loveliest and most heartwarming tales ever written.

PROVIDENCE

Genesis 45:4–8 *(cont'd)*

(xvi)

The first two or three sentences which Joseph addressed to his brothers after telling them who he was are, with a couple of similar sentences of his in 50:19–20, the most important in the whole epic. They demand some further thought on our part. Let us remind ourselves of what he said:

> And now do not be distressed, or angry with yourselves, because you sold me here; for God sent me before you to preserve life. For the famine has been in the land these two years; and there are yet five years in which there will be neither ploughing nor harvest. And God sent me before you to preserve for you a remnant on earth, and to keep alive for you many survivors. So it was not you who sent me here, but God.

Let us also, a little prematurely, consider what he said, again to his brothers, in chapter 50:

> Fear not, for am I in the place of God? As for you, you meant evil against me; but God meant it for good, to bring it about that many people should be kept alive, as they are today.

These two little speeches express in the colourful language of story the essence of what the theologians in their more technical language term the doctrine of Providence. Under this heading are grouped some of the knottiest problems of theology. How does God govern and maintain the world he created? How does his activity relate to the laws of nature, the forces of history, the freedom of the individual? What is the connection between his general providence over the universe and in the events of history, and what may be called his "special" providence in the life of his own people, those who believe that they have been called by him, if you like, his "Church"? Under what circumstances does God break, as it were, his own rules and work a miracle? Most troublesome of all perhaps, where is there a place for evil within the idea of a loving Providence?

The two statements of Joseph home in on what to the believer must be the central support and stay of any such doctrine, namely that God is able so to organize his world as to bring good out of evil. They express in their own way the conviction which St. Paul puts so memorably in the famous twenty-eighth verse of Romans chapter 8. We are most familiar with this in the Authorized Version:

> We know that all things work together for good to them that love God

but I think that J. B. Phillips spells it out more precisely:

> We know that to those who love God everything that happens fits into a pattern for good.

(xvii)

There is no doubt that the way Joseph speaks about God's activity in these two passages is more congenial to us today than the way that activity has been presented to us in the earlier parts of Genesis.

The two former Patriarchal epics think on the whole in terms of God interfering in and with the normal, appearing "out of the blue" and compelling Abraham to break with his past life, crudely challenging him to believe that a son could be born to him when his wife was well past the child-bearing age, speaking directly to him and on occasion confronting him in the form of an angel or even another human being, calling upon him out of heaven to sacrifice his "only" son to him, giving his partisan blessing to Isaac and Jacob and excluding Ishmael and Esau, coming down to assure Jacob of his protection, overlooking his ambitious scheming, wrestling with him face to face at the ford of the Jabbok, and so on. Their eye is in the main on God's "special" providence, and other peoples are mentioned only as they impinge, for the most part hostilely, on the life of his chosen people. The God of these stories is expected to appear and disappear suddenly, to perform miracles, to be felt and experienced in the unusual and the abnormal.

The Joseph epic, on the other hand, tries hard to take a more comprehensive and subtler view of the divine activity. It invites us to think of God as working always behind the scenes, controlling but not forcing the pace of events, permitting things to happen rather than directly causing them to happen, achieving his purpose through men's actions rather than upon or in spite of them. Thus he does not send the famine; it simply "began to come" (41:54). Contrast this with the picture of him raining down brimstone and fire on Sodom and Gomorrah out of the sky (19:24). Again, note how it is emphasized that the attack of the brothers upon Joseph was motivated by their own human jealousy and hatred. Though God was in what they did, they were free agents. They meant to do Joseph harm, and they did him harm, and God let them do him harm; but all the while he was planning to use that harm for his own ends, and gradually things turned out not as they, but as he wanted.

Nor, moreover, is it only Jacob's small clan that are saved, though it is they who are spoken of in the words "remnant" and "survivors". These are two of the Bible's most distinctive words. See 2 Kgs. 19:30–31; Isa. 10:20–23; 46:3–4; Joel 2:30–32; Amos 5:14–15; Mic. 7:18–20. By their use we are being told that God's provision for his people in this story was a deliverance from disaster and judgment as "miraculous" in its own way as any of his great acts of salvation to come in future days. Yet it is not an "exclusive" event. "All the earth" (41:57) comes to Egypt to buy as well as the sons of Jacob, Joseph's arrangements benefit the Egyptians and the Canaanites and many another nation as well as the Hebrews, and they as well as Jacob's clan are included among the "many people" who are kept alive.

In a very real sense, then, in this epic tale "all things" are seen to work together for good and "everything that happens" is fitted into the pattern of God's plan, though it may be only his people, the equivalent of Paul's "those who love him", who are able to appreciate the fact—and even they can only do so with the benefit of hindsight. This is so like the quiet and considered way so many of us today arrive at the assurance that God and not any other force, human or mechanical, is in charge of our lives and the lives of those around us that we are bound to be warmed and encouraged by it. We look back over our lives and we know that it is so. We do not often experience those shattering confrontations with the divine that people in the

Bible seem always to be experiencing. Our experience is much more like Joseph's and his brothers', a realization every now and again that events we once thought had no purpose in them, events perhaps that were calamitous in their immediate consequences, events even in which we ourselves acted meanly and shamefully, were in fact blessings in disguise, part and parcel of a larger and ongoing divine plan for us and ours. It is in the last resort that realization, never continuous, always partial, but none the less real, that enables us to grit out teeth in hope and press onwards in the battle of faith. Our times are in his hand. As old Jacob said, "It is enough".

Being human, we sometimes long in our ignorance and weakness for the burning certainties of God's saints, but our sincerest prayer is that which echoes George Croly's great hymn:

> I ask no dream, no prophet-ecstacies,
> 　No sudden rending of the veil of clay,
> No angel-visitant, no opening skies;
> 　But take the dimness of my soul away.

If God's Spirit can teach us to see the signs of a good Providence at work in troublous times and, we might add, can teach us to hang on when we do not see these signs, are we entitled to expect more?

(xviii)

I don't think we are. And yet from the Christian standpoint there is something more that must be said. It does not change the need for us to have faith and trust, nor to pray earnestly for the Holy Spirit to "enable" (as the mediaeval hymn has it) "the dulness of our blinded sight". No more than the story of Joseph does it solve the intellectual problems that are raised in profusion by the doctrine of Providence. Indeed, if anything, it sharpens the ambiguous clash between good and evil in the world's life which that doctrine is so concerned to reconcile. But at the same time it brings the strangest comfort to our souls.

That something more has to do with the Cross of Christ. It is why we Christians glory in it, and do not find it tragic. The crucifixion of Our Lord was not only the most savage instance of human cruelty and sin, indeed of the Devil's power, that could be imagined. It was also the most glorious evidence of God's overruling Providence, of his amazing ability to bring good out of evil and, when everything was pointing to the contrary, to make the "wrath of men" to praise him (Ps. 76:10). This in the final analysis is what the doctrine of divine Providence is all about.

INTO EGYPT

Genesis 46:1–27

1 So Israel took his journey with all that he had, and came to Beer-
2 sheba, and offered sacrifices to the God of his father Isaac. And God spoke to Israel in visions of the night, and said, "Jacob, Jacob." And
3 he said, "Here am I." Then he said, "I am God, the God of your father; do not be afraid to go down to Egypt; for I will there make of
4 you a great nation. I will go down with you to Egypt, and I will also
5 bring you up again; and Joseph's hand shall close your eyes." Then Jacob set out from Beer-sheba; and the sons of Israel carried Jacob their father, their little ones, and their wives, in the wagons which
6 Pharaoh had sent to carry him. They also took their cattle and their goods, which they had gained in the land of Canaan, and came into
7 Egypt, Jacob and all his offspring with him, his sons, and his sons' sons with him, his daughters, and his sons' daughters; all his offspring he brought with him into Egypt.

8 Now these are the names of the descendants of Israel, who came
9 into Egypt, Jacob and his sons. Reuben, Jacob's first-born, and the
10 sons of Reuben: Hanoch, Pallu, Hezron, and Carmi. The sons of Simeon: Jemuel, Jamin, Ohad, Jachin, Zohar, and Shaul, the son of
11 a Canaanitish woman. The sons of Levi: Gershon, Kohath, and
12 Merari. The sons of Judah: Er, Onan, Shelah, Perez, and Zerah (but Er and Onan died in the land of Canaan); and the sons of Perez were
13 Hezron and Hamul. The sons of Issachar: Tola, Puvah, Iob, and
14, 15 Shimron. The sons of Zebulun: Sered, Elon, and Jahleel (these are the sons of Leah, whom she bore to Jacob in Paddan-aram, together

with his daughter Dinah; altogether his sons and his daughters
16 numbered thirty-three). The sons of Gad: Ziphion, Haggi, Shuni,
17 Ezbon, Eri, Arodi, and Areli. The sons of Asher: Imnah, Ishvah,
Ishvi, Beriah, with Serah their sister. And the sons of Beriah: Heber
18 and Malchi-el (these are the sons of Zilpah, whom Laban gave to
Leah his daughter; and these she bore to Jacob—sixteen persons).
19, 20 The sons of Rachel, Jacob's wife: Joseph and Benjamin. And to
Joseph in the land of Egypt were born Manasseh and Ephraim,
whom Asenath, the daughter of Potiphera the priest of On, bore to
21 him. And the sons of Benjamin: Bela, Becher, Ashbel, Gera,
22 Naaman, Ehi, Rosh, Muppim, Huppim, and Ard (these are the sons
23 of Rachel, who were born to Jacob—fourteen persons in all). The
24 sons of Dan: Hushim. The sons of Naphtali: Jahzeel, Guni, Jezer,
25 and Shillem (these are the sons of Bilhah, whom Laban gave to
Rachel his daughter, and these she bore to Jacob—seven persons in
26 all). All the persons belonging to Jacob who came into Egypt, who
were his own offspring, not including Jacob's sons' wives, were
27 sixty-six persons in all; and the sons of Joseph, who were born to
him in Egypt, were two; all the persons of the house of Jacob, that
came into Egypt, were seventy.

The culminating point of the Joseph epic has been reached and
passed, and its chief lesson highlighted. What remains owes as
much to Israel's chroniclers and genealogists as to her story-
tellers. Only a few scenes in these long final chapters belong
properly to the epic, notably those where Joseph meets his old
father, where Jacob is given an audience with the Pharaoh,
where he makes Joseph swear to bury him in Canaan, where
after his death Joseph has to assure his brothers once more that
he is genuinely concerned for their welfare and, of course,
where Joseph's own death is recorded. The rest comprises lists
of names and sayings which for the most part concern the tribes
of Israel rather than the sons of Jacob as individuals. The
reader should not let these parts colour too much his picture of
the real human beings whose long series of traumatic adven-
tures is now being brought peaceably to its close.

The appearance of God to Jacob as he prepares to leave
Canaan is the only direct confrontation between the divine and

the human in the whole epic. The writer breaks from his usual habit of keeping God in the background in order to mark what is to him (and would have been also to his Hebrew audiences) a unique occasion. The ancestors of Israel are quitting the land of promise, and it will be a long time before they return to it. God therefore shows himself in "visions of the night" to the aged patriarch and renews the promise that his descendants will become a great nation; and he assures him that he will bring him back to Canaan again. This assurance is to Jacob personally and strictly speaking refers to his burial in the ancestral tomb at Machpelah (50:13). But it carries a hint, which the audience would not miss, that Israel herself would one day return to Canaan too.

The list of names which follows purports to be that of the people who accompanied Jacob into Egypt. But apart from a reference to Dinah in brackets, it mentions only sons and grandsons, and Benjamin, the innocent young man whose fate was so recently engaging us, has no less than ten sons. The list is in fact a list from a much later date of the twelve tribes of Israel and their constituent clans. It need not detain us.

THE PHARAOH UPSTAGED

Genesis 46:28–47:12

28 He sent Judah before him to Joseph, to appear before him in
29 Goshen; and they came into the land of Goshen. Then Joseph made ready his chariot and went up to meet Israel his father in Goshen; and he presented himself to him, and fell on his neck, and wept on
30 his neck a good while. Israel said to Joseph, "Now let me die, since I
31 have seen your face and know that you are still alive." Joseph said to his brothers and to his father's household, "I will go up and tell Pharaoh, and will say to him, 'My brothers and my father's
32 household, who were in the land of Canaan, have come to me; and the men are shepherds, for they have been keepers of cattle; and they have brought their flocks, and their herds, and all that they have.'
33, 34 When Pharaoh calls you, and says, 'What is your occupation?' you shall say, 'Your servants have been keepers of cattle from our youth

even until now, both we and our fathers,' in order that you may dwell in the land of Goshen; for every shepherd is an abomination to the Egyptians."

So Joseph went in and told Pharaoh, "My father and my brothers, with their flocks and herds and all that they possess, have come from the land of Canaan; they are now in the land of Goshen."
2 And from among his brothers he took five men and presented them
3 to Pharaoh. Pharaoh said to his brothers, "What is your occupation?" And they said to Pharaoh, "Your servants are shepherds as
4 our fathers were." They said to Pharaoh, "We have come to sojourn, in the land; for there is no pasture for your servants' flocks, for the famine is severe in the land of Canaan; and now, we pray you, let
5 your servants dwell in the land of Goshen." Then Pharaoh said to
6 Joseph, "Your father and your brothers have come to you. The land of Egypt is before you; settle your father and your brothers in the best of the land; let them dwell in the land of Goshen; and if you know any able men among them, put them in charge of my cattle."
7 Then Joseph brought in Jacob his father, and set him before
8 Pharaoh, and Jacob blessed Pharaoh. And Pharaoh said to Jacob,
9 "How many are the day of the years of your life?" And Jacob said to Pharaoh, "The days of the years of my sojourning are a hundred and thirty years; few and evil have been the days of the years of my life, and they have not attained to the days of the years of the life of my
10 fathers in the days of their sojourning." And Jacob blessed Pharaoh,
11 and went out from the presence of Pharaoh. Then Joseph settled his father and his brothers, and gave them a possession in the land of Egypt, in the best of the land, in the land of Rameses, as Pharaoh
12 had commanded. And Joseph provided his father, his brothers, and all his father's household with food, according to the number of their dependents.

(i)

The meeting of Joseph with the father he had not seen for upwards of twenty years is briefly but dramatically related. Indeed, the scene is so touching a one that we have to shake ourselves to realize that it is the very opposite of what Joseph's second dream in chapter 37 might have led us to expect. The first dream he had there, of the brothers bowing down to him, has already been fulfilled, but Joseph himself almost rushes to prevent this one being fulfilled. He is in effect admitting that it had been due to his own youthful pride and not to divine guidance (see further the commentary to 37:5–11, *Dreams*). So with a new found humility the grand vizier of Egypt throws his arms around the old peasant from Canaan and embraces him. The final act of reconciliation has taken place.

(ii)

Joseph then arranged for his father and brothers to be presented to the Pharaoh. He was clearly a little apprehensive about how the great king might react, and he told them to say to him that they were cattlemen rather than shepherds (they were, of course, a bit of both), adding that the Egyptians abominated shepherds. We have no evidence from any Egyptian source of this prejudice, but it is quite likely to have been true. Cattle were a mainstay of the Egyptian economy and flourished in huge numbers all along the banks of the Nile, whereas the shepherd's life would be associated by them with the nomadic peoples from outside who were always (and especially now while the famine was raging) pressing against their borders. He obviously wanted his kinsmen to be allowed to settle in the rich eastern pastures of Goshen which they had now reached, and was afraid the Pharaoh might be tempted, for all that they were his relatives, to move them more into the centre of the country.

He need not have worried. Indeed, the five brothers whom he selected to introduce to the Pharaoh ignored his advice and told the king proudly that they were shepherds. And in spite of that the Pharaoh welcomed them warmly and acceded to their request to be allowed to stay where they were in Goshen. He even suggested to Joseph that he withdraw some of them from time to time and employ them to tend the royal herds.

There follows Jacob's meeting with the Pharaoh, who is deeply impressed with the venerable patriarch and asks how old he is. The age put in Jacob's mouth by the story-teller is in terms of the epic quite impossible and must be an attempt by him to keep in touch with the tradition that Jacob was one hundred and forty-seven when he died (47:28). In the time-scale of the epic Joseph was at this juncture just approaching forty and his father, therefore, presumably somewhere in his eighties. But it is the second part of Jacob's reply that should especially interest us. With it he shows a quiet dignity he had been quite incapable of only a month or two before. In the best Hebrew fashion he acquiesces in the shortness (in God's sight) of his own and, by implication, of every human life, describing it as an uncertain pilgrimage often dogged with suffering and evil. His cantankerous complaints are behind him, and he can now look death straight in the face, unafraid and at peace. For, as he had said to Joseph when they met, "Now let me die, since I have seen your face, and know that you are still alive".

(iii)

These two little scenes in which Joseph meets Jacob and Jacob meets the Pharaoh are shot through with irony, but there is no great malice in it. The erstwhile proud son pays proper respect to the father he had once dreamed would bow before him (see also 48:12). The efficient prime minister is at a loss how to approach his king. A feared monarch is more gracious then he gave him credit for. The brothers, not long since in abject terror, can hold their heads high again. A crabbed old man finds serenity at last. And perhaps most delightful of all, the mighty are amiably but effectively put down from their thrones (Luke 1:52). The aged sojourner, lord of nowhere, blesses the all-powerful Pharaoh, not the other way round, and a clan of shepherds, whom the Egyptians despised, are by that same Pharaoh's permission given Egypt's best land to settle in. All this too, we remark with a smile of pleasure, was part of God's providence.

TYRANNY

Genesis 47:13–27

13 Now there was no food in all the land; for the famine was very severe, so that the land of Egypt and the land of Canaan languished
14 by reason of the famine. And Joseph gathered up all the money that

was found in the land of Egypt and in the land of Canaan, for the grain which they bought; and Joseph brought the money into
15 Pharaoh's house. And when the money was all spent in the land of Egypt and in the land of Canaan, all the Egyptians came to Joseph, and said, "Give us food; why should we die before your eyes? For
16 our money is gone." And Joseph answered, "Give your cattle, and I will give you food in exchange for your cattle, if your money is
17 gone." So they brought their cattle to Joseph; and Joseph gave them food in exchange for the horses, the flocks, the herds, and the asses: and he supplied them with food in exchange for all their cattle that
18 year. And when that year was ended, they came to him the following year, and said to him, "We will not hide from my lord that our money is all spent; and the herds of cattle are my lord's; there is nothing left in the sight of my lord but our bodies and our lands.
19 Why should we die before your eyes, both we and our land? Buy us and our land for food, and we with our land will be slaves to Pharaoh; and give us seed, that we may live, and not die, and that the land may not be desolate."
20 So Joseph bought all the land of Egypt for Pharaoh; for all the Egyptians sold their fields, because the famine was severe upon
21 them. The land became Pharaoh's; and as for the people, he made
22 slaves of them from one end of Egypt to the other. Only the land of the priests he did not buy; for the priests had a fixed allowance from Pharaoh, and lived on the allowance which Pharaoh gave them;
23 therefore they did not sell their land. Then Joseph said to the people, "Behold, I have this day bought you and your land for Pharaoh.
24 Now here is seed for you, and you shall sow the land. And at the harvests you shall give a fifth to Pharaoh, and four fifths shall be your own, as seed for the field and as food for yourselves and your
25 households, and as food for your little ones." And they said, "You have saved our lives; may it please my lord, we will be slaves to
26 Pharaoh." So Joseph made it a statute concerning the land of Egypt, and it stands to this day, that Pharaoh should have the fifth; the land of the priests alone did not become Pharaoh's.
27 Thus Israel dwelt in the land of Egypt, in the land of Goshen; and they gained possessions in it, and were fruitful and multiplied exceedingly.

Then all at once the atmosphere changes. It is difficult to see what could have been the purpose of this strange and very off-putting passage, which cuts so suddenly into the epic's happy

ending and seems almost to exult in Joseph's achievement in
reducing the whole citizenry of Egypt to penury and serfdom.
There is abundant evidence from Egyptian sources that the
Pharaoh was considered to be the real owner of everything in
Egypt and the population to possess what they did—cattle,
land, even their own freedom—only by his grace and favour.
But why does the writer claim that this situation came about
through Joseph taking advantage of the famine and, like the
cruellest bailiff of mediaeval feudalism, squeezing the life-
blood from an exploited and cringing peasantry? He even has
him granting exemption to a pagan priesthood.

Is he simply reporting without comment what was in the
tradition? Does he intend us to admire Joseph for his punctili-
ous devotion to duty, even though it furthered the rise of a
tyrannous system of government? Or is he suggesting that he
had to act like this in order to preserve his position and be able
to protect his kinsmen? Or worse, that, though recently humbled, he still had too much of the arrogant ruler in him? It is
impossible to say.

My own view is that the passage should be read in conjunc-
tion with a sinister allusion at the end of the previous passage
which most of us probably missed. There we had a report of
Joseph settling his family in Goshen, but the area is given its
later name of the land of Rameses. Having had the anachron-
ism pointed out to us, we might be inclined to let it pass as
carelessness, but a Hebrew audience would be more likely to see
it as deliberate. For Rameses or Ramses was one of the two
store-cities which the descendants of Jacob's clan would one
day be drafted to build by sweated slave labour when a less
accommodating Pharaoh than the present one succeeded to
Egypt's throne. See Exod. 1:11. It is a gentle hint that there was
a time coming when Israel would not be, as she was now, safe or
happy in Egypt. In this passage, however, the author takes the
opportunity to rub that lesson in much more crudely by
picturing Egypt itself as paralysed by dictatorship and at a
single man's beck and call. He is implying that if the Egyptians
themselves were little better than slaves, what hope could there

be for foreigners like the Hebrews when their high ranking kinsman was no more and a nastier and more authentic Pharaoh held the reins of power.

If I am right in this interpretation, the point he is making is certainly a valid one. The Bible occasionally allows us to smile, but it never does so for long in case we should become too complacent. But does he not tend to overdo it? Should not the ominous but subtle little reference to Rameses have been enough? Obviously the author himself does not think so, and he is prepared to labour his point even at the risk of having Joseph do some very questionable things and of impairing the agreeable atmosphere of reconciliation and unity which he has in the last couple of chapters been at such pains to build up. He senses that his audience may be relaxing a little too much and administers this dose of realism to correct the balance. Who of us, knowing how often we are tempted to lapse into sentimentality when reading the Bible, can say that he may not have been justified?

A Note on Dating the Patriarchal Age

If we put together all the features of the Joseph epic which connect it authentically with conditions in ancient Egypt, the list is quite an impressive one.

The names Potiphar in 37:36 and (a longer form of the same) Potiphera and Asenath in 41:45 are recognizably Egyptian, containing respectively the divine elements Re (the sun-god) and Neith (a goddess). The name assigned to Joseph by Pharaoh in 41:45 has given more trouble to Egyptologists, but the custom of re-naming which lies behind it is well attested. The phrase translated "Bow the knee!" (41:43) is probably, that translated "a father to Pharaoh" (45:8) certainly, Egyptian. The words for "reed grass" (41:2), "magician" (41:8), and "linen" (41:42) are borrowed from Egyptian. The organization of the royal court and the officers mentioned or alluded to—captain of the guard, chief butler (cup bearer) and baker, magicians and wise men, steward, director of the palace, grand vizier—are in accord with what we know of Egyptian practice. So are the great store set by dreams and the respect accorded to those who could interpret them. References to religious matters

(41:45; 47:22, 26), taboos and prejudices (43:32; 46:34), and feudal methods of government (47:13ff.) are either known to be or likely to be accurate.

Even more significant are the parallels in Egyptian sources to two events which are integral to the epic's plot, the seven-year famine and the promotion of a foreigner to a position of high eminence.

Famine in Egypt resulted from the failure of the Nile to inundate and water the surrounding countryside. It is a disaster not infrequently mentioned and loudly bewailed in Egyptian literature; twice the records actually tell of cannibalism among the inhabitants. Generally speaking the Nile was a beneficent river, but it was by no means predictable, and on occasion there could be not just a lessening but a complete absence of inundation. Rarely can this have occurred for as many as seven years in succession, but there is an inscription from the area of Aswan which recalls just such a time in the distant past. Experts are doubtful about the inscription's reliability, but it at least shows that a seven-year famine was not unthinkable.

Perhaps the most persuasive text of all, however, is one from the 12th century B.C. which names a "Syrian" who in years of drought had subjected the country to taxation. Israel had by that time escaped from Egypt and settled as a nation in Palestine, but what happened then could well have happened previously too.

Though no Egyptian source so far discovered mentions Joseph—or for that matter Moses, who was equally prominent in Egypt's court in his time—these indirect indications that there is a solid historical basis to the stories in the latter part of Genesis are very welcome, especially when we remember that the stories themselves were not composed with the modern historian's needs in mind but for quite other purposes.

A large number of scholars are of the opinion that the stories may most appropriately be accommodated within the period called by Egyptologists the Second Intermediate Period, which lasted from the beginning of the 18th to the middle of the 16th centuries B.C. This was a period of uncertainty and collapse not only in Egypt but all through the Near East, and for that reason is not surprisingly very deficient in surviving records. But we know that for much of it Egypt was ruled by a dynasty of foreign origin called the *Hyksos*. This name, thought once to mean "shepherd kings", is now usually rendered "rulers of foreign lands". From their personal names they seem to have been mainly Semites, though Hurrian names are also found. These Hurrians (Biblical Horites), whose own records have helped us on several occasions to explain some of Genesis' social customs, originated in Armenia and began to penetrate Syria and Mesopotamia in the 18th century. They were probably a contributory cause of the downfall of the Babylonian empire of Hammurabi. Some of them, it appears, as they moved southwards, combined with disaffected Semitic adventurers and succeeded in wresting control of a weakened Egypt and holding on to it for over a century (see Map 4). They were at no time more than a ruling elite of warriors and they seem in most respects quickly to have adopted Egyptian ways. But one noteworthy contribution of theirs of which we have information was the introduction of horses and chariot warfare. This may account for the references to chariots in 41:43 and to horses in 47:17.

I find myself agreeing in the main with these scholars. The whole period of which we are speaking, indeed, a period when peoples of various races were constantly on the move southwards towards Egypt, supplies an excellent backcloth not only for the rise of a Hebrew slave like Joseph to high office in Egypt and for the emigration of his family to join him there, but for the earlier journey of Abraham and his tiny clan from Mesopotamia to Palestine. Within it there is room even for the expedition of the four northern kings to the region of the Dead Sea related in chapter 14, an expedition which it is difficult to place in earlier or later periods, for which our sources are fuller.

If I were asked to suggest precise dates, I would—very tentatively—do so as follows:

circa 1700	Abraham leaves Harran
early 17th cent.	The expedition of the four great kings
circa 1640	Jacob goes to Mesopotamia
circa 1600	Joseph is sold into slavery and taken to Egypt
circa 1580	Jacob and his clan settle in Egypt.

DEATH-BED SCENES I

Genesis 47:28–49:32

The epic ends appropriately with (in the final verse of chapter

49 and in chapter 50) accounts of the death and burial of Jacob
and of Joseph's own death and the embalming of his body. But
before that we have (in the last part of chapter 47 and in
chapters 48 and 49) three death-bed scenes recording in considerable detail the charges of the dying Jacob to his sons and his
parting blessings on them and on his two grandsons, Ephraim
and Manasseh. Probably not a great deal of these two and a bit
chapters belonged originally to the epic, for the chief focus of
interest in them is not so much on the sons and grandsons as
individuals as on the tribes which they were supposed to have
fathered. The chapters are full of antiquarian information
about the tribes and their early fortunes on Palestinian soil after
the Conquest, information which the patriarch Jacob could not
possibly have known. This information is of great value to
historians of Israel, and readers who would like to find out
more about how they go about their work and how much they
can squeeze out of the ancient and enigmatic poems which are
preserved here may wish to consult some of the books mentioned in the list for Further Reading. They will find it a
fascinating experience. Our main concern, however, as it has
been all through this Commentary, is with the real "live"
individuals whom we call the Patriarchs and not with the ethnic
and tribal traditions which later generations have read back
into Patriarchal times. It is enough for our purposes that the
chapters be printed and a few necessary explanatory notes
added.

Jacob asks to be buried with his forefathers in Canaan (47:28–31)

28 And Jacob lived in the land of Egypt seventeen years; so the days of
Jacob, the years of his life, were a hundred and forty-seven years.
29 And when the time drew near that Israel must die, he called his son
Joseph and said to him, "If now I have found favour in your sight,
put your hand under my thigh, and promise to deal loyally and truly
30 with me. Do not bury me in Egypt, but let me lie with my fathers;
carry me out of Egypt and bury me in their burying place." He

31 answered, "I will do as you have said." And he said, "Swear to me";
    and he swore to him. Then Israel bowed himself upon the head of his
    bed.

Jacob blesses the two sons of Joseph (48:1–22)

1   After this Joseph was told, "Behold, your father is ill"; so he took
2   with him his two sons, Manasseh and Ephraim. And it was told to
    Jacob, "Your son Joseph has come to you"; then Israel summoned
3   his strength, and sat up in bed. And Jacob said to Joseph, "God
    Almighty appeared to me at Luz in the land of Canaan and blessed
4   me, and said to me, 'Behold, I will make you fruitful, and multiply
    you, and I will make of you a company of peoples, and will give this
    land to your descendants after you for an everlasting possession.'
5   And now your two sons, who were born to you in the land of Egypt
    before I came to you in Egypt, are mine; Ephraim and Manasseh
6   shall be mine, as Reuben and Simeon are. And the offspring born to
    you after them shall be yours; they shall be called by the name of
7   their brothers in their inheritance. For when I came from Paddan,
    Rachel to my sorrow died in the land of Canaan on the way, when
    there was still some distance to go to Ephrath; and I buried her there
    on the way to Ephrath (that is, Bethlehem)."
8, 9   When Israel saw Joseph's sons, he said, "Who are these?" Joseph
    said to his father, "They are my sons, whom God has given me here."
    And he said, "Bring them to me, I pray you, that I may bless them."
10 Now the eyes of Israel were dim with age, so that he could not see. So
    Joseph brought them near him; and he kissed them and embraced
11 them. And Israel said to Joseph, "I had not thought to see your face;
12 and lo, God has let me see your children also." Then Joseph
    removed them from his knees, and he bowed himself with his face to
13 the earth. And Joseph took them both, Ephraim in his right hand
    toward Israel's left hand, and Manasseh in his left hand toward
14 Israel's right hand, and brought them near him. And Israel stretched
    out his right hand and laid it upon the head of Ephraim, who was the
    younger, and his left hand upon the head of Manasseh, crossing his
15 hands, for Manasseh was the first-born. And he blessed Joseph, and
    said,

        "The God before whom my fathers Abraham and Isaac walked,
        the God who has led me all my life long to this day,
16 .   the angel who has redeemed me from all evil, bless the lads;

and in them let my name be perpetuated, and the name of my
fathers Abraham and Isaac;

and let them grow into a multitude in the midst of the earth."

17 When Joseph saw that his father laid his right hand upon the head
of Ephraim, it displeased him; and he took his father's hand, to
18 remove it from Ephraim's head to Manasseh's head. And Joseph
said to his father, "Not so, my father; for this one is the first-born;
19 put your right hand upon his head." But his father refused, and said,
"I know, my son, I know; he also shall become a people, and he also
shall be great; nevertheless his younger brother shall be greater than
20 he, and his descendants shall become a multitude of nations." So he
blessed them that day, saying,

"By you Israel will pronounce blessings, saying,
'God make you as Ephraim and as Manasseh' ";

21 and thus he put Ephraim before Manasseh. Then Israel said to
Joseph, "Behold, I am about to die, but God will be with you, and
22 will bring you again to the land of your fathers. Moreover I have given
to you rather than to your brothers one mountain slope which I took
from the hand of the Amorites with my sword and with my bow."

Jacob foresees the future fortunes of the twelve tribes (49:1–28)

1 Then Jacob called his sons, and said, "Gather yourselves together,
that I may tell you what shall befall you in days to come.

2 Assemble and hear, O sons of Jacob,
and hearken to Israel your father.

3 Reuben, you are my first-born,
my might, and the first fruits of my strength,
pre-eminent in pride and pre-eminent in power.

4 Unstable as water, you shall not have pre-eminence
because you went up to your father's bed;
then you defiled it—you went up to my couch!

5 Simeon and Levi are brothers;
weapons of violence are their swords.

6 O my soul, come not into their council;
O my spirit, be not joined to their company;
for in their anger they slay men,
and in their wantonness they hamstring oxen.

7 Cursed be their anger, for it is fierce;
   and their wrath, for it is cruel!
   I will divide them in Jacob
   and scatter them in Israel.

8 Judah, your brothers shall praise you;
   your hand shall be on the neck of your enemies;
   your father's sons shall bow down before you.

9 Judah is a lion's whelp;
   from the prey, my son, you have gone up.
   He stooped down, he couched as a lion,
   and as a lioness; who dares rouse him up?

10 The sceptre shall not depart from Judah,
   nor the ruler's staff from between his feet,
   until he comes to whom it belongs;
   and to him shall be the obedience of the peoples.

11 Binding his foal to the vine
   and his ass's colt to the choice vine,
   he washes his garments in wine
   and his vesture in the blood of grapes;

12 his eyes shall be red with wine,
   and his teeth white with milk.

13 Zebulun shall dwell at the shore of the sea;
   he shall become a haven for ships,
   and his border shall be at Sidon.

14 Issachar is a strong ass,
   crouching between the sheepfolds;

15 he saw that a resting place was good,
   and that the land was pleasant;
   so he bowed his shoulder to bear,
   and became a slave at forced labour.

16 Dan shall judge his people
   as one of the tribes of Israel.

17 Dan shall be a serpent in the way,
   a viper by the path,
   that bites the horse's heels
   so that his rider falls backward.

18 I wait for thy salvation, O Lord.

19 Raiders shall raid Gad,
    but he shall raid at their heels.

20 Asher's food shall be rich,
    and he shall yield royal dainties.

21 Naphtali is a hind let loose,
    that bears comely fawns.

22 Joseph is a fruitful bough,
    a fruitful bough by a spring;
    his branches run over the wall.
23 The archers fiercely attacked him,
    shot at him, and harassed him sorely;
24 yet his bow remained unmoved,
    his arms were made agile
    by hands of the Mighty One of Jacob
    (by the name of the Shepherd, the Rock of Israel),
25 by the God of your father who will help you,
    by God Almighty who will bless you
    with blessing of heaven above,
    blessings of the deep that couches beneath,
    blessings of the breasts and of the womb.
26 The blessings of your father
    are mighty beyond the blessings of the eternal mountains,
    the bounties of the everlasting hills;
    may they be on the head of Joseph,
    and on the brow of him who was
    separate from his brothers.

27 Benjamin is a ravenous wolf,
    in the morning devouring the prey,
    and at even dividing the spoil."

28 All these are the twelve tribes of Israel; and this is what their father
said to them as he blessed them, blessing each with the blessing
suitable to him.

Jacob repeats his request to be buried in Canaan (49:29–32)

29 Then he charged them, and said to them, "I am to be gathered to my

people; bury me with my fathers in the cave that is in the field of
30 Ephron the Hittite, in the cave that is in the field at Mach-pelah, to
the east of Mamre, in the land of Canaan, which Abraham bought
with the field from Ephron the Hittite to possess as a burying place.
31 There they buried Abraham and Sarah his wife; there they buried
32 Isaac and Rebekah his wife; and there I buried Leah—the field and
the cave that is in it were purchased from the Hittites."

DEATH-BED SCENES II

Genesis 47:28–49:32 *(cont'd)*

(i)

The first matter demanding comment is the notice that Jacob's
death took place seventeen years after he reached Egypt. This is
most improbable. When he left Canaan (45:28), he was obviously expecting to die soon, and wished only to see his son
before he did. His words to Joseph in 46:30 are along the same
lines. Most tellingly of all, in the next scene (chapter 48)
Joseph's sons, who were born before the onset of the famine
(41:50), are still young children when taken to receive his dying
blessing. The notice looks like yet another attempt to bring the
epic into agreement with genealogical traditions about the life-
span of the Patriarchs. It will be remembered that because of
these traditions Abraham and Isaac were also both credited
with many years of life following scenes in which they seemed to
be on the point of death. See at 47:9 and in particular the first
part of the commentary on the blessing scene in chapter 27. I
think that we can reasonably assume that Jacob died, aged
about ninety, not long after the removal of his clan from
Canaan to Egypt.

(ii)

When Jacob felt his time was near, he extracted a promise from
Joseph not to bury him in Egypt but with his fathers in the
homeland. To stress the solemnity of the occasion he asked him
to put his hand under his thigh, a procedure that Abraham had

also adopted with his servant when he sent him to Mesopotamia to find a wife for Isaac (24:2). To be buried with their ancestors was for the Hebrews the ideal conclusion to life, a symbolic extension beyond the grave of the fellowship of the family. Nothing was more abhorrent to then than to have no proper burial place, as the moving little story of Rizpah in 2 Sam. 21:10ff. so clearly shows. Satisfied with Joseph's oath, Jacob "bowed himself upon the head of the bed", a quaint phrase which probably means no more than that he acknowledged it with a faint nod from his pillow.

(iii)

Soon thereafter Jacob took a turn for the worse and Joseph brought his two sons, Manasseh and Ephraim, to see him. The long emotional story which ensues, though it is a very human one, probably had as its main purpose the enhancing of the status of the tribal groups which later bore these names. Properly speaking half-tribes, they seem during the settlement period to have quickly outstripped most of the other full tribes in numbers and extent of territory (see Map 5); and of the two, Ephraim became in course of time the more important and influential, so that after the split in the monarchy its name could be used (like the title Israel itself) as a designation of the whole northern kingdom. See for example Isa. 7:1–9, 17. These future events are presented here as the outcome of prophecies spoken by the dying Jacob. The two grandsons are in effect being adopted by Jacob as his own and given a share of the inheritance along with Reuben, Simeon and the rest. And Ephraim's precedence is underscored by his dramatic gesture in crossing his hands as he blessed them, so that his right hand landed on the head of the younger boy and his left hand on that of the older. There is, perhaps not surprisingly, no mention of the fact that they had an Egyptian mother.

There are touches of the genuine Jacob in this story, notably his plaintive invoking of his dear Rachel's memory and—would he ever learn?—his insistence to the bitter end on showing partiality. There is also in the last verse of the chapter a probable allusion to 33:19, which recorded his purchase of some land in the area of Shechem (the Hebrew word translated "slope" is the same as the name of the city; it means literally "shoulder"). Nor is it in historical terms at all unlikely that Joseph would take his sons, born far away from their grandfather's encampment, to be blessed by the old chief before he died. But because of the heavy overlay of tribal associations, we would be unwise to make too much use of this chapter as an authentic Patriarchal source.

(iv)

The same is true of the series of poetic verses in chapter 49, which purport to be Jacob's final blessings to his twelve sons but which in fact, when properly understood, tell us more about the vicissitudes of the twelve tribes of Israel in Canaan following the invasion under Joshua. See Map 5 for an outline of the areas of settlement.

The tribes represented by the three oldest brothers were not strong in later times. Reuben succeeded only in occupying a small territory east of the Jordan, and Simeon and Levi were in the end unable to capture any land at all. Simeon was scattered partly in Judah and partly in the north, and Levi became an elite priestly caste. These happenings are set forth as a reckoning for the misdeeds of Jacob's sons related in 35:22 (Reuben's incest) and in chapter 34 (Simeon and Levi's terrible vengeance on Shechem), which is on the face of it fair enough. But why was there no allowance made for Reuben's generous conduct in 37:21ff. and 42:37ff., which Jacob must have known or learned about? And why was Levi's fate in the event more honourable than Simeon's? The verdicts are not as just as they seem and look more like attempts to account for tribal fortunes that were common knowledge than genuine forecasts of a shrewd old father.

The tribes which settled in Transjordan (Gad) and in the north of Palestine (Zebulun, Issachar, Dan, Asher, and Naphtali) are likewise given short shrift. All that is said of Zebulun is that it lived close to the sea, though in fact Asher's territory was nearer the Mediterranean. Issachar's "forced labour" is thought to allude to the troubles it experienced from having the powerful Phoenicians of Sidon as near neighbours. The verses on Dan probably have in mind the sorry story of Judg. 18, which tells of its violent and unsuccessful attempts to find territory in southern Palestine and its eventual migration to the far north. The pious and in context rather despairing prayer, "I wait for thy salvation, O Lord", which follows Dan's "blessing", may reflect the poet's disapproval of this particular tribe. Gad, a Transjordanian tribe, would be constantly exposed to Bedouin raids. Asher's prosperity in the north would have resulted from trade with the Phoenicians, though no doubt it also shared some of Zebulun's discomfiture from the same quarter. Naphtali's blessing seems to be a simple notice of its independent character as a mountain tribe in Galilee.

The large space given to the prophecies about Judah and Joseph (that is, Manasseh and Ephraim together) accurately represents the dominance of these two tribal groups in the Judges period and in the following monarchical period, when they supplied the nuclei of the two Hebrew kingdoms. Joseph's blessing dwells on its large population and the fertility of central Palestine where this confederation settled, while Judah's waxes eloquent about its right to staff and sceptre and its glorious, if rather bloody, victories over its enemies, including the other tribes. It would be no surprise if this section owed its enthusiastic tone to a Judaean poet who knew about the rise of David and his and Solomon's magnificent, if short-lived, success in creating a Hebrew empire. The rendering of verse 10 "until he comes to whom it [the sceptre] belongs" is based on the ancient Greek version. It has a distinct messianic ring to it, and this verse was in fact often treated as a hidden prophecy of Christ by the early Church, which used the Septuagint. Protestant circles dependent on the AV ("until Shiloh came"), which follows the Hebrew, were fortunately not able to employ the verse in that sense. I hope that no-one will be tempted to do so today on the strength of the RSV's translation. Not only is the phrase still argued about by scholars, but the whole passage in which it is set smacks of an unsavoury triumphalism. The proud tribe from which David came is in effect looking back and seeing its success foreshadowed in the dying words of Jacob.

Benjamin was a small but important tribe in later times and gave the new nation its first king in Saul. It had a reputation for warlike fierceness (see 1 Chr. 8:40; 12:1–2), and it is this which is celebrated in its blessing. It does not seem to worry the poet that the Benjamin of the Joseph epic was, on the contrary, a meek and uncomplaining young man.

(v)

With a very few exceptions these blessings and prophecies put in Jacob's mouth have little connection with the character of Joseph and his brothers as portrayed in the epic. They supply a host of valuable clues about Israel's later history but next to nothing that helps us to understand the real wishes of the dying patriarch. Perhaps one that does is the circumstance that *all* his sons were called to his death-bed. He has his favourites among them, but this time no Ishmael and no Esau is excluded and left in the darkness outside. This is worth thinking about. It by no means allows us to cast aspersions on God's cruel choices on these previous occasions—that we have no right to do—but it does place the aged Jacob in a more agreeable light. He had learned something from his own youthful experience and did not carry his likes and dislikes, strong though they were, too far. This more tolerant attitude was achieved via a life that was largely governed by intolerance, his own or others', but it was achieved. It is a pleasure to note it and also to note how it fits in beautifully with the general emphasis of Genesis' third and last epic cycle which, as we have seen, has been on God's providence rather than God's grace.

NOTHING IS HERE FOR TEARS

Genesis 49:33–50:14

33 When Jacob finished charging his sons, he drew up his feet into the

1 bed, and breathed his last, and was gathered to his people. Then Joseph fell on his father's face, and wept over him, and kissed him.
2 And Joseph commanded his servants the physicians to embalm his
3 father. So the physicians embalmed Israel; forty days were required for it, for so many are required for embalming. And the Egyptians wept for him seventy days.
4 And when the days of weeping for him were past, Joseph spoke to the household of Pharaoh, saying, "If now I have found favour in
5 your eyes, speak, I pray you, in the ears of Pharaoh, saying, My father made me swear, saying, 'I am about to die: in my tomb which I hewed out for myself in the land of Canaan, there shall you bury me.' Now therefore let me go up, I pray you, and bury my father; then I
6 will return." And Pharaoh answered, "Go up, and bury your father,
7 as he made you swear." So Joseph went up to bury his father; and with him went up all the servants of Pharaoh, the elders of his
8 household, and all the elders of the land of Egypt, as well as all the household of Joseph, his brothers, and his father's household; only their children, their flocks, and their herds were left in the land of
9 Goshen. And there went up with him both chariots and horsemen; it
10 was a very great company. When they came to the threshing floor of Atad, which is beyond the Jordan, they lamented there with a very great and sorrowful lamentation; and he made a mourning for his
11 father seven days. When the inhabitants of the land, the Canaanites, saw the mourning on the threshing floor of Atad, they said, "This is a grievous mourning to the Egyptians." Therefore the place was
12 named Abel-mizraim; it is beyond the Jordan. Thus his sons did for
13 him as he had commanded them; for his sons carried him to the land of Canaan, and buried him in the cave of the field at Mach-pelah, to the east of Mamre, which Abraham bought with the field from
14 Ephron the Hittite, to possess as a burying place. After he had buried his father, Joseph returned to Egypt with his brothers and all who had gone up with him to bury his father.

The death of Jacob is related with some panache. The description of him drawing his feet up into his bed and breathing his last is very effective. On the peculiar phrase "gathered to his people" see at 25:8 (Abraham). His body is embalmed for the journey to Machpelah, and not only Joseph but the Egyptians mourn his passing. A large party of Egyptian courtiers accompany the cortège and the local Canaanites are amazed at the "very great and sorrowful lamentation" (we are told indeed that they named a place after the event!). Jacob's body is finally taken to the cave near Hebron which Abraham had bought from the Hittites (chapter 23) and deposited there with those of Abraham and Sarah, Isaac and Rebekah, and his own wife Leah. This was what he had requested (49:29–32). His fathers' sepulchres were there, and it was more appropriate that he be buried alongside them than with his beloved Rachel on the road to Bethlehem, though personally he must have wished for that above all else.

It is a remarkable procession, and Hebrew audiences must down the ages have returned to this passage time and again to savour its every nuance. It told of the passing of him who was given the name Israel as a second name and who more than any of the other Patriarchs embodied in his person the hopes and fears, the contumelies and the strivings, the whole embattled and magnificent faith of their race. He was not a man whom we can easily bring ourselves to like, but he was no less than Abraham a giant among men, a far more heroic figure than Isaac and more heroic too, I think we can admit, than Joseph, who in spite of a year or two of cruel suffering had altogether an easier pathway through life. It is gratifying to think that even this doughty warrior of the spirit, whose manhood was passed in opposing everyone in sight, even God, and whose old age in recrimination and complaint, was able as he died to rest in an overarching divine Providence and to speak generously not only of the God "before whom my fathers Abraham and Isaac walked", but of the God "who has led me all my life long to this day" (48:15). It took him nigh on ninety years, but at his life's close he too knew "that to those who love God everything that happens fits into a pattern for good".

I would not wish to compare Jacob too closely with another Hebrew schemer and rapscallion who also attained a dignity in death that escaped him in life. There are far more differences between him and Samson than there are similarities. But the parallels are perhaps close enough for us to be permitted to quote as Jacob's epitaph the words used of Samson by John

Milton in his great poem *Samson Agonistes*. Milton invites us to forget the unworthy things in Samson's earlier life and to concentrate on his heroic death as he brought down the pillars of Dagon's temple on himself and his country's enemies. We should be prepared, seeing things as we now do in these final chapters of Genesis from the standpoint of a loving God who ordered them all for his higher purposes, to pronounce the same verdict on Jacob:

Nothing is here for tears, nothing to wail
Or knock the breast; no weakness, no contempt,
Dispraise or blame; nothing but well and fair,
And what may quiet us in a death so noble.

ALL PASSION SPENT

Genesis 50:15–26

15 When Joseph's brothers saw that their father was dead, they said, "It may be that Joseph will hate us and pay us back for all the evil which 16 we did to him." So they sent a message to Joseph, saying, "Your 17 father gave this command before he died, 'Say to Joseph, Forgive, I pray you, the transgression of your brothers and their sin, because they did evil to you.' And now, we pray you, forgive the transgression of the servants of the God of your father." Joseph wept when 18 they spoke to him. His brothers also came and fell down before him, 19 and said, "Behold, we are your servants." But Joseph said to them, 20 "Fear not, for am I in the place of God? As for you, you meant evil against me; but God meant it for good, to bring it about that many 21 people should be kept alive, as they are today. So do not fear; I will provide for you and your little ones." Thus he reassured them and comforted them.

22 So Joseph dwelt in Egypt, he and his father's house; and Joseph 23 lived a hundred and ten years. And Joseph saw Ephraim's children of the third generation; the children also of Machir the son of 24 Manasseh were born upon Joseph's knees. And Joseph said to his brothers, "I am about to die; but God will visit you, and bring you up out of this land to the land which he swore to Abraham, to Isaac, 25 and to Jacob." Then Joseph took an oath of the sons of Israel,

saying, "God will visit you, and you shall carry up my bones from
26 here." So Joseph died, being a hundred and ten years old; and they
embalmed him, and he was put in a coffin in Egypt.

By contrast Joseph's death is much more crisply and, for a
Hebrew tale, more characteristically related. He died an old
man, having seen his great-grandchildren born, was embalmed
and "put in a coffin in Egypt". No funeral procession carried his
body to Canaan, nor was there loud lamentation among the
Egyptians, though he had done more for them than ever Jacob
had. He gathered his clan around him and encouraged them to
look to the future, to a day when God would "visit" (a great
Biblical word this; compare Gen. 21:1; Exod. 4:31; Isa. 29:6;
Luke 1:68) his people and lead them back to the land "which he
swore to Abraham, to Isaac, and to Jacob". But many generations were to pass before that day dawned, and only then were
his own remains returned to the homeland which he left as a
mere youth and saw but once briefly again in the flesh. See
Exod. 13:19; Josh. 24:32. See also Heb. 11:22, where this scene
is chosen as the example of Joseph's "faith".

The Patriarchal stories of Genesis thus end with their face
turned resolutely, if a little plaintively, towards the far horizon
and with a renewed emphasis on the need for a pilgrim faith, the
kind of faith that Abraham had shown as they began, when he
set out on the journey from Harran to Palestine. But there is, as
there was not in Genesis 12, a backwards perspective as well.
There are achievements to be celebrated, not men's achievements which, as these stories know only too well, are no real
achievements, but God's. God's Gospel has been set in motion,
and some of the gloom of Genesis' first eleven chapters has been
lifted. Proof has been given that God could defeat sin and evil
and save his people *now*. It is fitting that this should also be
emphasized in Genesis' last chapter.

The brothers are afraid that, with Jacob gone, Joseph will at
last reap his vengeance on them, and he has to reassure them
that their malice towards him those twenty and more years ago
was forgiven and forgotten. One wonders whether Jacob had in

fact, as they claimed, told Joseph to forgive them, or whether they made this up in order to bring more pressure to bear on him. Be that as it may, for the first time openly they ask his pardon and he, though not quite so openly, confesses that he had been tempted to "play God" towards them. But, as he reminds them and as they seem finally to accept, it was not their intention—or his—that mattered. God had been in all that had happened, and he had meant it all for good, "to bring it about that many people should be kept alive, as they are today".

So does an epic that had opened in hatred close with hatred swallowed up in love. And it was God's doing. It has been a heartwarming tale of God's providential care, of his influence for good where evil had seemed all-powerful, of his bringing peace and unity to a family split wide open by fierce and unlovely emotions. Sometimes we may feel that it lacks the realism and the existential clash of the Abraham and Jacob epics. There could be truth in that assessment. But read carefully and with an eye for its ironies, the epic of Joseph is not sentimental. It is cathartic. We relive as we read it those rare but blessed moments of perception in our own soiled lives when all our strivings ceased and we were able to glimpse through the darkness the controlling hand of a gracious and benign Providence. Yes, we need a pilgrim faith, for there is a long way to go before God's full salvation comes. But just as much we need these moments of purifying insight if we are to go on at all.

To sum up this ultimate lesson of Genesis, I turn once more to Milton's *Samson Agonistes,* invoking the master of English epic—though his theme is Biblical—to help us understand an older and equally masterly Hebrew epic. As Samson's father and a few friends prepare his burial, they begin to see the tragedy of his death in a new light. The last word is given to the Chorus:

> All is best, though we oft doubt
> What the unsearchable dispose
> Of Highest Wisdom brings about,
> And ever best found in the close.

Oft He seems to hide His face,
But unexpectedly returns,
And to His faithful champion hath in place
Bore witness gloriously; whence Gaza mourns,
And all that band them to resist
His uncontrollable intent:
His servants He, with new acquist
Of true experience from this great event,
With peace and consolation hath dismissed,
And calm of mind, all passion spent.

FURTHER READING

Books marked * are more suitable for initial study.

COMMENTARIES

*R. Davidson, *Genesis 12–50* (The Cambridge Bible Commentary on the New English Bible) (Cambridge University Press, 1979)

S. R. Driver, *The Book of Genesis with Introduction and Notes* (Westminster Commentaries, 1904)

*A. S. Herbert, *Genesis 12–50, Introduction and Notes* (Torch Bible Commentaries) (SCM Press, 1962)

*D. Kidner, *Genesis: An Introduction and Commentary* (Tyndale Old Testament Commentaries) (Inter-Varsity Press, 1967)

G. von Rad, *Genesis* (Old Testament Library) (SCM Press and Westminster Press, Second Edition, 1963)

J. Skinner, *A Critical and Exegetical Commentary on Genesis* (The International Critical Commentary) (T. and T. Clark, Second Edition, 1930)

E. A. Speiser, *Genesis: Introduction, Translation and Notes* (Anchor Bible) (Doubleday, 1964)

*S. G. Stevens, *Genesis* (Layman's Bible Book Commentary) (Broadman Press, 1978)

B. Vawter, *On Genesis: A New Reading* (Geoffrey Chapman, 1977)

OTHER STUDIES

*Y. Aharoni and M. Avi-Yonah, *The Macmillan Bible Atlas* (The Macmillan Company, 1968)

*E. Auerbach, "Odysseus' scar", Chapter 1 of *Mimesis: The Representation of Reality in Western Literature* (Princeton University Press, 1946) (a famous comparison of Homeric and Hebrew epic style)

*E. M. Good, *Irony in the Old Testament* (The Westminster Press, 1965), especially Chapter IV, "Genesis: The Irony of Israel"

 S. Herrmann, *A History of Israel in Old Testament Times* (SCM Press, 1975)

 B. Mazar (editor), *The World History of the Jewish People,* Volume II *Patriarchs* (W. H. Allen, 1970)

*S. Sandmel, *The Enjoyment of Scripture: The Law, the Prophets, and the Writings* (Oxford University Press, New York, 1972), especially Chapter IV, "The Pentateuch"